THE BEGINNINGS

OF THE

NEW YORK CENTRAL RAILROAD

G. W. Featherstonhaugh

THE BEGINNINGS

OF THE

NEW YORK CENTRAL RAILROAD

A HISTORY

BY

FRANK WALKER STEVENS

G. P. PUTNAM'S SONS

NEW YORK   LONDON

The Knickerbocker Press

1926

Copyright, 1926
by
FRANK W. STEVENS

Published April, 1926

Made in the United States of America

PREFACE

THE judicious reader will most likely desire to know upon what authorities the statements in this book are based. Such a desire is natural and commendable and since foot notes are practically impossible, it can only be met in the preface. First it is well to understand what has not been used. Statements made years after an event and based upon memory alone almost without exception have been found unreliable and have been discarded. Interesting examples may be cited. A good old lady recently remembered vividly that the first train to run over the Utica and Schenectady was the so-called DeWitt Clinton train and she saw it pass. As the chapter on the Mohawk and Hudson shows, the DeWitt Clinton locomotive was scrapped in 1835, and the aforesaid first train passed over the Utica and Schenectady in 1836.

The popular authority for the origin of the Mohawk and Hudson is a paper read by Joel Munsell, an Albany annalist, before the Albany Institute in 1875. He says that in 1831 C. C. Cambreling was president of the company. Mr. Cambreling was never its president. He says the DeWitt Clinton locomotive arrived in Albany July 25, 1831, and was put upon the road July 27. David Matthew, the engineer who helped build it, came to Albany with it and operated it exclusively in 1831, says it left New York where it was built June 25 and that he ran it on the road July 2. Munsell says the much talked of first trip over the road was August 13, that the train was moved by

▼

horse power only and that the grand excursion in which the DeWitt Clinton was used occurred September 24. Matthew, the engineer who operated the engine, and Brown, the artist who made the silhouette, say the event occurred August 9 and Brown says the silhouette was cut immediately thereafter and publicly exhibited in Albany. Munsell says the silhouette is a truthful portraiture of the train. The Company's journal under date of August 17 records payment of $103.87 "in full to G. W. Veeder for sundry expenses attending celebration opening 12 miles of the railroad as per voucher No. 343."

Munsell says the extension from Gansevoort Street to Ferry Street was opened in 1839. The books of the company show it was in 1841. June 15, 1841, the Board passed a resolution beginning, "Resolved, that as soon as the extension of the main Rail Road to Ferry Street in the city of Albany is completed," etc. On September 3, 1841, the Board passed another resolution to adjourn to Saturday, September 11, at the Eagle Tavern in Albany "after which they will unite in the celebration of the opening of the new section to Ferry Street."

Munsell says "a number of stage coach bodies were placed upon trucks for temporary use affording seats for fifteen or eighteen passengers each." These six coach bodies were constructed by James Goold of Albany for permanent use at a cost of $310 each after plans prepared by John B. Jervis, could by no possibility seat even fifteen persons, and are rated in the Company's inventory as nine passenger capacity. They were contracted for in April, two to be delivered July 1 and the remaining four by August 1.

Another source of information which has been wholly rejected is popular articles and popular works assuming to present historical data. A book of the latter class published in 1906 records the following interesting item under date of August 1, 1853: "New York Central railroad and the Hudson River railroad consolidate under plan of Edwin Dean Worcester of this city," and on the same page informs us "New York Central Railroad organized on plans by Edwin Dean Worcester of this city" under date of April 1, 1853. This latter date was eleven days previous to the preliminary meeting held at Syracuse, April 12, to consider consolidation. As to plans by Mr. Worcester, he was in 1853, assistant cashier of the Albany City Bank, had nothing to do with the consolidation and did not enter the service of the Central until about January 1, 1854.

Another writer within the past two years in describing the consolidation of 1853, gravely informs us "In this movement Commodore Vanderbilt was the leading spirit." This, it is perhaps needless to say, will not be found in the account this book gives of that consolidation.

Surviving books of each company, publications contemporary with the event described preserved in many cases in scrap books kept by the Utica and Schenectady, original letters and memoranda, official reports, comprise the sources used, all of which, however, has been subjected to careful checking. So multifarious are these matters that it has found foot notes showing the source of each statement would be useless and afford no real means in most cases of checking up its accuracy. Great effort has been made to obtain absolute accuracy and it is hoped success has crowned the effort but it must be considered possible that errors have crept in although everything has been gone over many times.

It is greatly regretted that in some important respects the book is incomplete or fragmentary. Data does not exist in such cases for making a complete and trustworthy account. An incomplete account of many things is sure to be misleading, if not absolutely erroneous, and in all such cases where the most diligent effort was unable to present the subject adequately the result has been silence. Without the minute books of the directors the financial growth of a company cannot be traced, and without full account books the minutes are practically useless for that purpose.

The illustrations presented have been chosen with care to illustrate and not with intent to present a mere picture gallery.

The book is written with the belief that a historical account should embody what happened, how it happened and why it happened as well as the direct results of what happened. Anything which tells us merely what happened does not rise above the dignity of a mere chronicle. That the standard thus set has not always been attained is freely admitted, although every effort has been made to work toward it. This has led to the presentation of very great detail in some cases, which on reflection was deemed to be advisable.

Acknowledgment should be made to George W. Featherstonhaugh of Schenectady, a grandson of the originator of the Mohawk and Hudson and to Mrs. William Gorham Rice and Mrs. Charles S. Hamlin, daughters of John V. L. Pruyn for valuable information and data.

The author desires to give full and grateful recognition to Ernest J. Van Droskey, his assistant, who has borne the burden of searching for information not only in the dusty records of the companies, but also in numerous public libraries and from many persons. He has also been indefatigable in checking the manuscript prepared.

INTRODUCTION

THE New York Central Railroad Company came into existence as a corporate entity in 1853, by the consolidation of ten railroad corporations existing under the laws of the State of New York. Seven of these were at the time owners of roads in active operation, the road of one was in process of construction and nearly completed, and two were organized with routes established but with no construction commenced. One, the Albany and Schenectady, was incorporated with the name Mohawk and Hudson, changed to Albany and Schenectady in 1847. One, the Rochester and Syracuse, was formed by the consolidation in 1850 of the Auburn and Syracuse and the Auburn and Rochester. One, the Buffalo and Rochester, was formed in 1850 by the consolidation of the Tonawanda and the Attica and Buffalo. One, the Rochester, Lockport and Niagara Falls, was a reorganization and extension of the Lockport and Niagara Falls.

The earliest of these roads both in incorporation and construction was the Mohawk and Hudson incorporated April 17, 1826, and opened for operation August 9, 1831. The year 1926, accordingly, completes a full hundred years since the inauguration of the series of enterprises which have resulted in the New York Central Railroad and its subsidiary roads, known as the New York Central Lines, and to commemorate those early roads, which by their legal union in 1853 united in forming the Central and to record their early

ix

problems, trials, successes, failures and growth, is the purpose of this volume.

To assist in the development of an understanding why the consolidation of 1853 was an economic necessity forced by the location, history and business of the roads, the accompanying map has been prepared which will, if carefully studied, make plainer the gradual leading up to the inevitable result. A tabulation of the names, date of incorporation and year of opening for operation, arranged in order of the opening, will also assist the reader, and here it follows:

	Incorporated	*Opened*	
Mohawk and Hudson	1826	1831	Albany to Schenectady
Utica and Schenectady	1833	1836	Utica to Schenectady
Tonawanda	1832	1837	Rochester to Batavia
Lockport and Niagara Falls	1834	1838	Lockport to Niagara Falls
Syracuse and Utica	1836	1839	Syracuse to Utica
Auburn and Syracuse	1834	1839	Auburn to Syracuse
Auburn and Rochester	1836	1841	Auburn to Rochester
Schenectady and Troy	1836	1842	Schenectady to Troy
Attica and Buffalo	1836	1842	Attica to Buffalo
Rochester, Lockport and Niagara Falls	1850	1852	Rochester to Niagara Falls

These roads were pioneers, and encountered difficulties incident to all new enterprises. The first steam railroad, the Stockton and Darlington, in England was not opened until 1825. Railroad construction in that country was not an assured success until 1829. In 1826 no railroad had been constructed or commenced in the United States. Between 1826 and 1830, steam railroads were projected in South Carolina and in Maryland and a few miles of road constructed. With the question of priority in time, this work is not concerned, it being of no practical importance. It is intended to throw such light as may be obtained from scattered and imperfect records upon the serious questions which were encountered and solved with varying degrees of success by those engaged in initiating the gigantic and all embracing system of transportation by steam railroads upon which the very existence of the greater part of the world now depends.

The track, the motive power, the methods of operation were at the outset crude and extremely imperfect. Even a short railroad involved in its construction an amount of expense which severely taxed the financial resources of the times. The buffetings of the severest financial panic which this country up to that time experienced, had to be borne. The strain of reconstructing the entire track was inescapable.

The roads which are the subject of our investigation also had a problem peculiar to themselves. They derived their existence and their powers from the state of New York. In 1825, that state had completed at great expense, the Erie Canal, one of the great enterprises of the first half of the nineteenth century and was carrying a debt incurred in the work, which it hoped to meet from the use of the canal through the charging of tolls upon the freight conveyed thereon. Accordingly there was, as will be explained in detail later, a prohibition, total or partial, upon the carrying of freight by these roads in competition with the canal, which was not wholly removed until 1847, and from 1844 until December 1, 1851, a large portion of the freight they did carry was compelled to pay in addition to the charges of the railroads, such sum in tolls to the state as it would have paid if carried upon the canal.

It is true that these roads in their way so served the public that it constantly demanded the increase of their facilities. Such increase demanded additional capital and such capital could not be obtained without the prospect of a reasonable return thereon coupled with safety against loss of the principal through legislative action. But the capital required to the public of that day seemed gigantic and the fear of monopoly and the oppression which it was thought would necessarily follow such tremendous aggregations of money, was an obsession with many which added to other burdens difficult to carry. To some the consolidation of 1853 threatened the civil liberties of the people and was a forerunner of the destruction of the state.

When rightly understood, the story of the first twenty years of steam railroading is of thrilling interest. The solution of great problems is always attended with pain and toil. No industry has ever presented as many and as great problems as those which for a full hundred years have been developed by steam transportation. Great as are the unsolved and pressing problems of to-day, they are no more difficult than those which were faced by the pioneers and which they dealt with according to their light and ability.

To bring to mind the situation as it then existed, to make a permanent record of the events which transpired, in short to make a history of things which should not be forgotten is the purpose of this work.

CONTENTS

ILLUSTRATIONS

xv

THE BEGINNINGS OF THE NEW YORK CENTRAL RAILROAD

CHAPTER I

THE MOHAWK AND HUDSON

ON the 28th day of December, 1825, there appeared in the Schenectady Cabinet, a newspaper of that city, a brief notice as follows:

> APPLICATION will be made to the legislature of the state of New-York, at the approaching session, for an act to incorporate the Mohawk and Hudson Rail Road Company, with an exclusive grant for a term of years, for the construction of a Rail Road betwixt the Mohawk and Hudson rivers, with a capital of three hundred thousand dollars, to be increased to five hundred thousand dollars, if necessary; and to receive such certain tolls on the same, as may seem fit for the legislature to grant.—Dated December 19, 1825.

This unsigned notice was inserted by George William Featherstonhaugh of Duanesburgh, Schenectady county, New York, to whose persistent and indefatigable exertions the first railroad of the many scores now composing the New York Central Lines owed its existence. In forwarding him proof of the publication of the notice for six successive weeks, the printer wrote "If the application succeeds my bill for advertising will be $1.56—if it does not succeed—nothing." A petition in accordance with the notice was duly filed with the legislature by Stephen Van Rensselaer, the old Patroon, and Featherstonhaugh. The application seems to have met with some opposition. The Albany and Schenectady Turnpike Company feared the pro-

1

posed road would interfere with its rights and business, and certain citizens of Albany were greatly perturbed, as witness the following letter from Mr. Van Rensselaer, who at that time was serving as representative in Congress of the Albany district:

Ho. Rept., March 15, 1826.

DEAR SIR:

I have brought an old House about my ears by signing the petition. I have written I will withdraw my name if necessary, the Albanians think the city will be ruined and the trade diverted to my land below the overslaugh. You must help me out of the difficulty.

Your friend,

S. VAN RENSSELAER.

To GEO. W. FEATHERSTONHAUGH, ESQ.

The bill was drawn by Featherstonhaugh but was amended in its progress through the legislature in particulars which came near wrecking the enterprise and which occasioned two years delay before by a new act of the legislature they were eliminated as will more fully appear later. However, he labored strenuously for his measure, overcoming all objections, and it passed the Assembly March 29, 99 voting for and 8 against it, and finally became a law April 17, 1826, being Chapter 253 of the Laws of that year. At that time there was, of course, no general law authorizing the incorporation of railroad companies and any such incorporation could be obtained only by special act of the legislature. By this act "Stephen Van Rensselaer and George William Featherstonhaugh with such other persons as shall associate with them for that purpose, be and are hereby constituted a body politic and corporate by the name of The Mohawk and Hudson Rail Road Company for the purpose of constructing a single or double rail road or way betwixt the Mohawk and Hudson rivers."

The name of Stephen Van Rensselaer, he being a resident of Albany of high character, great wealth and large influence, seems to have been thought of great value to the enterprise, but his actual connection with the same appears to have been almost perfunctory, although he was elected first president of the Company and held that position until 1832. He rarely attended meetings of the directors, so far as can be ascertained performed no executive duties, did not assist in developing the plans or details of the work, and at the outset subscribed for only 100 shares of stock of a par value of $10,000, but on May 16, 1828, he addressed the following letter to Featherstonhaugh at Duanesburgh.

DEAR SIR:

I have disposed of the greatest part of my stock not finding it convenient to pay the instalments that may be required; my faith is still strong if the business is well managed it will be profitable to the stockholders. I regret Madam's indisposition and pray for her recovery.

Yours truly,

S. VAN RENSSELAER.

The transfer book of the Company shows that June 30, 1828, Van Rensselaer transferred 40 shares to John I. DeGraff and 40 shares to James Strong; on each share only three dollars had been paid. Thus he retained only 20 shares. In May, 1830, he acquired 4 additional shares, making 24 shares his total holding during the actual construction of the road.

The scheme originated with Featherstonhaugh alone. He drew the act and procured its enactment. By his exertions, representations and influence, he interested and procured the early stockholders. It is fitting there should be some account at this place of his history up to 1826. George William Featherstonhaugh was born in London, April 9, 1780, and was in 1826, 46 years of age. His father died a few days after his birth and his mother removed with him to Scarborough in Yorkshire where he grew to manhood. He was graduated at Oxford, and having abundant means, traveled for five years on the continent of Europe, acquiring the French, German, Italian and Spanish languages. In 1806 he came to America for further travel, and in 1808 married Sarah Duane, daughter of James Duane, who had been a member of the first and second Continental Congresses, a state Senator of the state of New York, first mayor of New York City after the revolution, and a district court judge of the United States. By this marriage he became connected with some of the leading families of the state and formed acquaintance or business connection with most of the prominent men. He also came into possession of a large tract of land in Duanesburgh of which he improved about one thousand acres; erected a large mansion on the banks of Featherstonhaugh lake, filling it with valuable furniture, paintings and books. He became a practical and experimental farmer, importing blooded cattle and sheep, having at one time a flock of over one thousand merino sheep. It is said he organized the State Board of Agriculture. For several years prior to 1825, he was greatly interested in the subject of railroads, procuring all the current publications on that subject and also writing articles for the press. He became impressed with the feasibility and desirability of such a road from Schenectady to Albany. Short lines of road from mines and quarries to canal or tidewater had been constructed in England for some years, but the motive power was that of animals and no road using steam power for general traffic was in existence until the Stockton & Darlington was opened in England in September, 1825.

Among the papers in his handwriting which have survived until this time there is a carefully prepared estimate of cost and anticipated results from operation of a railroad from Albany to Schenectady made up by him in 1825, which possesses great interest as disclosing calculations and theories upon which the earliest railroad building in this country was based. The following is a complete transcript thereof:

Estimate for a railway of 16 miles, made for 4 Lines or a double Track.

		Per Mile
18 Feet wide is 2¼ Acres per Mile......	$40.	$100.
Fencing both Sides 640 rods at.........	50 Cts.	320.
Leveling and dressing the road........		300.

Sleepers 12 feet long ⎰
to underlay both tracks ⎱

| Every 10 Feet 1 Sleeper gives 528 pieces per Mile at...................... | $1. | 528. |
| Cartage 100 Loads................... | $1.50 Cts. | 150. |

Timber Beds for iron rail

---

528 pieces per mile, sawed to form...................	$1.	4 times is	2112.
Cartage to the Ground 66 Loads..................	$1.50	4 times is	396.
Seasoning and laying the Timber Beds 150 Dollars per mile.		4 times is	600.
Laying the Sleepers, letting in, and fastening the Timber Beds...................	$100.	4 times is	400.

Flooring

Hemlock Plank 3 inches thick 3 Feet wide ⎰
each Track. Double Floor and double track. ⎱

$4906.

	Per Mile
Brought forward per Mile.....................	$4906.
15840 Feet per Mile at 125 Cts. per 100 Feet, $198.	
2 Tracks......................................	396.
Double Floor.................................	396.
Battens to the Floor per Mile..................	100.
Carpenters Work at Floor per Mile..............	200.
Nails and Pegs................................	200.

Iron Rail 1 Inch Square

5280 Feet per Mile
 528 do Plus 1/10th for ends to bend and fasten
_____
5808

   3 lbs. to each Foot
_____

17424 lbs. Say 8 tons at 90 Dolls. $720. 4 times is	2880.
Transportation of iron 32 Tons per mile ⎞	
two tracks 20/ ⎠	80.
Blacksmith's Work per Mile....................	100.
	$9258.

| $9258 per Mile for 16 miles gives................ | $148128. |

$148128 at $6 per Cent per annum..............	8887.68
18000 for 300 Waggons at $60 at 6%...........	1080.
	$9967.68

Wear and tear of Waggons 3% on $18000.........	540.
Repairing the Wood Work.....................	450.
50 Horses at $70 each........ $3500.	
50 Gearings—12.50 Cts. each.. 625.	
To last 6 years........... $4125 pr annm	687.50
60 Hired Men and Boys at $150................	9000.
Salaries to Managers, Engineers, &c.............	2354.82
	$23000.

In this Estimate for a rail road of 16 miles every thing is considered but stores at the ends of the Road contiguous to Water

Carriage, and the Profits on these Branches more than compensate the investment.

___

Suppose Horse Power

___

A Horse goes 3 Miles an hour with 6 Tons, allowing 100 Feet
of Way to every mile . . . .
$52 \times 6 = 312$ Tons.   Miles $16 \times 312 = 4992$ Tons.
3 Times a day $3 \times 4992 = 14976$.   2 Tracks, 29952 Tons.
29952 Tons per diem for 300 days 8,985,600 Tons every Year.
This 8,985,600 represents the Capacity of transportation on
such a road, travelling 3 times a day.
Which at a Toll of 2 Cents per Ton per Mile is for 16 Miles
$2,875,392 Dollars per ann^m
or Two Millions, Eight hundred Seventy five thousand 392 Dolls.

But as the actual transit by the Canal last Year was 157,000
Tons:
Abstract from this . . . . 100,000 Tons
Also abstract from Land   }
    travelling during Winter }   100,000 Tons
                                ___
                                200,000 Tons . . . .

One fourth of this being ascending Trade, pays per Ton per Mile
3 cents, and two Cents freight betwixt Schenectady & Albany.

50,000 Tons at 3 Cts. Toll   150000
          at 2 Cts. Freight   100000
                                  ___
                                  250000

150,000 Tons descending Trade pays)
    1½ Cts. Toll on the Canal and 2 Cts. }
    freight—or 3½ Cents. . . . .)   525000
                                              ___
                                              $7750.00 per Mile.

which for 28 miles is . . . . $217,000.

By Conducting 200,000 Tons on a rail road at 3 Cents pr Ton
per mile, would be
                $96,000
                $121,000 gain to the Publick
                ___
                $217,000

3 Cents per Ton per Mile on 200,000 Tons is per
Mile... $6,000.

Per 16 miles 6000 × 16 =...................... $96,000.
Deduct Annual Charge=...................... 23,000.

Profit.................................... $73,000.

By the act of incorporation the capital stock of the
corporation was fixed at $300,000 with liberty to in-
crease it to $500,000 at any time within six years, and
Van Rensselaer, Featherstonhaugh and Lynde Catlin
were appointed commissioners to receive subscriptions
to the capital stock at suitable places in the cities of
Albany and New York within six months from the
passage of the act, giving twenty days public notice of
the time and place of receiving subscriptions in a public
newspaper in each of said cities. Lynde Catlin was
then the president of the Merchants' Bank in New York
City. The first day appointed was June 29th, in the
city of Albany; that in New York was early in July and
a meeting for the election of five directors was appointed
by the commissioners for the 27th day of July at the
Merchants' Bank in the City of New York, and at
that time, Stephen Van Rensselaer, Lynde Catlin, G.
W. Featherstonhaugh, Peter Augustus Jay and Andrew
Edmeston were elected the five directors prescribed
by the charter. The first meeting of directors was held
July 29th at the Merchants' Bank in New York. The
only business transacted was the postponement of the
election of president and vice president until the next
meeting; the appointment of Lynde Catlin as treasurer;
the appointment of Peter Fleming as engineer for one
year from June 10, 1826, at a salary of $1500, he to
proceed immediately to Great Britain to acquire information respecting the construction and management of
railways; that Fleming be allowed his actual expenses

Estimate of the Expense of the
Mohawk and Hudson Railroad

To Jermury Road per mile $ 1500
To Metal on Surface — making path} 1500
a 12/. per Cubic yard ———}
To Beam timber @ $12. per 100 ft. 2534
To Oak plank Sleepers ——— 1508
To Workmanship of Timber @
$ 20 per 100 feet ——————— 1056

To Iron Rails and Chairs 82 Tons
@ $65 ——————— 5330
14428
To Carreye of Materials
@ 5 pr cent ——— } 721
15149
20
Amount for 20 miles — 302.980
Additional Rack Rails ——— 6150
Passing places throryt the lines — 3075
312.205

To 10 per cent for Contingencies
surveys — superintendence &c — } 31.220
Total amount for } $ 343.425
20 Miles ———}

Peter Fleming
Civil Engineer

New York
25 July 1826.

FIRST ENGINEERING ESTIMATE FOR COST OF MOHAWK AND HUDSON.

9

while absent, not exceeding $700, and that $700 be advanced him on account of his salary and expenses.

The next meeting of the directors was held at the Merchants' Bank September 7, 1826, at which only four directors were present, it being recited in the minutes, "Mr. Andrew Edmeston having unfortunately died since the last meeting of the Directors." To fill the vacancy thus occasioned, Nicholas Fish was elected. Stephen Van Rensselaer was elected president and G. W. Featherstonhaugh, vice president. The following resolution was adopted:

Resolved: That Col. Fish and Mr. Jay be a committee to prepare a petition to the Legislature for amendments to the act of incorporation.

Here we get an intimation of the first trouble of the new corporation which nearly wrecked the enterprise and in fact delayed all construction for over two years. The 15th section of the act of incorporation made the stockholders and directors "jointly and severally and personally liable" for all debts contracted by the corporation or its agents, and authorized suit against them to recover. The 17th section is so peculiar that it should be quoted in full:

17. And be it further enacted, That the grant in this act contained, is made and shall be deemed to be taken on the condition, that if the legislature of this state shall, at any time within five years from the time of the completion of the said rail road, make provision by law for the repayment to the said company of the amount expended by them in constructing said rail road, with interest, after deducting therefrom the amount of the tolls received thereon, then the said grant shall become null and void, and the said rail road shall vest in and become the property of the people of this state.

With these two sections in force it was clear the stockholders would never undertake what was at that time a clearly speculative enterprise on terms which made them personally liable for all losses in addition to the amounts paid on their stock, and that with a provision that in case of success the state could step in and absorb all the profits. It will be noted that in case the state took over the road, the company was to receive "the amount expended by them in *constructing* said railroad with interest *after* deducting therefrom the amount of tolls received thereon." Observe that the deduction is the tolls received and not the tolls received less the expenses incurred in operation. So that if successful the stockholders were at least liable to lose all the expenses of operation for five years.

A bill was introduced into the legislature of 1827 amending the charter in respect to these two sections, but for some reason which is not ascertainable at this time, it failed to become a law. Doubtless the presence, energy and enthusiasm of Featherstonhaugh had he been present would have carried it through as it did a year later, but he was absent in England, having sailed September 24, 1826, with his wife and son for a visit there and to investigate with Engineer Fleming the methods of railroad construction and operation in use in Great Britain. He had representatives endeavoring to get the bill through the legislature. A letter to a friend written while in England is of great interest in disclosing his relation to the enterprise and the imminent danger of total failure arising from the objectionable charter provisions which had been thrust into the act.

SCARBOROUGH, Dec. 18, 1826.

MY DEAR SIR:

I was only 17 days and a few hours in crossing the Atlantic with my Family, and have not yet got over the extreme surprise of finding myself in so short a period in so interesting a country as England. . . . As to railways, considered here as the greatest improvement of modern times, and now extending themselves in all directions, I did think it was a subject I was pretty well informed upon before I left home, having with great care studied all the written information on that subject: but if we had constructed our Rail Road upon the information in our possession, it would all to have been done over again, as has been the case with a great many here, at the expense of £50, and £75,000 Stg. The construction of canals is considered here a very simple operation, but the proper adjustment of a railway, on a system which admits of no derangement, is deemed the highest production of art and science. To this may be added the singular mechanical contrivances for loading and unloading = the general economy of the locomotive system—the adjunct branch for the safety and comfort of passengers, &c, &c, &c, &c, &c. A letter is very insufficient to give a tolerable notion of the beauty of all these arrangements and the perfection of the results produced by them. My Engineer, Mr. Fleming whom I sent to this country, in August last has been very industrious; he has just left me on an excursion to the South, and in a few days, after passing Xmas with my aged Mother now 76 years old, I go to Scotland to examine everything there; and it is my settled purpose to return to New York with drawings and models of everything here, of value to our country. Adding the knowledge to be acquired here, to that which we possess of our climate, &c, it is my opinion we shall be able to construct a better Rail road than any now in existence: the experiment then will be a fair one, and the whole of the U. S. will have the benefit of it. An imperfect experiment might injuriously retard the introduction of this valuable improvement. To effect all these desirable results, I shall spare no expense. Our Rail road company does not allow me a single dollar to that end. I did not wish it. I had no mercenary views in originating the project, satisfied to do what I know will eventually be a blessing to the country. But the Legislature must be just and generous too and repeal the 17th and 15th clauses of the bill, the first resuming the Charter after 5 years; the other making us personally liable as if we were a Bank, or my friends will not sustain me, and *the experiment will not be tried.* I wrote to you before on this subject, thro' Mr. Mather. God bless

you my dear Sir; my best remembrances to all my friends
from

Your faithful St.
G. W. Featherstonhaugh.

General Theodore Sill,
Assembly Chamber,
Albany,
New York.

The italics are those of Mr. Featherstonhaugh and show
exactly the peril attending his scheme.

But as already stated the legislature of 1827 passed
no amendatory act and as a result nothing was done
toward construction in that year, the project was
dormant, except Fleming was retained as engineer,
and Featherstonhaugh remained in England.

At a directors' meeting held January 7, 1828, a
petition addressed to the legislature asking for the
desired amendments was adopted. They also asked
for an increase in the number of directors. The petition states that they have employed a skilful engineer
and been to the expense of sending him to Great Britain,
etc., and that he has returned "with a large mass of
valuable information." That they have caused accurate surveys for the road to be made and are prepared
to commence their operations "with full confidence of
forming a road which will be eminently useful and
honorable to the state."

An amendatory bill was drafted and introduced into
the legislature and there for some months it remained
dormant. Featherstonhaugh at this time was still in
England, but returning home in the late winter or early
spring, he seems to have gone to Albany and taken the
matter vigorously in hand and procured the passage of
the bill, since it became a law March 28, 1828, Chap.
122 of that year. The 15th, or personal liability

section, was unconditionally repealed, nine directors were authorized and the 16th and 17th sections were repealed so far as repugnant to the provisions of the amendatory act with reference to a purchase of the road by the state. These new provisions having been in effect accepted by the Company in building its road and never acted upon by the State in taking over the road within fifteen years after its completion, need not be detailed here. But the whole episode in all its details is well worthy of careful study by one interested in the legislative treatment which has been extended to railroads.

Five days after the passage of the law a meeting of the Board of Directors was held in New York. Featherstonhaugh was present and reported the action of the legislature and the Board disclosed its views concerning what had brought it about by adopting the following:

Resolved, that the thanks of this Board be presented to G. W. Featherstonhaugh for his exertions in obtaining the last mentioned act.

At this meeting Featherstonhaugh presented a bill for expenses incurred by him in obtaining the act of incorporation, the amendatory act, and in certain surveys by John Frost, the latter amounting to $180.57, and Featherstonhaugh's personal expenses being $1600.50, a total of $1781.07. Nothing was included for his expenses to England. The bill was ordered paid and was paid May 7. And thus the obstacle which had held up the project for two years was removed.

Nine directors now being required, a stockholders' meeting was called for the 29th day of May at the Bank Coffee House in the City of New York at which Stephen Van Rensselaer, George W. Featherstonhaugh, Nicholas

Fish, Herman Le Roy, John Jacob Astor, David S. Jones, Lynde Catlin, James Duane and Peter A. Jay were elected directors. The Board met June 2nd at the house of Mr. Jay in New York and elected Van Rensselaer, president, Featherstonhaugh, vice president, Catlin, treasurer, and Jay, secretary. But the remainder of the year 1828 passed without any substantial action. No further meeting of the directors was held until October 15th and the next thereafter was held January 26, 1829. The driving power was in some manner incapacitated. When Featherstonhaugh was not on duty nothing was done. As already stated he returned from an absence abroad of a year and a half, probably early in March, 1828. In June of that year, his wife, to whom he was greatly devoted, died. We may reasonably infer that his extensive and long neglected farming operations required great attention and much time.

In January, 1829, the directors appointed a committee consisting of Featherstonhaugh, John Jacob Astor and Lynde Catlin "to report on the measures which will be proper to be taken preparatory to commencing the construction of the Rail Road." The committee was to have power to employ agents for the purchase of land on the proposed route on and near the Mohawk and Hudson rivers.

At a meeting of the directors held February 17, 1829, Featherstonhaugh and Catlin of the committee made a report, Astor having declined to serve on account of his health. They recommended the adoption of various measures and also submitted an estimate of the probable expense of constructing the road prepared by Engineer Fleming, the total of which was $275,366.29. It is short and well worth inserting here as showing the views of construction obtaining after all the study which

had been given the subject by Fleming and Featherston-haugh in England and elsewhere.

Estimate of Expense

First Estimate p^r Mile for construction of Railway—

To Beams—Oak 7 x 7—7,040 cubic feet	at 25/100	$1,760.
To 1,760 Sleepers 9 feet 8 x 4 at every 6 feet, each 2 cubic feet	at 12½/100	440.
To Blocks between each two sleepers		85.
To 3,520 Brackets—Oak 1/6 ft.	25/100	146.87
To Longitudinal plank below sleepers 3,960 C. ft. 9 x 3—	12½/100	445.
To top planking—oak 1¼ inches for 4 lines at p^r mile p^r 100 ft.	$2.50	528.
Flemings compound rail for four lines, p^r Yard	$4.	7,040.
Laying of Frames & Rails & fencing the same—per foot	25/100	1,320.
Tracking path of State at p^r Yd.	25/100	440.
Sideboard for do		210.
Forming the route 25 feet wide at surface		2,237.
Puddling 1,760 Yards at	50/100	880.
Per Mile		15,531.87

Local estimates	
Passing Places ¼ mile	$4,000.
Double railway along canal ¼ mile	4,000.
Engine Machinery & self acting plane	10,000.
Bridges	750.
Wharf at Canal and the Hudson	5,000.
	23,750.
To 16-1/5 miles of Railway	251,616.29
Total amount	275,366.29

The Board took prompt and decisive action thereon as is shown by the following extract from the minutes of the meeting.

The foregoing Report having been read the following Resolutions were unanimously agreed to—

Resolved, that contracts be made without delay for the timber contained in the Estimate of the Engineer, to be delivered at places to be designated by him.

Resolved, that measures be taken to acquire the title to the real estate necessary for the Railway.

Resolved, that the engineer be instructed to prepare the line and divide it into sections of a convenient length, to the end that contracts may be made for leveling and graduating the line of the Railway.

Resolved, that Mr. Featherstonhaugh be authorized to advertize for and receive proposals for the contracts mentioned in the foregoing resolutions; and that any three Directors be a committee with the approbation of a majority of whom he may conclude such contracts.

Resolved, that Mr. Featherstonhaugh and Mr. Catlin be a committee with power to purchase, or to take legal measures for acquiring the real estate necessary for the Railway, and also such additional ground at or near the terminations of the railway as they may think expedient, and to employ counsel and agents for that purpose.

Resolved, that three dollars on each share of the capital stock of this corporation be, and the same is hereby required to be paid by the subscribers, to Lynde Catlin, Esq., the treasurer at the Merchants Bank in the City of New York on the first day of April next under the penalty of the forfeiture of all previous payments thereon.

Adjourned till Tuesday next the 24th Feb. inst. at 5 o'clock P.M.

The 24th of February, one week later, Featherstonhaugh reported that he had caused advertisements to be published and hand bills put up inviting proposals for contracts, and the secretary reported he had given notice of the assessment.

During the ensuing two weeks something happened. What it was, the records of the company give not the slightest indication, nor has it been found possible to obtain information from other sources. On the 13th

day of March, the directors met at 398 Broadway,
New York City, six only being present, Van Rensselaer,
Featherstonhaugh and Duane being absent, and passed
resolutions (1) suspending the making of all contracts
heretofore ordered; (2) rescinding the resolution levying an assessment of $3 per share on the stock; (3)
levying a new assessment of $1 per share payable May
1st then next. April 1st the Board met again but
transacted no business. April 3rd a new election of
directors was ordered to be held on the fourth Monday
(25th) of May following. The election was held as
ordered and resulted in the election of Peter A. Jay,
Stephen Van Rensselaer, John Jacob Astor, Nicholas
Fish, Herman Le Roy, David S. Jones, George W.
Featherstonhaugh, James Renwick and John I. De
Graff. The new members were Renwick and DeGraff,
succeeding Duane and Catlin, retired.

At the first meeting of the new Board on July 14th,
Van Rensselaer was re-elected president, Nicholas Fish,
vice president, and James Renwick, secretary. Only
Fish, Astor, Le Roy, Jones and Jay were present at this
meeting. One week later, July 21st, another meeting
was held, the same five being the only ones present, and
the minutes show the following as the first business
transacted.

On motion of Mr. Astor—

Whereas G. W. Featherstonhaugh, Esq., who at the late election was chosen a director of this incorporation has alone of all
the directors resident in New York or its vicinity not taken his
seat at the Board: Resolved that the Secretary be directed to
address him a letter enquiring whether it be his intention to
serve as a director or not.

At this meeting Lynde Catlin was again elected
treasurer.

August 1st, Featherstonhaugh in a brief communication dated July 31st, resigned his position as director and the resignation was accepted. Churchill C. Cambreling was two days later elected to the vacancy. At a meeting held November 29, 1829, a letter was received from Featherstonhaugh tendering his stock to the Company. He then owned 601 shares, just one share more than one fifth of the entire capital stock. His proposition was accepted, he discharging all the claims he had against the Company. Thus ended all connection of the originator and sole promoter of the project with the Company for which he had worked so long and faithfully. What was the reason? Brief description has been given of his family and his remarkable estate at Duanesburgh. It now must be added that in March, 1825, he lost his two daughters by death within a few days of each other. As already noted, his wife died in June, 1828, shortly after their return from Europe. In June, 1829, just after his last election as director, his noble mansion at Duanesburgh and all its contents were destroyed by fire. This succession of misfortunes seems to have temporarily broken his spirit for he determined to abandon what he termed "the tomb of all his hopes" and in December following he removed to Philadelphia and began a new career at the age of fifty. The man was so remarkable and the new career so distinguished that they deserve further notice. As the originator of one of the first steam railroads in America, his name should not be forgotten.

Fortunately the withdrawal of Featherstonhaugh did not result in a disruption of the Company, although for some months indecision and vacillation seem to have been in the saddle. Apparently there was no master spirit to guide the uncharted course but in the end faith in the importance and great desirability of the work in view triumphed.

July 21, 1829, the engineer was directed to prepare forthwith "working draughts of the stationary and locomotive engines, of the machinery of the inclined planes, of the wagons for goods and passengers proposed to be used upon the most approved plans now used in England." August 3rd, Messrs. Renwick, Cambreling and DeGraff were appointed a committee to examine and report a proper location for the railroad "and in general to report to the Board such plans and measures as may be necessary to carry the objects of the incorporation into effect." All this ground had been gone over before, but in the entire absence of experience in such work, we may assume that a review of the subject for their better information was the purpose of the Board rather than dissatisfaction with conclusions previously reached. September 22nd the Board received from the engineer the plans and drawings called for by the resolution of July 21st. The engineer also submitted a letter containing a comparison of the various proposed routes. At this meeting the committee appointed August 3rd submitted a report which was referred to a meeting of the stockholders called for September 25th.

A meeting of the stockholders was held at the City Hotel in New York the 25th of September at which 15 were present. There were then about 40 stockholders. The action taken was significant of the feeling prevailing. The report of the committee was read and the Committee was requested to make contracts for the ground situated at the two extremities of the engineer's line "*subject to the contingency of the Railway being carried into effect.*" On motion of John Jacob Astor, further proceedings in relation to the report were sus-

pended until a future meeting. The meeting then adjourned to meet again at the call of the committee.

The action of this meeting and of the directors at this time affords clear indication of indecision whether or not to go on with the enterprise. Mr. Jay resigned as director in September; Mr. Jones in November. Another stockholders' meeting was held November 7th at which but 10 were present. The atmosphere had cleared decidedly as shown by the resolution adopted: "Resolved, unanimously, that the Board of Directors be requested to take decisive measures to carry the objects of this incorporation into effect." The report of the committee was also accepted and approved. Unfortunately no record of this decisive report can be found.

In the minutes of a meeting of the directors held January 8, 1830, appears the following, "A letter from P. Fleming, late engineer of the Company, was laid before the Board." How and when his employment was terminated is not known.

His successor was John B. Jervis, who later became known as one of the leading engineers of the country. The first mention of him in the records of the Company is an entry in the minutes of February 17, 1830, showing the receipt of a letter from him. That day a committee was appointed with power to choose and engage a principal engineer of the Company. At the meeting of March 30, 1830, the committee reported they had employed Mr. Jervis on condition that he should devote one half his time to the service of the Company, in alternate months beginning on the 1st day of May then next and serving in May, July, September, November, January and March; that he should organize and distribute the work in such a way that no delay should arise in the execution in consequence of his absence; that his compensation should be two thousand dollars for the six months in the year ending May 31st, 1831, in full of salary and personal expenses while upon the line and while passing thither and thence from and to the other work in which he is engaged. A letter from Mr. Jervis was read at this meeting "pointing out the mode of carrying into effect the objects of the incorporation."

A resolute attempt to start work was made at this meeting by giving the chief engineer power to form a corps of resident engineers and necessary assistants and by ordering an assessment of $3 per share on the capital stock payable at the Merchants' Bank in New York the 4th of the following May. April 30th, the chief engineer was authorized to employ a surveyor to mark out and make plans of the grounds necessary to be occupied by the Company. May 22nd C. C. Cambreling was appointed the commissioner and a committee appointed to confer with the commissioner "with powers to assign his duty and fix the terms of his engagement." July 25th the committee reported they had conferred with him and "have assigned to him the duties of locating the road agreeably to the survey and map of Mr. Jervis, the engineer; to make agreements and contracts for the purchase of or obtaining the land which will be required for the road, to procure deeds and titles for the same, to advertise for and enter into contracts for grading and forming the Road and for the materials for the same, to make arrangements with the Corporation of the City of Albany to lay out a street to facilitate the construction of a lateral road to a central part of the City for transporting passengers, to exercise a general superintendence of the concerns of the Company and to recommend to the Board such measures as may promote the interest of the Company and expedite the accomplishment of their object."

Cambreling was a representative in Congress and for the performance of the aforesaid duties up to the meeting of Congress he was to receive $2000. "The Committee is impressed with the belief [says the report] that all the important agreements, contracts and arrangements may be completed within that time," which clearly shows how little good business men like Astor, Catlin and Renwick knew about the problems involved in building even sixteen miles of railroad.

From this time until the commencement of operation on the road the action of the Board of Directors consisted chiefly in levying assessments upon the capital stock, the last one completing full payment being ordered June 13th, 1831, and made payable September 1st following. There were in all fifteen assessments for the original capital stock of $300,000.

The practical work of supervising and constructing the road was carried on for the directors by C. C. Cambreling under the supervision of the general or executive committee composed of Astor, Catlin and Renwick. These committeemen being residents of New York, it may perhaps be assumed that they did not trouble themselves over details and that the commissioner was the real guiding and deciding power.

The precise date of breaking ground for construction is not as certain as the cost of the entertainment of the guests which latter is recorded in the accounts of the Commissioner as $99.26. The date is stated in the Albany *Argus* about a year later as being July 27th, 1830. Bloodgood, Secretary of the Albany Institute, in his elaborate account of the road written in September, 1831, says it was August 12th. Joel Munsell in an account of the "origin, progress and vicissitudes" of the road prepared in 1875 and read before the Albany Institute April 20, 1875, says it was July 29th but cites no authority for that date. It being a matter of no consequence which is correct no attempt has been made to determine which is right. It is mentioned here in detail merely to show the difficulty always attending the effort to fix historical dates by the memory of individuals unaided by contemporary written data. Thus far the effort made has been to present a faithful picture, so far as existing data will permit, of the origin of the experiment and the troubles which hindered and delayed for four years the commencement of construction. It will be better to consider the road itself, its location and construction in another place. It is well, however, at this point in a general way to relate some interesting and instructive matters which have not been directly touched as yet.

This was not a local enterprise in the sense of being undertaken and pushed by local men. Albany and Schenectady men took but little part. Other than Featherstonhaugh of Duanesburgh, and perhaps one or two from Schenectady, the active influential stockholders were mostly residents of New York City or its vicinity. The original subscribers to the 3,000 shares of capital stock were 33 in number, but only 12 took 100 shares or more and those 12 were the holders of 2321 of the 3000 shares. They did not all hold on until the road was completed and in operation. The following list gives their names, the first column the number of shares originally subscribed for by each, the second column the number of shares held of record by each September 15, 1831.

	Original Shares	Shares Held Sept. 15, 1831
George William Featherstonhaugh	621	
John Jacob Astor	500	180
Nicholas Fish	200	150

	Original Shares	Shares Held Sept. 15, 1831
Andrew Edmeston..............	200	
Daniel C. Verplanck...........	100	
Samuel Jones.................	100	
Lynde Catlin.................	100	140
Peter A. Jay.................	100	30
Stephen Van Rensselaer........	100	24
Peter Remsen................	100	
George Griswold..............	100	20
David S. Jones...............	100	125
	2,321	669

The first transfer of stock was made June 28, 1828. The total number of different stockholders down to September 15, 1831, was 142. The total number September 15, 1831, was 61. Transfers were very numerous after June 28, 1828, the total number down to September 15, 1831, being 657, the total number of shares transferred 11,155. Details are as follows:

	No. of transfers	No. of shares transferred
1828........................	8	270
1829........................	8	412
1830........................	168	3,556
1831, to Sept. 15.............	473	6,917
	657	11,155

September 7, 1831, additional stock to the amount of $200,000 was authorized and between September 15 and November 18, transfers were as follows:

	No. of transfers	No. of shares transferred
Old stock......................	118	2,740
New stock	157	2,752
	275	5,492

As early as October 1, 1830, two months after construction was commenced, stock began to be handled on the New York Stock and Exchange Board, the asking price being 110. October 27 as high as 123 was bid and December 17, the bid was 129½, while 131½ was asked. November 3, 70 shares were sold at 124 and December 17, 5 shares were sold at 129¾. The price crept up through the 30's during the remainder of the month until December 31, 20 shares sold at 140. January, 1831, the price dropped back into the 30's, the last sale that month being of 30 shares on the 25th at 139. February 28, 1831, 25 shares were sold at 143 and on March 10, 134 shares at 163½, March 17, 20 shares at 171¼. During June and July sales were made at 174 and in August the peak price was 179, and September 14, 196¾ was reached for 6 shares. The determination of the Board of Directors made September 7, as soon as known, brought the price down to 145 and to 148 the last days of that month.

To grasp the significance of the foregoing figures of prices and transfers, it should be kept in mind that construction did not begin until July, 1830, and operation until August 10, 1831, and that the total number of shares was but 3000.

Before the commencement of operation, the financial results thereof could only be conjectured and accordingly transfers and prices could have been only upon a purely speculative basis. They show, however, the anticipations which were entertained as soon as construction was commenced. After August 10, a more substantial basis of calculation obtained since it was possible to ascertain the demand for service, the amount of service rendered, the rates charged, the receipts and expenditures. Not that the Company published in detail any of these things, for it did not so far as can be ascertained, but approximate estimates could readily be made. True, such estimates in many cases are purely grotesque. Thus the Albany *Daily Advertiser* of August 19, ten days after operation commenced indulged itself and the public with the following:

The travel amounts to 3 and 4 hundred persons a day and is as yet only commenced. The income of this company from present appearances will be about $140,000 a year for passengers only and the stock instead of being worth 70 per cent advance is worth 6 or 7 hundred per cent.

The effect of such publications as this may well be traced in the rush for incorporations of railroads in the winter of 1832 to which consideration will be given later. The actual results of operation during 1831 as they appear on the books of the Company are of significance and should now be considered.

Summary of Net Earnings

Of the Mohawk and Hudson Railroad Company
from August 10 to December 31, 1831

Date	Receipts from Passengers and Baggage	Expenses Operating Road	Net Earnings Deposited in Bank	Operating Ratio
1831	$	$	$	%
Aug. 10 to Sept. 30	6,610.58	2,442,20	4,168.38	36.9
Oct. 1 to 31	4,902.50	1,624.53	3,277.97	33.8
Nov. 1 to 30	3,869.87	2,024.08	1,845.79	52.3
Dec. 1 to 31	936.84	1,386.32	def. 449.48	150.0
Total	$16,319.79	$7,477.13	$8,842.66	45.8

does it seem possible to ascertain whether it was ever surveyed. There were also other considerations than grades which certainly to some extent had weight in fixing the location.

After many and very natural changes of view, the route recommended by John B. Jervis was finally adopted, not by the Board of Directors, for their minutes do not disclose any decisive action with reference thereto on their part. The minutes of April 30, 1830, contain the following:

> Mr. Jervis principal engineer of the company attended and received the instructions of the Board. On motion Resolved, that the principal engineer be authorized to employ a surveyor to mark out and make plans of the grounds necessary to be occupied by the company.

On May 22, Messrs. Astor, Catlin and Renwick were appointed a standing committee to carry into effect the objects of the incorporation. It would seem that Jervis mapped out the location and this committee approved it. This location was required by the charter to commence at the Hudson river at any point within the bounds of the city of Albany or within half a mile north of the same and extend to any point in the city of Schenectady or within half a mile west of the same.

The problem was solved by locating the easterly end of the road on the bank of the Hudson at Gansevoort street on the south line of the city of Albany, thence along the center of Gansevoort street and private lands to South Pearl street, thence on a tangent in a northwesterly direction to Dove street, as then laid out; thence after curving to the north on a tangent to Ontario street, thence curving a trifle southerly to an intersection with Lydius street, now Madison avenue, and the Western Turnpike, now Western avenue, just northerly of their crossing, passing on this course about 600 feet southerly of the Albany penitentiary as it now stands, thence generally in a northwesterly direction to the city of Schenectady. The location near and in that city can not be described understandingly without the aid of a map. Generally speaking, it was northeasterly of the existing right of way.

The total length of the main line as originally constructed was 15.875 miles, ending at Mill Creek in Schenectady near the old Erie canal. Afterwards the inclined planes at each end were discontinued as will be shown later and new routes adopted at both ends, that at the Albany end passing down the valley of Patroon's Creek, its present location, and at the Schenectady end following the present location. The length of the original line disused at Schenectady was 2.053 miles; at Albany 5.55 miles, making a total of 7.60 miles, and leaving 8.275 miles still in use for railroad right of way.

The route having been surveyed and staked out was divided into thirty sections for grading, which would make an average length of about one-half mile. The actual length of each is not known. The material to be handled was largely sand with some clay. Prices paid were for excavation of sand, seven cents per cubic yard; for clay nine cents; for embankment of sand, eight cents, of clay, eleven cents. What is known as the two way method of estimating quantities was used, that is, quantities taken from a cut and placed in an embankment were given a unit price for excavation and then for placing in the embankment. No record has survived showing the yardage handled.

Ground was broken at Schenectady with some ceremony, and of course, with a liberal supply of that speechmaking which seems indispensable to all public works.   There were six principal embankments between the two inclined planes.   The greatest height of embankments was 44 feet and greatest depth of cut 47 feet.

The slopes of both cuts and embankments were sodded, a process then termed rampering.   There seems to have been paid for rampering up to June 30, 1832, $8,435.56.   Whether this work was done to preserve the slopes from wasting, or to beautify the appearance of the way, according to the English practice, does not appear.   If the latter, the practice seems soon to have disappeared almost wholly from railroad construction.

The First Track

The early idea of the railroad was to build a "permanent" superstructure or one as nearly permanent as possible.   To make an expected enduring track of rigid supports in the road bed, therefore, pits two feet square and spaced three feet apart, center to center, were excavated under each line of rails.   In each pit about nine cubic feet of broken stone were placed and rammed down to form a solid mass.   This stone, which was principally granwacke, was broken into pieces that would pass through a ring two inches in diameter and cost $2.00 per cubic yard.   With this as a foundation, stone blocks were set thereon, each stone block was sixteen inches high, with a top surface of fifteen inches by sixteen inches.   These stone blocks were quarried either on the Erie Canal about twelve miles from Schenectady or at Sing Sing on the Hudson River and cost 45 cents each.   The blocks were brought to their level by a heavy rammer, "handled by four stout men," as Mr. Jervis expressed it.   On the top of the surface of each block two holes were drilled into which small plugs

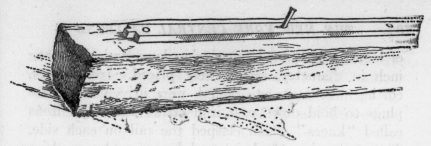

WOOD RAIL AND IRON STRAP. FROM PHOTOGRAPH.

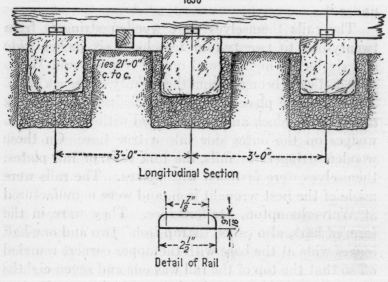

TRACK WITH RIGID SUPPORTS
Constructed by John B. Jervis for
MOHAWK & HUDSON R.R.
1830

Ties 21'-0"
c. to c.

3'-0"   3'-0"

Longitudinal Section

$1\frac{7}{8}$"

$\frac{9}{16}$"

$2\frac{1}{2}$"

Detail of Rail

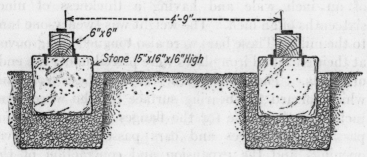

4'-9"

6"x6"

Stone 15"x16"x16"High

Transverse Section

of locust wood about four inches long, and about one
inch in diameter were loosely placed. Iron spikes,
costing nine cents per pound, were driven into these
plugs to hold down cast iron chairs and angle irons
called "knees" which clasped the rail on each side.
The proportion of chairs and knees used was three
knees to each chair. These chairs, sometimes called
"double chairs" were long enough to pass beneath the
rail, while the cast iron knees sometimes called single
chairs, were on each side of the rail but did not pass
under it.

The rails themselves were wooden stringers from
twenty-one to twenty-four feet long, six inches wide
and six inches high, hewed out of Norway and White
Pine and were brought from the vicinity of Seneca Lake.
The rails were placed on the iron chairs longitudinally
on the stone block and were wedged with small wooden
wedges on the outer side into a true line. On these
wooden stringers or rails, the iron rails, or rail plates,
themselves were fastened with spikes. The rails were
made of the best wrought iron, and were manufactured
at Wolverhampton, Staffordshire. They were in the
form of bars, also called "strap iron" two and one-half
inches wide at the base with the upper corners rounded
off so that the top of the rail was one and seven-eighths
of an inch wide and having a thickness of nine-
sixteenths of an inch. The weight was twenty-one tons
to the mile. These bars were also tongued and grooved
at their ends and iron plates were placed under the ends
or joints. The iron spikes securing these iron rails
which formed the bearing surface for the wheel con-
tacts and the guide for the flanges of the wheels for
passing locomotives and cars passed through oval
openings and the expansion and contraction of the
metal were thus provided in these openings and by

the tongues and grooves at the rail ends where they formed the rail joints.

At a distance of twenty-one feet, tie pieces or "cross sleepers" were laid down as a further security to bind the rails together and to keep them parallel. These cross sleepers or ties were rounded timber seven inches in diameter and eight feet long, or when split were of size to equal the same quantity of timber, and cost twenty cents each. On embankments the stone blocks were not at first laid, in order to give time for the fill to settle. At these places a timber foundation was adopted by laying down a longitudinal sill timber under the wooden rail stringer upon which cross sleepers were laid.

Broken stone was also laid down between and at the sides of the rail and this was again covered with earth so that practically the whole of the wood work of the track was covered with broken stone and earth.

As thus constructed the iron rail merely formed the bearing surface and guide for the wheels and the wooden stringers as a separate piece acted as a girder and supplied the strength for carrying the weight of the rolling stock and its load.

The track was also provided with a path between the rails for horses, in case it was necessary to use them in place of a locomotive on rainy days, or when the locomotive boilers would not make sufficient steam, which at first was a frequent occurrence.

Experience proved that this form of construction was too rigid and inelastic as well as too expensive, and when Mr. Jervis was engaged in 1832 in constructing another road—the Saratoga and Schenectady Railroad —he discarded the type of stone blocks set upon broken stone supporting stringers, and introduced the use of cross ties upon which the stringers were placed to support the small strap iron rails. The road bed was ballasted with sand upon which the cross ties rested. The superstructure thus constructed was flexible and the road bed was elastic. This is the principle now followed in the construction of all steam railroads throughout the country.

The character of the first and rigid construction of the Mohawk and Hudson Railroad is well illustrated in the accompanying drawing.

The thin strap rail, all of which for some years was imported from England or Wales, continued to be used although it proved highly unsatisfactory. Although the rail joints were strengthened by the additional plate placed under the rail ends, it was found that the iron rail wore faster at these points than at others and had the dangerous tendency of separating from the wooden stringers and curling up under the impact of the rolling wheels of locomotives and cars. When so separated from its support and curling backward upon itself, the loosened rail occasionally penetrated the floor of a car passing over it, and it is said many accidents or narrow escapes were experienced by passengers from these "snake heads" as the rail was called when it came through the floor of a car.

The Use of Horse Power

It probably has been generally supposed that the motive power on the Mohawk and Hudson was from its opening, steam. On the contrary, the charter contained a provision permitting the use of animal power as well as steam. The road was constructed with a broken stone pathway between the rails to permit the use of horses. On the second exhibition excursion, Sept. 24, 1831, there were two trains, one of three coaches drawn by the steam locomotive, DeWitt Clinton,

another of seven coaches, each drawn by a single horse.
These trains ran only from Western Avenue in Albany
to the head of the inclined plane at Schenectady, a
distance of about twelve miles. The trip was performed by the locomotive in forty-six minutes and by
the cars drawn by horses in seventy-five minutes. The
return trip, being generally a down grade, was performed by the locomotive in thirty-eight minutes and
by the horses in sixty-eight minutes. A careful and
detailed account of the road published by S. DeWitt
Bloodgood of Albany, Nov. 8, 1831, says: "Passengers
are carried upon this road in coaches drawn by horses
and by locomotive engines whose powers are not yet
conclusively tested."

The road was operated from Aug. 10, 1831, to
Dec. 31, 1831, when operation was suspended until
April 19, 1832. The following is an analysis of the
operating expenses during this period made up from the
books of the company.

	Horse Power	All Other Expense	Total
Aug. and Sept............	$2,100.86	$341.34	$2,442.20
Oct.....................	942.70	681.83	1,624.53
Nov....................	840.95	1,183.13	2,024.08
Dec....................	875.73	510.59	1,386.32
Total.................	$4,760.24	$2,716.89	$7,477.13

In 1840 and certain succeeding years before the
elimination of the inclined planes, the cost of horse
power used in operation was as follows:

1840............	$6,033.75	1842............	$3,992.95
1841............	6,904.07	1843............	3,440.72

In the inventory of January, 1840, the Superintendent reports 34 horses of different prices valued at $2,840. In that of January 1, 1833, appears a list of 28 horses, showing their names and value, the most valuable being Alexander, $140, while Bill stood lowest at $65, the average of all being $95. In 1839 locomotive steam power cost $5,727.62, whereas the cost of horse power was $10,095.93. In 1838 horse power cost $9,973.72, locomotive steam power $17,769.57. In a superintendent's report on the expenses of 1838, the following details concerning horse power appear:

Horse power for branch road, including drivers'
    wages, etc.................................... $7,203.26
Horse power from junction to head W. I. plane..... 1,108.16
Horse power foot W. I. plane to Schenectady...... 1,662.30

Total...................................... $9,973.72

This with other data clearly indicates that horse power alone was used on the State street branch, at the west end in Schenectady from the foot of the inclined plane, and to some extent in transportation of passengers between the inclined planes on the main line.

There were stables on Maiden Lane at the junction of the State street branch and in Schenectady. After the discontinuance of the State street branch the use of horse power was greatly reduced and after the present line came into use on the abolition of the inclined planes it was wholly abandoned.

EARLY LOCOMOTIVE ENGINES

The great distinctive feature of a railroad is its motive power. As already pointed out, railroad tracks had existed in England for a considerable number of

years before 1825, but the motive power used was
animal power. Yet the railroad era is universally
recognized as beginning in 1825, upon the Stockton &
Darlington, with the first use of steam locomotive
power. The locomotive is the heart of the road.
Upon its power and speed depend the efficiency and
extent of the transportation afforded. Nothing in the
early history of steam railroads can be of greater interest
than the characteristics of the first locomotives and we
are warranted in going into as great detail as our data
will justify in drawing a picture which will enable one
to see them exactly as they were and to know their
powers and limitations.

During the first ten years of its existence, the
Mohawk and Hudson purchased and used to a greater
or less extent, five steam locomotives each of which
received a name by means of which its history can be
traced with some detail. These were the DeWitt
Clinton, John Bull, Experiment, Mohawk and Hudson.

The earliest on the road was the DeWitt Clinton.
It was constructed in the spring and early summer of
1831, upon the order of John B. Jervis, the engineer,
at the West Point Foundry, situate at the foot of Beach
street, New York City. According to a very careful
and minute account of the road prepared for *Silliman's
Journal* of October, 1831, the plans were drawn by a
Mr. Hall of whom no further trace can be found. The
engine was the third constructed by the West Point
Foundry, the two former having been built for a South
Carolina railroad. It was shipped by water to Albany,
June 25, in charge of David Matthew, who had been
engaged in its construction and was its first engineer.
He at once set it up and commenced experimenting with
its operating efficiency. Its weight was 6,758½ pounds,
length 11 feet 6 inches, mounted on four wheels of 4 feet

6 inches diameter. It had two cylinders, one on each side of the engine at the rear end of the boiler, of 5½ inches diameter and 16 inches stroke, connected with the axle of the front wheels, the piston and connection being on the inner side of the wheels. It was rated at 10 horse power or over. The wheels were all drivers, power being applied to the axle of the front pair and the two pairs joined by outside connecting rods. The boiler was tubular with a drop furnace, having two fire doors, one above the other, and was supplied with copper tubes 2½ inches in diameter and about 6 feet long. The cylinders were on an incline and the pumps worked vertically by bell crank. The tender was mounted on smaller wheels than the engine and carried a square box with an awning upon it, constructed with an iron tank for water and a place for fuel.

The general appearance and details of this locomotive and tender are well represented in the cut of a silhouette made of its appearance August 9, 1831, by William H. Brown, a skillful artist in that kind of work, who took part in the excursion of that day. It is also faithfully reproduced in most details in the replica constructed in 1893 by the New York Central and Hudson River Railroad Company for the World's Exposition of that year at Chicago, and now on exhibition in the gallery of the concourse of the Grand Central Terminal in New York City.

Experiments with this locomotive developed some troubles. The steam supply pipe leading to the cylinders probably terminated in the upper part of the boiler, for the surging of the water in the boiler was so great that it passed over into the cylinders. This was remedied by building a high steam chamber within the dome shown in the cut over the top of the boiler and the end of the supply pipe was placed toward the top of this

REPRODUCTION OF BROWN'S SILHOUETTE OF DEWITT CLINTON TRAIN.

chamber.   The draft was bad, and the chimney, as the smokestack was then called, itself was too large.   An effort was made to use anthracite, but it was found to pack and required a blast.   An artificial blast was given and then the heat seemed too great in one place and too little in others and melted the grates.   Resort was then had to wood and that was the fuel used on the exhibition excursion of August 9.

What it did not have in the way of the very simplest appliances which were soon found to be indispensable on locomotives, is somewhat remarkable.   There was no headlight, no bell, no whistle, no spark arrester in the stack, no cab.   The engineer stood on a small platform at the rear of the boiler without protection from the sun or weather, nor was there any covering or protection for any of the levers or machinery.   The fuel had to be passed by the fireman into the furnace over this small platform on which the engineer stood, having no seat so far as can be learned, and how the two could do their work in the narrow space is something of a mystery.

It is said its average speed, drawing three loaded cars of about eight tons weight, was 15 miles an hour, but that it frequently accomplished 30 miles an hour with the same load.   It was used only between Western avenue in Albany and the head of the inclined plane at Schenectady, a distance of but little over 12 miles.   It was first used in the carriage of passengers, August 9, on which day an exhibition excursion was given.   An interesting account of this excursion is given by Mr. Brown, the silhouette artist, in his book, *First Locomotives in America,* he being one of the passengers.

On this first excursion, on the 9th day of August, 1831, as no such officer as a conductor had been required upon the road, where hitherto no connected train of cars had been run, but where each driver officiated as collector of fares, Mr. John T. Clark, as the first passenger railroad conductor in the North, stepping from platform to platform outside the cars, collected the tickets which had been sold at hotels and other places through the city. When he finished his tour, he mounted upon the tender attached to the engine, and, sitting upon the little buggy-seat, as represented in our sketch, he gave the signal with a tin horn, and the train started on its way. But how shall we describe that start, my readers? It was not that quiet, imperceptible motion which characterizes the first impulsive movements of the passenger engines of the present day. Not so. There came a sudden jerk, that bounded the sitters from their places, to the great detriment of their high-top fashionable beavers, from the close proximity to the roofs of the cars. This first jerk being over, the engine proceeded on its route with considerable velocity for those times, when compared with stage-coaches, until it arrived at a water-station, when it suddenly brought up with jerk No. 2, to the further amusement of some of the excursionists. Mr. Clark retained his elevated seat, thanking his stars for its close proximity to the tall smokepipe of the machine, in allowing the smoke and sparks to pass over his head. At the water-station a short stop was made, and a successful experiment tried, to remedy the unpleasant jerks. A plan was soon hit upon and put into execution. The three links in the couplings of the cars were stretched to their utmost tension, a rail, from a fence in the neighborhood, was placed between each pair of cars and made fast by means of the packing-yarn for the cylinders, a bountiful supply being on hand (as the present brass-ring substitute had not then been invented). This arrangement improved the order of things, and it was found to answer the purpose, when the signal was again given, and the engine started.

In a short time the engine (after frightening the horses attached to all sorts of vehicles filled with the people from the surrounding country, or congregated all along at every available position near the road, to get a view of the singular-looking machine and its long train of cars; after causing thus innumerable capsizes and smash-ups of the vehicles and the tumbling of the spectators in every direction to the right and left) arrived at the head of the inclined plane at Schenectady, amid the cheers and welcomes of thousands, assembled to witness the arrival of the iron horse and its living freight.

After some time passed in the ancient city of Schenectady, and ample refreshments had been afforded, the word was given by conductor Clark to prepare for the return. The excursionists resumed their seats, and in due time, without any accident or delay, the train arrived at the point from which it had first started, the head of the inclined plane at Albany.

The Clinton was used again September 24 on another exhibition excursion, but how much more in the operating period ending December 31, we have no means of knowing. Something didn't work right, for April 14, 1832, before operation was resumed May 1, there was paid the West Point Foundry Association $700 "for 2 pair wheels of wood with iron tires and eccentrics for Locomotive Engine DeWitt Clinton per Agreement." In 1832 it was undoubtedly used either with or without the new wheels but again with unsatisfactory results, for October 22 its condition was such as to bring it to the attention of the Board of Directors who thereupon resolved, "That the engineer by and with the advice and consent of the Directors of this Company residing in Albany be authorized and requested to have the Locomotive Engines put in complete order and if necessary to procure a new boiler for the DeWitt Clinton and to improve the John Bull by the addition of wheels or otherwise." This action clearly indicated that the Clinton was not in order and to put it so might require a new boiler. At that time and subsequently all repairs and alterations to the locomotives were debited to them and credited to the shop doing the work, but no charge appears on the books in 1832 for any repairs to or new boiler for the Clinton. January 1, 1833, the locomotive engines were appraised and the value of the engine was fixed at $1500 and of the tender at $300, being $1800 for both. Their original cost cannot be ascertained owing to lack of detail in a large account with the West Point Foundry Association, covering them and other machinery, but it is certain that it was very much greater than the appraised value. June 4, 1833, it was charged with $1.31 "work by sundry persons" during May and "Wood Shop" was credited with that amount. November 1, 1833, the Board of Directors authorized the superintendent to dispose of the locomotive engine DeWitt Clinton. Nothing further appears either of debit or credit until April 20, 1835, when the DeWitt Clinton is credited with $400 for parts sold "as per day book." The day book entry is well worth transcribing in full for it discloses the fate of this locomotive beyond any question.

Sold to F. J. & G. W. Eddy the following parts of the
   Locomotive De Witt Clinton—The Boiler, Smoke
   —Steam & Exhaust pipes, two working pumps, one
   hand pump, one shackle bar shoe and eccentric, one
   six in. cylinder and piston, for which rec^d. from
   them check in part $300.00
Their Note for Balance, dated 10 April 1835, payable
   6 months from date at the New York State Bank
   with Interest 100.00

April 30 the Clinton is charged with $3.00 "work this month" and "Machine Shop" is credited with the same. Obviously this work was taking down the Clinton. Messrs. Eddy were doubtless needing a stationary engine and bought one cylinder of the locomotive and the boiler and stack, leaving the wheels, one cylinder and other parts on hand.

Two remaining book entries bring us to the end.

September 13, 1836, a year and a half later, the day

DEWITT CLINTON TRAIN AND MODERN LOCOMOTIVE.

book says "Received Cash of Mr. Dwelley for one Cylinder and seventeen pieces castings from **L. E. Dewitt Clinton**, $65," and the Clinton is credited with the same. The same year, October 29, the day book says:

Ward & Ross

To Locomotive Engine De Witt Clinton for 1 Set common Eliptical tender Springs sold them this date.. $20.00

And this is the last we know of the Clinton except that in 1893 one of the old original wheels was found lying in some junk heap at the West Albany Shop[1] and is referred to on the drawing for wheels used in constructing the replica. The record shows clearly that its active use on the road was confined to 1831 and 1832 and that it was dismantled, and $485 realized from the sale of the parts named. For practical use it proved wanting; it was too light to handle loads of adequate size; its wheel rigidity was injurious on curves to either itself or the track or both; it was so constructed as to make impracticable the remedying of its defects. But these defects were of service in leading to improvements in newer engines and it will ever be remembered as the first locomotive engine used on the New York Central system.

The second locomotive engine bought by the Mohawk and Hudson was the John Bull, manufactured by Robert Stephenson & Company at Newcastle on the Tyne in England from their own design and presumably was of a pattern similar to those that firm was putting up for the Liverpool and Manchester Railway. It was delivered in New York late in August, 1831, and

[1] Statement of A. Buchanan, Jr., one of the builders of the replica, to the writer.

was at once transshipped to Albany where it was set
up and put upon trial. Its cost at Albany was as
follows:

Cost and charges f.o.b. ship............	$3,763.32	
Custom house bonds for duty..........	1,017.25	
Freight from Liverpool to N. Y........	88.67	
Weighing............................	12.00	
Freight N. Y. to Albany..............	30.00	$4,911.24

Shortly after its arrival at Albany four new wheels
and two axles with eccentrics were ordered from the
manufacturer at the following cost:

Cost and charges....................	$733.49	
Custom house bonds for duty..........	201.50	
Freight from Liverpool...............	4.77	939.76

There were also exchange and interest on the
remittance for cost and charges of both above items
amounting to   449.67

Thus making total expenses............ $6,300.67

John Hampson, the engineer who first handled this
locomotive on the road, in a letter written in 1849,
says it had four wheels of the size of those of the Clinton,
cylinder diameter 10 inches and stroke 14 inches. He
notes a marked contrast in the appearance of the two
engines. "The contrast between this engine and
the American one was great, the latter being a beautiful
light race horse looking machine, while the former
looked heavy and 'elephantic.' However, it proved to
be an excellent machine and the writer has (in 1831) on
the Mohawk and Hudson Railroad frequently driven it
with a train of cars behind it, 5 miles in 12 minutes."
He also says, "it was immediately christened John

Bull," and so it appears in the accounts of the Company. Some notices which have appeared apply this name erroneously to another locomotive. It was originally intended to call it Robert Fulton, but the popular fancy to name the English locomotive John Bull and later another of American manufacture (the Experiment) Brother Jonathan, prevailed.

Bloodgood in his careful and painstaking account of the road prepared in September, 1831, and finally put in pamphlet form the same year, says it was of

compact appearance and weighed 12,742 pounds, of which eight thousand seven hundred and forty-five rested on one pair of wheels. The frame is as long as that of the DeWitt Clinton (11 feet 6 inches) and is mounted on wooden wheels strongly bound with iron. There are two cylinders each of 10 inches diameter and 14 inches stroke, these are in the lower part of the chimney and are kept warm by the smoke and hot air. The pistons are connected with the axles of the hind wheels. The fire is made in a cylindrical furnace hanging down between them and the heat passes through eight rows of horizontal tubes of the length of the boiler. The steam pipe passes through the boiler just above the tubes and by a simple contrivance the steam passes to the top of the steam chamber and there enters a funnel mouthed tube connected with the steam pipes. Any bad effects of the surging of the water are of course prevented. The safety valve is of the ordinary kind. The eduction [exhaust] pipes are carried partly up the chimney and powerfully assist the draft. The engine has been tried and found to succeed admirably. As great weight renders its usefulness somewhat problematical upon a wooden rail, there are yet some accurate experiments to be made on these subjects.

He also quotes from an original description of the engine written by Robert Stephenson,

As to the power of the engine it would take twenty tons without difficulty but with twelve it would be much better. The small inclination of one to two hundred and twenty-five (about 23 feet to the mile) will affect the motion of the engine very little.

In a letter written in 1859, John T. Clark, who was a resident engineer in constructing the road, speaking of the John Bull concurs with Bloodgood that "The Spokes and rim or felloes were made of wood and secured by wrought iron flanged tires" and says, "It is, perhaps, needless to say that after this engine was put in use those parts of the wheels made of wood gave audible complaint of hard service. The 'shrieking' of the machine caused no little merriment among the knights of the whip, etc."

Whatever the reason the Company found it advisable to order new wheels and axles at once as already noted. The rigidity described in connection with the Clinton and hereinafter more fully detailed in connection with the Experiment caused Jervis to seek a remedy and, after the operation of that locomotive in 1832 disclosed that an adequate remedy had been found. In October, 1832, the directors as already noted authorized and requested the engineer "to improve the John Bull by the addition of wheels or otherwise." These improvements were made in the Company's shops in the winter and spring of 1833 at considerable expense and it would seem consisted among other things of placing in front a two wheel truck since the superintendent's day book for May 24, 1833, about the end of the work, contains the following, "M[achine] shop gives engine J. B. 1 set (32 in.) wheels, $60." The most minute items that went into these repairs are specified in this day book but there is no mention of other wheels.

In a letter to the editor of the *American Railroad Journal* dated July 18, 1833 (see issue of July 20, 1833), Mr. Jervis says,

I made a plan for a six wheel engine for the Mohawk and Hudson road, which was completed and in operation before I made the plan for the Saratoga engine. This engine proved satisfactory so far as regarded the principle of a six wheeled carriage and was an important pioneer for the second plan. The superior ease with which this engine moved, both for its own machinery, and the road led to the determination to alter the English engine on the Mohawk road so that it could be placed on a six wheeled carriage. As the engine was particularly arranged for four wheels, this could not be conveniently done in any other way than by communicating the power through the intervention of a bell crank which was very successfully done by Mr. Whitney. This engine is now working on six wheels and the ease and smoothness of her motion over that she had when on four wheels is very striking. The arrangement of six wheels does not admit of the wheels under the main frame being connected with those under the small frame: consequently we can obtain the adhesion of only one pair of wheels. This, however, is hardly of any importance when high speed is required.

He also says in this letter,

Thus the English engine belonging to the Mohawk and Hudson Company was such as to render the motion very unfavorable to the engine and severe on the road.

The John Bull was continued in active service until 1838, when it was entirely rebuilt except the boiler. The report of the superintendent, Asa Whitney, for the year 1838 contains the following with reference thereto:

The disbursements for "locomotive steam power" have been increased by an improvement made on the engine John Bull, the cost of which, $3,676.37, has been expended over and above what would be ordinarily required to keep each engine in repair. This engine was put on the road in the summer of 1831, on four wheels as imported and was altered during the winter following by putting it on six wheels; since then it has not had any material repairs until the last year when it was entirely rebuilt, except the boiler and is now the most efficient engine on the road: its effective power on an ascending grade has been increased full one third by the alteration.

The rebuilt John Bull remained in service for some years, but having nothing of the original construction left except the boiler, its historical interest ceased in 1838 and its further history need not be traced.

From every point of view the locomotive most entitled to lasting interest, placed upon the Mohawk and Hudson, was the Experiment, later known as Brother Jonathan. The interest in the DeWitt Clinton lies in the facts that it was American built and was the first used on the road. The latter fact gives it a dramatic appeal which should not be under-rated. It was, however, built after the general design then used in England having four drivers fixed to a rigid frame with no other supporting wheels. This method of constructing, lacking flexibility and power of adjustment to curves and inequalities in the track, resulted in preventing desired speed and in severity to track or engine, or both. This defect being disclosed by the tests made with both the Clinton and John Bull became at once the subject of great considera-tion by John B. Jervis, chief engineer, and Horatio Allen, then chief engineer of the Charleston and Ham-burg Railroad in South Carolina. Mr. Allen had been an assistant to Mr. Jervis on the Delaware and Hud-son canal and spent the summer of 1831 with him at Albany.

Mr. Jervis in an interesting letter published in *The Railroad Gazette* of December 23, 1871, p. 396, gives a carefully detailed account of the problem which engaged his attention. He says,

We were both very interested to ascertain some method by which the weight of an engine could be spread on more wheels, work more favorably and thus save our weak railroads from an action they could not safely support.

He frankly states what they both knew had been accomplished by practically coupling two cars or two engines on separate trucks together and says,

The question with Mr. A. and myself was not, Could two separate cars or trucks be so connected as to run on a railroad? but, Could this be done in a way that would secure the requisite speed for passengers?

The two engineers differed as to the solution of this problem. Mr. Allen had constructed an engine upon his plan, but that plan was never adopted in other engines. As to his own plan, Mr. Jervis says,

I was content to have a simple truck, all wheels alike as a support, guide and to give more steady motion. Would such an engine keep the track or rail at high speed? This was the question. The English called it "bogie" or scarecrow. The Eastern railroads would not use it and up to 1836 most of their engines were four wheeled, English made or on English pattern.

Again on the question as to the precise credit he was entitled to, Mr. Jervis says,

I have shown that neither Mr. Allen nor myself is entitled to the credit of originating the truck principle, or that principle by which two cars or trucks may be connected by a common frame and made one machine, either in cars or locomotives. All we are entitled to is our respective plans for adapting this principle to passenger speed which had not previously been done.

This problem was successfully solved by Mr. Jervis backed by the faith and money of the directors of the Mohawk and Hudson in the construction of the Experiment. This name first given it shows just what it was —a costly attempt to solve a serious problem, the success or failure of which could only be learned by actual trial. The name given the truck used in that solution, "bogie" indicates the feeling toward it until it proved equal to the emergency for which it was designed. Then it came into universal use in America. Mr. Jervis is entitled to credit for the idea adopted; the directors of the Mohawk and Hudson are entitled to credit for putting up the money to make the experiment possible. Begun with the belief that it could be constructed for $300,000, their road had cost them nearly double that sum, but the enthusiasm which followed the successful opening of the road had its

JERVIS' LOCOMOTIVE EXPERIMENT, BUILT 1832.

proper effect, and November 4, 1831, they authorized the executive committee, consisting of John Jacob Astor, Lynde Catlin and James Renwick, to purchase another locomotive engine "provided they consider it expedient to do so."

The executive committee deemed it expedient, Mr. Jervis prepared his plans for the new locomotive embodying the experiment he desired to make, contract for the work was let to the West Point Foundry Association, and in August, 1832, the completed machine was shipped to Albany in charge of David Matthew to set up and run it, the man who had performed the same duties for the DeWitt Clinton. As to results, we will first take Mr. Matthew's testimony.

I left New York in August, 1832, with the engine in charge to place on the road and run it. This was the first bogie engine or truck used under the front part ever built in this country or any other. . . . With this engine I have crossed the Mohawk and Hudson Railroad from plane to plane, fourteen miles in thirteen minutes, making one stop for water. I have tried her speed upon a level, straight line, and have made one mile in forty-five seconds by the watch. She was the fastest and steadiest engine I have ever run or seen and she worked with the greatest ease.

Thirty-seven years later, Mr. Jervis remarked with justifiable pride,

I regard it as the greatest point that an American engineer, in the face of English practice, should have devised a plan, which at the time was considered very radical, of introducing a truck to support the end of the frame and guide the motion of the engine and which after thirty-seven years of experience, is now adopted on every engine of nearly fifty thousand miles of railroad in America.

As already noted, the performance of the Experiment brought about the addition to the John Bull in the following spring of a leading truck with two wheels.

The general appearance of the Experiment is shown in the accompanying cut copied from a cut published in *The Railroad Gazette* for February 1, 1872, which was made from a drawing furnished by Mr. Jervis. The details we have regarding it are meager. Its cylinders were of 9½ inches diameter and 16 inches stroke. It was about 15 feet in length. The leading truck had four wheels, was placed under the front end of the boiler for support, attached by a strong pin and worked upon friction rollers so as easily to follow the curves of the road. The furnace was five feet long with three inch tubes and was made to burn anthracite. The two driving wheels were of five feet diameter. Except as noted, it does not seem to have included any improvements over the then prevailing construction. It was with its tender placed in the inventory of January 1, 1833, at $5028.60 which was undoubtedly its cost as may be inferred from but not precisely shown by the books of the Company.

It remained in service many years under the name, Brother Jonathan, but when retired is not known.

Early in 1833, the directors became greatly interested in the demand for transportation of freight, and anticipating a great increase in that demand and recognizing the necessity of increasing their motive power to meet it, on July 19th, authorized the President to procure from England two new locomotives. An order was placed for them with Robert Stephenson & Co. One, the Mohawk, arrived about May 1, 1834, the other, the Hudson, about June 1st. No description of these locomotives conveying any adequate idea of their construction has been found. The total cost of the two delivered at New York, including customs duties and freight seems to have been $12,545.22. Before being placed in service, both received considerable work of some character not disclosed by the records, amounting to nearly $1,100.

No other locomotives were purchased until after 1840. In the inventory of January, 1840, the four described, John Bull, Brother Jonathan, Mohawk and Hudson, were valued at $7,000 each and are the only ones inventoried.

Early Passenger Coaches

The first passenger coaches used in 1831 were merely the ordinary stage coaches slightly modified and placed upon a four wheel truck as may be seen from the engraving of the DeWitt Clinton train. These, of course, were at once found all wrong for use on a railroad and the Schenectady Whig, as quoted by the Buffalo *Journal* and *General Advertiser* of April 25, 1832, published the following:

Mohawk and Hudson Rail Road—The transportation of the materials for the other track of this road, for which the travel was suspended last fall, being completed, and the damage by the flood having been repaired, the road, we are informed, will be put in operation this day for the transportation of passengers. The company are now having constructed in this city, and intend putting on the road in a short time, a number of carriages of a new and very beautiful and convenient kind. These carriages are of a square form, fifteen feet long, with the separate compartments, and will contain 18 persons with ease. We consider them a great improvement upon the kind heretofore used, —as passengers, at the same time they have more room, will be protected from the smoke and coals of the engine. One of these carriages, bears the name of our new sister city, Utica— a compliment which the citizens of that place will undoubtedly return, by a frequent resort to its soft cushions and panelled walls, and thus find themselves in "Utica," though an hundred miles from home.

It is not known if these coaches were ever actually put upon the road, although it is probable they or something similar were put in use in 1832 or 1833.

STATE STREET BRANCH

The operation of the road had barely begun before the Company entered upon the construction of a branch from the crossing of Madison avenue with the Western Turnpike, now Western avenue, down that avenue and State street to a point near Capitol Square, and thence down State street to the Hudson river. This branch was completed prior to January 1, 1833; a passenger station and later a stable were erected at State and Eagle streets, the station being used as the exclusive passenger terminus of the road in Albany until September, 1841, when upon completion of an extension of the main line from Gansevoort street along Broadway to Ferry street, it was ordered that the State street branch be discontinued and taken up. Horse power was used exclusively upon the branch. The history of this branch is one of the interesting episodes of the road and deserves a somewhat detailed account as illustrative of one of the numerous problems attending a new enterprise wholly without precedent throwing light upon the proper course to pursue.

Prior to 1826, there was a turnpike road from Albany to Schenectady, owned and operated by the Albany and Schenectady Turnpike Company, chartered in 1802. This had never been a very lucrative enterprise and when the bill to incorporate the Mohawk and Hudson was introduced in 1826, the Turnpike Company made more or less opposition to the same and to protect its interests, the following language was made a part of the 11th section of the railroad charter:

And provided also, That nothing in this act shall authorize the said corporation to interfere with the rights granted in the act entitled "An act to incorporate the Albany and Schenectady turnpike."

The charter of the Mohawk and Hudson, however, contained the following in its first section:

and by that name, they and their successors shall be, and they are hereby vested with the sole and exclusive privilege of constructing, erecting, building, making and using a single or double railroad or ways, for the purposes aforesaid, from and to any points comprised within the limits above mentioned.

So long as the Mohawk and Hudson remained practically dormant, the turnpike company remained quiescent, but apparently watchful of its intended competitor. The activity manifested toward starting construction in 1829 roused it to action and in the winter of 1830, it procured the passage of Chapter 319 of the laws of 1830, passed April 20th, by which the Company were authorized to extend their road east to the Hudson river "and to convert about eighteen feet of their turnpike in the said county of Albany, into a rail-road or way: and to transport and carry persons and property upon the same, by the power and force of steam or animals or of any mechanical power, or of any combination of such power and force." Other provisions of the act made it lawful to "ask, demand and receive the same rates of toll for using the same" as the Mohawk and Hudson was authorized to demand and receive. This was directly in violation of the exclusive right conferred upon the Mohawk and Hudson within the limits prescribed for it, which limits included the turnpike in the county of Albany and raised a nice question of law upon which, of course, the two companies differed. This difference between the companies excited them both to activity and both sought relief from the legislature of 1831. The turnpike company sought to be given authority to extend their proposed railroad west to the Erie Canal in the city of Schenectady. The Mohawk and Hudson people not only opposed this, but also asked for an extension of their road along Washington street to a point near the capitol. Against this the turnpike company vigorously protested and a sharp warfare seems to have been conducted, resulting in a draw, since the legislature took no action on either request. The turnpike company seeing its financial ruin impending in 1831, voted both by its directors and stockholders to avail itself of the privileges conferred by the act of 1830, and to increase its capital stock $400,000 for that purpose. September 21st it issued a circular to its stockholders explaining the details of the plan and calling upon them to elect whether they would take the additional shares of stock to which they were entitled. The directors also levied an assessment of $20 on each share payable on or before the 1st day of November. This vigorous action aroused the attention of the railroad company and Commissioner Cambreling addressed a letter to the turnpike people requesting a conference; the latter responded; the correspondence was laid before the railroad board and October 17th it appointed a committee of three to confer with a committee of the turnpike company and also adopted the following:

Resolved, That such Committee be authorized to propose to construct a branch railway for the accommodation of the citizens of Albany to run along the Western turnpike to Capitol Square and to the river should this Company so determine. To increase the Capital of this Company One Hundred Thousand Dollars which shall be subscribed by the stockholders of the Albany and Schenectady Turnpike Company. To appoint three Directors among the citizens of Albany, one of whom shall be the Mayor. And to unite with the Turnpike Company in an application to the Legislature for an Act authorizing these measures.

Catlin, Cambreling and DeGraff were appointed the committee and acting promptly came back four days later with a report of a conference and a written proposition from the turnpike people. October 24th answer was made to this proposition and very shortly the answer of the turnpike company was received. October 29th a substantial agreement had been reached, a contract embodying its terms was directed to be drawn. November 9th the draft of the contract was approved and ordered transmitted to the turnpike company. November 24th the contract had been fully perfected. All the various propositions are set out in the minutes. The contract is exceedingly detailed and long. It resulted in the passage by the legislature the following spring of Chapter 79 of the laws of 1832, passed April 2nd. This authorized (1) the Mohawk and Hudson to construct a branch from its railroad at or near its intersection with the great western turnpike to Capitol Square in Albany and thence to the Albany basin, (2) an increase of $100,000 in the capital stock which should be divided into shares of $100 each which might be subscribed and paid for at par by the stockholders of the turnpike company in proportion to the stock held by them respectively in the turnpike company. In case any stockholder failed to take his share, the turnpike company itself could take and pay for the same and in case it did not do so the directors of the Mohawk and Hudson could distribute and dispose of the unsubscribed shares as they saw fit.

Other provisions of the act need not be mentioned at this time. The branch authorized was constructed before January 1, 1833, from near the crossing of Western avenue and Madison avenue down Western avenue to State street, thence down State street to Eagle and across both to a lot purchased by the

Company abutting on State and a little east of Eagle.
For the use of the western turnpike an annual rent
of $25 was paid. The right of use covered so much of
the turnpike as was necessary, "say about thirty feet"
and the track was to be on the northerly side of the
street to its intersection with State street. State
street was occupied by permission of the city and
nothing has been found showing any compensation paid
therefor.

Subscription books were opened for the $100,000
of stock on the 5th day of June, 1832, and on the 9th of
June, the treasurer reported that the entire amount
had been subscribed for. Twenty-five per cent was
required to be paid at time of subscription and further
installments of 25 per cent in sixty, ninety and one
hundred and twenty days thereafter. We may reasonably infer from the promptitude of subscription that all
this block of stock was taken by stockholders of the
turnpike company with great satisfaction, they getting
it at par, since on the preceding April 12th another
block of stock to the par amount of $150,000 had been
sold at public auction in the city of New York and
realized a premium of over 28 per cent as will be elsewhere told.

A question arose whether the branch upon leaving
Western avenue should go down Washington street or
State. The Board decided in favor of State, July 21st,
and on the same day approved the contract with the
Western Turnpike Company and appointed a committee to negotiate with the Albany Academy for
certain lots on State street near to its intersection with
Eagle. September 21st, the committee reported the
Academy had declined disposing of the property at
private sale, but had put it up at auction August 11th,
and that at such auction they had bought it for $15,500,

possession to be delivered May 1, 1833. These were the lands used for a passenger station. The minutes of the directors for April 3, 1833, show that the branch was completed to Capitol Square January 1st. The continuation to Albany Basin was not undertaken at this time. October 20, 1832, the engineer was directed to survey the best route to the Basin. Nothing further seems to have been done about this continuation until July 19, 1833, when a committee was appointed to confer with the president of the Albany and Schenectady Turnpike Company "on the propriety of abandoning the construction of the remainder of the branch and to propose in lieu thereof the construction of the road from near the foot of the eastern inclined plane through Court, Market and Quay streets to State street or as much further along Quay street as may be deemed useful."

Evidently the directors were anxious to escape from their contract with the Turnpike Company to build the branch from Capitol Square to the Basin. On July 23rd, immediately after inspecting the main line at the river, they adopted a resolution that in case the Turnpike Company consented to release the Company from its obligation to continue the branch to the Basin, the engineer was instructed to continue without delay the railroad from Gansevoort street (the terminus of the main line at the river) to the Basin and to Maiden Lane. July 22nd the committee to confer with the president of the Turnpike Company made a report accompanied by a letter from said president. Neither report nor letter can be found but their tenor may be clearly inferred from the action taken.

The branch down State street was constructed pursuant to a previous order of the Board made May 9, 1833. The engineer being instructed to proceed without delay, we may assume the work was done in the summer of that year. The next we learn of it is interesting. At a meeting held June 13, 1835, the Board of Directors were informed that the Grand Jury in the Mayor's Court of Albany had indicted as a nuisance that part of the road from the State street depot to the river. Counsel were engaged to defend. On the 19th of August the directors were advised that the trial of the indictment had resulted in finding the Company guilty and that the nuisance was ordered to be absolutely abated. The Board discussed the contract with the Turnpike Company and also the order of abatement at some length and finally determined to let matters take their course by resolving to take no measures at present. Obviously they didn't propose to do anything which might be construed as a violation of their contract with the Turnpike Company. On the 18th of September, it was reported to the Board that the Mayor's Court had been moved for a further order in the case, the Company not having abated the nuisance. Counsel for the Company attended and explained that the Company intended no disrespect, but the road had been constructed under very peculiar circumstances and the Company had been advised by counsel to take no steps under the order already made. The superintendent submitted an affidavit showing what it would cost to take up the track between the Basin and the depot. The Court then entered an order directing the Sheriff to take up the track and fined the Company $350, being the estimated cost of doing the work, with about $30 added for sheriff's fees, etc. The Court said if the expense proved to be less than the fine, the difference would be remitted on application. The Sheriff then employed the Company's superintendent to take up the track and replace the street in its original condition. It was reported that the work had been commenced and was nearly done. No record has been found of the payment of the fine and one would be glad to know all the outside maneuvering which led to this indictment and conviction. So ended the road from the depot to the river. What happened to the branch from the main line to the State street depot will be better understood in another connection.

EXTENSION IN SCHENECTADY

The original termination of the road in Schenectady was on the southerly side of Mill Creek about 900 feet southerly from State street and 300 feet easterly from the Erie Canal. The legislature in February, 1831, granted a charter to the Saratoga and Schenectady Rail Road Company, which soon thereafter commenced construction. A connection of the two roads was obviously desirable and on September 22, 1832, the directors resolved, "That when Mr. John I. DeGraff shall execute to this Corporation free of expense a complete title to the Land required to construct the line of the Rail Road across the Erie Canal at Church street in the city of Schenectady to connect the Mohawk and Hudson Rail Road with the Saratoga and Schenectady Rail Road, this Company will proceed to construct the same, provided the Saratoga and Schenectady Rail Road Company consent to defray one half the expense of constructing the same." Work on this extension would seem to have commenced promptly, since on October 22nd, a committee was appointed to investigate and settle the accounts for construction, to examine the title to the land covered by the extension, to audit and settle the accounts with the Saratoga and Schenectady and to direct the Treasurer to pay any balance justly due that road. This committee reported

April 1, 1833, that in December, 1832, they performed the duty assigned them and found the whole cost of the road beginning on the east side of the Erie Canal and terminating at the bridge across the Mohawk River (at Washington street) was $28,043.96, of which the Company's share was one half or $14,021.98. The Saratoga and Schenectady advanced nearly the whole moneys required for the work. In addition to the cost named, there was some additional work required which cost $204.38, making a total expenditure of $28,248.34 for a road substantially 2300 feet in length without equipment or accessories of any kind, but including a bridge over the Erie Canal. This first connection between two railroads in this country affords a very excellent example of the expense of construction in cities from the very inception of railroad building.

This extension disappointed the projectors very materially. The construction of the Utica and Schenectady made another connection possible and even imperative. Chapter 383 of the laws of 1837 authorized its discontinuance provided the Saratoga and Schenectady consented thereto. May 17, 1837, the Board appointed a committee to request the consent of the Saratoga and Schenectady, and if such consent be given to effect such discontinuance and make all necessary contracts for that purpose. On December 4, 1837, the Board instructed the committee to communicate with it and insist that it pay one half the expense attending the discontinuance. February 10, 1838, there was laid before the Board the consent of the Saratoga and Schenectady to such discontinuance and it also appeared that the legal proceedings to effect the discontinuance were progressing. March 29, 1838, the Board directed that the part of the right of way which the act of 1837 declared should remain open as a public street, should be released and conveyed to the city of Schenectady if such conveyance should be deemed necessary. Thus was concluded the first abandonment of constructed road.

EXTENSION TO FERRY STREET

As has already been shown, the main line was completed in 1831 only to the crossing of Western avenue and Madison avenue in the city of Albany. Some construction work had been done easterly of that point but how much, no records disclose. The eastern inclined plane was situate upon this incomplete part. The construction of the State street branch in 1832, the agreement with the Turnpike Company that all passenger coaches used on the road should be used exclusively on that branch and the main line westerly to Schenectady, and the extension by the legislature for two years of the time in which the road must be completed undoubtedly led to a suspension of all work upon this part of the road for a time. Indeed June 16, 1832, the Board ordered that the construction of a second track thereon be suspended for a time with a view to use the materials on hand in the construction of the State street branch. Freight business had not developed largely as yet and under the agreement this part of the road could be used only in handling freight. Early in May, 1833, however, the directors met at Albany and during several days made a careful inspection of the road and on the 9th directed the engineer forthwith to proceed to have the main road to the river completed and the superintendent was directed to report as soon as he conveniently could what additional accommodations were requisite for the transportation of goods and such passengers as may choose to travel in carriages for carrying property and generally to report other information needless to specify at this time. The superintendent made a report and the Board took the same into careful consideration in July and as a result thereof ordered the construction of a storehouse at the eastern termination on the river and sought to have the branch from Capitol Square to the Basin eliminated as hereinbefore related and an extension through Court, Market (now Broadway) and Quay streets to State street substituted therefor.

July 20, 1832, a committee on transportation submitted a lengthy and interesting report. It showed that the transportation of merchandise had already commenced in advance of expectation and of accommodation for its successful prosecution; that there had already been carried during that year 900 tons and that the fall business would probably double that amount; that the Company had received as toll ten shillings ($1.25) on each ton, and that the owner had been subject to a further charge of from four to six shillings a ton for bringing to and taking away from the road. The Company was restricted by its charter to charging no more tolls than were charged on the Erie Canal at the time of the passage of the charter. The committee reported that it was difficult to fix with precision the canal tolls, but found them to have been on down freight from 6 to $7\frac{1}{2}$ cents per hundred and on up freight from 10 to $12\frac{1}{2}$ cents. A most glowing picture was drawn of the advantages to be obtained from supp ying proper freight facilities.

Matters ran along for some time without change in the eastern terminal from the location at Gansevoort and Quay streets. Chapter 224 of the laws of 1838 is very persuasive as to the perturbation of mind which existed regarding both the inclined planes and the proper location of the freight and passenger terminals in

Albany. Section 1 authorized the Company to change the location of the Schenectady end of the road so as to do away with the inclined plane there. Section 15 authorized it with the consent of the Common Council of Albany to extend its main line north to such point or points as the council might authorize; also with like consent to build a new branch into the city, this latter provision being the one under which the change to the present route was ultimately made. No such law would have been asked for or passed unless there had been grave dissatisfaction both of the Company and the public with the existing facilities.

On September 1, 1838, the Board referred to a committee a report of the superintendent regarding changes necessary to be made in order to obtain exclusive use of locomotive power and directed it among other things to consider "the probable facilities for accomplishing the same without embarrassing the finances of the company." The road, as will be shown elsewhere, was then in a chronic state of financial embarrassment which continued to grow worse. September 29th, the committee was authorized, if it saw fit, to apply to the Common Council of Albany for its consent to the construction of the road up the river from Gansevoort Street. February 2, 1839, it was resolved to make application to the legislature to loan the credit of the State to an amount not exceeding $350,000 to enable the Company to extinguish its existing bonds "and to pay the cost of making any future improvements on the line of this road under the said act of April 16, 1838," (Chap. 224.). May 24, 1839, a committee was appointed "to confer with the Utica and Schenectady Rail Road Company and ascertain whether that company will in case it is determined on the part of this Company to make any alterations in the route of their road under the act of April 16, 1838, guarantee the payment of the bonds or obligations that this Company may issue for the purpose of raising the necessary funds to make such alterations."

As early as October, 1835, the Common Council of Albany had taken action to induce the Company to change the terminations of both the main and branch lines in the city and in that month the president was authorized to employ an engineer to examine the route for a railroad from the Company's main road down the Hudson street and Fox street ravines and report upon the practicability of the same.

Thus matters ran along without any practical result, except to demonstrate the impossibility at that time of constructing a new line into the city, until the 15th of June, 1840, when the Board adopted a resolution reciting that the Common Council of the city of Albany did on the 4th day of March, 1839, consent that the Company extend a line of railroad near the south bounds of the city north through Market street to the south side of Ferry street and that the Company's secretary did March 18, 1840, notify the city the Company accepted such license, recognizing and confirming the act of the secretary and declaring their intention to avail themselves of the rights and privileges thus vested in them. On the same day the Board directed its executive committee to cause the main track of the road to be extended to Ferry street.

The extension was completed at some time in the summer of 1841. On its completion the question arose whether the Company could, in view of its agreement with the Schenectady Turnpike Company discontinue operations of the State street branch and take up the tracks. Legal advice assured the directors they could do this under the provisions of the Act of 1838, and

accordingly on September 11, 1841, the directors
unanimously adopted a resolution declaring the State
street branch unnecessary for the transaction of the
business of the road and discontinuing the same, and the
superintendent was directed to take up the material.
Thus ended the branch to Capitol Square as an operating road, and began operation over the main line to
Ferry street.

CHANGE AT SCHENECTADY ELIMINATING INCLINED PLANE

It was early discovered that a railroad could not be
operated successfully and to the satisfaction of the
public with grades thereon too stiff to be overcome with
the use of locomotive power and which required
inclined planes with operation over them handled by
stationary engines and long ropes. The struggles
resulting from this discovery have received incidental
notice in the accounts given of the various branches
and extension of the Mohawk and Hudson. We are
now prepared to consider more fully the steps which
brought about the final changes of location and placed
the roadway in substantially its present location.

Those changes were authorized by Chapter 224 of
the laws of 1838, passed April 16th, and the passage of
this act shows that at that early date the desirability,
if not the necessity, of the elimination of the inclined
planes was apparent to the Company, the legislature
and the public. From that time on the questions were
not of legal power to make the change, but of financing,
locating feasible routes and obtaining the consent at
the eastern end of the city of Albany. Financing
afforded almost insuperable obstacles; the Company
was struggling with difficulties arising in part from the
panic of 1837, and its aftermath. The cost of the

changes would be very great and would throw a burden upon the Company in the way of fixed charges which might easily prove too great to be carried. The city of Albany was greatly interested in the project to obtain a railroad connection with Boston, over what is now the Boston and Albany, and ultimately pledged its credit to that end, to the extent of $1,000,000, a tremendous sum in those days for a city of but 33,000 inhabitants. Capital was not abundant. To get down from the top of the plateau to the valleys of the Hudson and Mohawk was not easy in view of the limited power of the locomotives of those days. Another impelling, if not compelling, consideration was the project of constructing the Schenectady and Troy Railroad which was opened for operation in 1842. The possibility of its diverting traffic from the west to Troy was believed in by that city which constructed the road, and also aroused the attention of the inhabitants of Albany and of those controlling the Mohawk and Hudson. How the problems indicated were solved will now receive our attention.

Shortly after the passage of the law of 1838, a controversy sprang up over the election of directors which was settled by the Supreme Court in August. During its continuance, no affirmative action was possible but at the first meeting of directors held after it was decided, the following resolution was adopted:

Resolved, that the report and plans heretofore submitted by the Superintendent for a modification of parts of the company's road with a view to the exclusive use of locomotive power for the conveyance of passengers be referred to the directors residing at Albany together with Mr. Davison, and that they be requested to consider the expediency of making such alterations or other improvements, and also the probable facilities for accomplishing the same without embarrassing the finances of the company and to report to the board at their next meeting or as soon as may be convenient and also that the Committee be authorized to take such professional advice as they may deem necessary and proper.

Much as one would like to see the plans of the superintendent, no trace of them has been found. Nor did the committee make any formal report to the Board. February 2, 1839, the Board adopted the resolution hereinbefore cited directing application be made to the legislature for a loan of State credit to the amount of $250,000, to be used among other things "to pay the cost of making any future improvements on the line of the road under the said act of April 16, 1838." The improvements thus alluded to naturally include the matters referred to the committee and we may infer the committee's investigations had disclosed otherwise insuperable difficulties in financing the project. Nothing came out of this move. Why it failed is not known.

The next move was the effort made May 24, 1839, to obtain a guarantee of the Company's bonds issued for alterations in the route of its road. This resolution has already been given and need not be repeated here. The failure of this appeal led to a period of doubt and inaction which finally resulted in the resolution of June 15, 1840, to extend the main line to Ferry street. This action seemingly administered a death blow to the elimination of the Albany inclined plane, since it contemplated the discontinuance of the State street branch and the carrying of all traffic down the main line to the river.

Matters then remained undisturbed until September, 1841, at which time the Ferry street extension had been completed. At a meeting of the directors held the third day of that month at the Company's office at the head of the western inclined plane, a long resolution was unanimously adopted, reciting the act of 1838, also containing the following preamble:

And whereas it is manifest to this Board that public opinion requires an abandonment of the inclined plane at Schenectady, and the interest of this Company would be greatly promoted by the immediate construction of a new section or route of rail road, so as to enable this Company to use and operate said rail road without the aid of stationary power, And whereas a rail road from the city of Troy to the city of Schenectady is in progress and is expected to be in operation in the course of the next year and that without this improvement the annual income of the road will be greatly diminished, And whereas the expense and cost of operating the said road from the head of the said inclined plane to the depot in Schenectady amount annually to the sum of ten thousand dollars: And whereas the practical operation of this new road will be a saving of the cost of maintaining and attending the engine and fixtures of the said inclined plane, together with the cost of all the horse power connected with the Schenectady depot and its attendance: and the yearly expenses now incurred from the head of the said plane to the said Schenectady depot are estimated to pay the interest at seven per cent on the whole cost of the proposed new section of said road, including the maintenance of the bridge at State Street, And this Board having examined the surveys, maps and estimates of the expense of the several proposed routes, and having duly considered the same: Do now here resolve, and the Executive Committee are hereby authorized to cause to be constructed a new section or route of rail road, so as to dispense with the stationary and horse power at the said west inclined plane and the aforesaid bridge.

A finance committee was also appointed with full power to borrow money to pay the cost of the improvement and to issue bonds bearing seven per cent interest for the same, said bonds to be signed by the president and secretary. Another committee was appointed to ask the Governor for the appointment of three commissioners to locate the new route agreeably to the provisions of the act of April 16, 1838.

And having performed such meritorious work, the Board was evidently in good spirits, for it then adjourned to meet at Albany on the 11th day of September and "unite in the celebration of the opening of the new section to Ferry street." The skies were apparently clearing beautifully. At the Albany meeting, they ordered the discontinuance of the State street branch as already related.

But unfortunately, if not trouble, at least severe annoyance was ahead. Many citizens of Albany were

PASSENGER STATION AT FERRY STREET, ALBANY. USED 1841–1844.

greatly displeased at the change of terminus in that city. A public meeting was held in the Capitol on the 16th of September, which proved to be highly intemperate in the language used and a committee was appointed, with Erastus Corning as its chairman, to ask a conference with the directors or a committee from them. Mr. Corning wrote to director LaSala, the president being absent, and Mr. LaSala answered on September 20th.   A part of his answer is too informative of what was going on to be omitted:

> While you invite the Company to an interview and a friendly meeting, in order to promote the interest of, and peace and harmony among your citizens and the Company, the latter is assailed by the other party, with opprobrious epithets, and all kind of abuse, and the directors are held up to the eyes of the public as monopolists, enemies of the prosperity of your City, &c, &c, because they in the faithful and honorable discharge of their duties towards the public and their constituents, have adopted measures, calculated to benefit both.   I therefore would advise to defer any negotiations until the disgraceful and unnatural war waging by your citizens against the Company, has ceased, and an excitement, raised by appealing to the passions of your working classes of people, has also subsided.

Another meeting of Albanians was held on the 17th of September at the Columbian Hotel, which sided with the Company.   All these matters being laid before the directors at a meeting held September 25th, some spirited resolutions were adopted which can not properly be omitted from any account of the transactions of those days.

> The Chairman then called the attention of the Board to the published proceedings of another meeting of citizens of Albany held at the Columbian Hotel in said City on the seventeenth day of September instant.   All which being read and discussed, it was thereupon unanimously resolved, That this Company, will most cheerfully extend to the citizens of Albany every accommodation and facility, in their power not inconsistent, with the rights, comfort and convenience of the travelling public, or adverse to the interests of the stockholders.
>
> Resolved, that while this company will pay respectful attention to the representations and wishes of their fellow citizens, they cannot recognize the right of "The Board of Trade and Commerce of the City of Albany" or of any person or persons, body politic or corporate to interfere in their concerns, and they

protest against all, also every species of dictation, and will firmly resist every attempt at coercion.

Resolved, that while this company are struggling to afford facilities to the travelling public, to the full extent of their means; by reducing their inclined plane at Schenectady; extending their main track to the Hudson river; substituting steam power for horse power; landing and receiving passengers, and their baggage at the steam boat wharf; they regret to experience such a gratuitous spirit of hostility, as is manifested by a small portion of the citizens of Albany, who seem to suppose, that the comfort, convenience, and expedition of the travelling public, and the best interest of this company, must be sacrificed to promote their own local advantage.

Resolved, that where it must be manifest to every person, that the convenience of the travelling public requires the eastern termination of the road, to be at or near the Steam Boat landings: and this company having without success, repeatedly petitioned the Common Council of Albany for leave to establish a more "convenient central depot" for their business; and when the present termination of the road, at the south side of Ferry street, is the point, designated by a resolution of the Common Council for that purpose, notwithstanding the urgent solicitation of this company, to be permitted to extend their road to the most central business part of the city, in the vicinity, of the landing of the Steam Boats; complaints from any section of that city appear to us unreasonable and unjust.

Resolved, that it appears from the published proceedings of the two meetings of citizens above referred to, that there exists a great diversity of opinion in Albany, in regard to the most suitable termination of the rail road; one portion being favorable to the present location of the Depot, and the other adverse; it would seem to this Board, that it was impossible for them to take any further steps in this matter, without giving dissatisfaction to a numerous and respectable portion of said citizens: It is manifest, therefore, that it would be unjust to treat with the representatives of one section of said city to the exclusion of the other. Whenever the present opposing interests shall unite in recommending another termination of said road, which will equally accommodate the travelling public, and promote the interest of the stockholders; this company will promptly and cheerfully comply with their wishes.

Resolved, that we sincerely regret to find those Directors of the Utica & Schenectady Rail Road Company, *who reside in the City of Albany*, arrayed against this company, in sustaining an adverse interest, and using their money, and their influence and exertions as such directors, to the prejudice of this company; and this regret is increased by the fact, that stockholders in the Mohawk & Hudson R. R. Co. are largely interested in the Utica Company. Had any portion of our Directors ever assumed the same hostile attitude towards the Utica Company, that these Directors now manifest towards us, their stockholders would have just grounds of complaint. But we feel the most entire confidence that the sense of justice of a majority of the Directors of that company will correct this evil.

Resolved, that in the spirit of conciliation, and with an anxious desire to preserve harmony, and cultivate peace, and good will, with and among every class of the citizens of Albany, the Executive Committee of this Board are hereby authorized to receive any proposition or communication from committees of the aforesaid meetings respectively; and should they deem it necessary to take any action thereon; then to report the same to this Board, at their next meeting.

Resolved, that the Secretary transmit a copy of the foregoing, to Erastus Corning, Esq., Chairman, &c, and also to the Chairman or Secretaries of the said meeting at the Columbian Hotel; and publish the same in the public newspapers.

Resolved, that Mr. Stevens be and hereby is authorized to obtain a conveyance of the right of this company to the depot, land and buildings in Schenectady.

Whereas—This Company having paid for the one equal half of the cost and expenses of the depot at the City of Schenectady, which is used in common by this company and the Utica & Schenectady Company,

Resolved, that the said depot be closed against all stage agents and runners, or any other person to solicit passengers, hostile to the interests of this company: and the superintendent, or any member of the executive committee of this company, is hereby authorized and directed to use all necessary means to carry this resolution into effect.

These resolutions and the firm stand taken seem to have closed the matter. The public had discovered the great local importance of railroad facilities and were ready to assert an extra legal control over their location on the narrow basis of the local interest, disregarding the broader interests of the road and the general public. This first attempt, unfortunately, has not proved to be the last of its kind.

The city of Albany took a lively interest in the elimination of the inclined planes and after a conference between the executive committee and a committee of citizens of Albany, Mr. Thomas W. Olcott, for the latter committee, submitted a letter to the Board April 8, 1842, containing three propostions. These were considered and rejected. The Board in turn submitted a proposition that the Company would make the contemplated improvements at both ends of the road and issue their bonds as theretofore proposed for $155,000, provided the city of Albany would advance $80,000 cash on the said bonds and guarantee the residue at par and pay all excess cost of said improvements over said $155,000. This was communicated to Mr. Olcott and rejected by him the same day.

June 17, 1842, the whole Board was appointed a committee to meet a committee from the Utica and Schenectady Rail Road Company and the citizens of Albany on matters not specified, being "an arrangement to be entered into between the two companies and the citizens of Albany" and presumably relating to the contemplated improvements.

The next day the Board declined to accept the proposition as made, expressing themselves as willing to enter into such an arrangement with some modifications. Negotiations with the city of Albany continued and resulted in the passage, August 15, by the Common Council of the city of the following resolution.

The President Mr. Banks presented to the Board a certified copy of a Resolution of the Common Council of the City of Albany, in answer to his letter of the 11th Instant, which resolution being read by the Secretary, was ordered to be entered on the minutes, which is hereby entered and is as follows, viz.:

Whereas an application has been made to the Common Council by the Mohawk & Hudson Rail Road Company requesting them to guarantee the Bonds of said company to an amount not exceeding one hundred thousand dollars for the purpose of dispensing with the Inclined plane at Schenectady.

And whereas such application is enforced by the petition of a large number of the influential citizens of Albany recommending that application to the immediate and favorable action of this Board.

Resolved therefore that his Honor the Mayor be authorized on behalf of this Board, and under the City seal to guarantee the Bonds of the Mohawk & Hudson Rail Road Company to an amount not exceeding one hundred thousand dollars for the purpose aforesaid. The said bonds to be payable in ten years, and the interest thereon to be paid by the said company semi-annually, upon the said Company's executing to this Board a Mortgage upon their Road and the property connected therewith for the sum aforesaid as security against such liability: and upon their furnishing satisfactory evidence, that there is no incumbrance or lien upon said Road and property now existing to an amount greater than one hundred thousand dollars.

Resolved that his Honor the mayor be requested immediately to transmit a copy of these Resolutions to the President of said Company.

It is reasonable to believe this action was induced by the building of the Schenectady and Troy. The entire situation points conclusively to this.

September 6, proposals were received and opened for reducing the inclined plane at Schenectady. The proposal of James and Charles Collins of $57,800 was accepted. The finance committee was authorized to negotiate bonds for $100,000 to be guaranteed by the city of Albany, and also to enter into all necessary contracts for reducing the western plane and to have control and superintendence of the work.

October 15th, the president reported a contract with the Collinses for reducing the western plane, they to find all the materials except the land and iron rails for $61,300. The books of the Company, however, show that the total cost of the new line eliminating the plane was $91,827.06, including all preliminary surveys and expenses.

ELIMINATION OF ALBANY INCLINED PLANE

December 2, 1842, a new committee was appointed to make and perfect an agreement with the corporation and citizens of Albany in regard to an extension of the main track, or to fix upon the central point of location at or as near the Hudson river as practicable so as to avoid the inclined plane and to be operated by locomotive steam power, or any other agreements the committee might deem to be for the interest of the Company. The wide powers given this committee indicate a great desire to change existing conditions and great uncertainty as to the change which should be made. Negotiations of some kind proceeded, but what they were is not known, since the committee on January 26, 1843, merely reported progress. March 6, bonds to be guaranteed by the city of Albany to the amount of $100,000 for reducing the inclined plane at Schenectady were ordered to be issued.

At the election of directors in June, 1843, practically a new Board was elected, and George Law, a new man on the Board, was made president and given extraordinary powers to reorganize the business and operations of the Company. Whether the old Board had become wearied and retired, or the stockholders had become dissatisfied and retired them, can only be inferred from the fact that out of 10,000 shares, only 4,709 voted, and there was no contest, except a very minor one over one of the new directors. June 27, the Board discussed at length the propriety of making an effort to change the location of the road at Albany so as to avoid the use of stationary power, and after such discussion adopted the following resolution:

Resolved 1. That on compliance with the terms herein-after mentioned, this Company will, on obtaining the consent of the Common Council of the City of Albany, proceed forthwith under the Act of the Legislature, concerning this Company passed April 16, 1838, to construct a new line of double track Rail-Road, one track of which at least shall be of the H rail, (and both if the Company see fit) commencing at some suitable point on the Company's main road, and running down the valley of the Patroon's Creek, and thence to some suitable point near the River in the central part of the City of Albany, so as to avoid the use of stationary power, with a track running to the Boston Rail Road Landing at the foot of Maiden Lane, on which new Road the Company's business shall be transacted.

2. The Corporation of Albany, or the Citizens of said City, are to advance on the Bonds of this Company secured by a Mortgage on the Company's Road and property, such amount as may be necessary to construct the said Road, not exceeding One hundred and twenty-five thousand Dollars, at four per cent interest payable semi-annually, the principal payable thirty years from the date of said Bonds; and also to furnish, without any charge therefor, the necessary lands for the route of such new Road and Depot-ground which shall be satisfactory to this Company, not less than 100 by 200 feet in extent.

Resolved that the President and Messrs. Banks and Mills, together with any two of the Directors residing at Albany who can make it convenient to attend, be a Committee to confer with the Common Council of the City of Albany, or any Committee thereof, or with the Citizens of Albany, in relation to the matters embraced in the foregoing resolutions.

On the 11th of July following, the Common Council of the city of Albany adopted the following resolution:

Resolved

That this Board will borrow, and loan to the President, Directors and Company of the Mohawk & Hudson Rail-Road Company, a sum not exceeding One hundred and twenty-five thousand Dollars for the term of twenty or twenty-five years, at an interest of five per cent. per annum, payable semi-annually, for the purpose of making a new double track branch Road to some central point in the City, at or near the Hudson River, in such a manner as to dispense with the inclined plane, and the payment of said loan to be secured by a Bond and Mortgage on the Road and Implements of the said Rail-Road Company; and that the Board will also procure the necessary land for the line of the Road, suitable for a double track and necessary Depot grounds, at least 100 by 200 feet, at a cost not exceeding the sum of Twenty-five Thousand Dollars, and grant the use thereof to the said Rail-Road Company, so long as the same are used by them for the purposes contemplated:—and that the Select Committee appointed by the Board to confer with the Directors aforesaid, be authorized and empowered on the part of this Board to arrange, prepare and adjust all necessary details to carry the foregoing into effect, and that the Mayor be authorized under the City Seal to execute all necessary agreements for that purpose, and that the Clerk of this Board transmit a certified copy of this Resolution to the President of the said Company.

Two days later on the 13th, the Board adopted the following resolutions:

Resolved That this Company will, in pursuance of the Act of the Legislature of this State relative to this Company, passed April 16, 1838, proceed as soon as practicable after the completion of the arrangement hereinafter mentioned, to construct a new double track of Rail-Road on what is called the Patroon's Creek route, in such manner as to avoid the use of stationary power, and terminating on Hudson's River at such suitable point near the central part of the City of Albany, as may be agreed upon between this Board and the Common Council of the City of Albany, with suitable Depot Buildings, on receiving from the said Common Council of Albany, a grant of the necessary Land for the line of the said Road and for the

Depot Buildings; the latter to be at least one hundred by two hundred feet in extent, and the location to be agreed upon by the Committee appointed by the said Common Council and this Board or a Committee thereof:—and that this Board will, for the purpose of constructing said Road and erecting the said Buildings, borrow from the City of Albany, the sum of One hundred and twenty-five thousand Dollars, at an annual interest of five per cent. payable semi-annually, to be secured by the Company's Bond or Bonds, and a mortgage on the Company's Road and property, payable at not more than twenty-five years from the date of such Bond or Bonds and Mortgage:—and that this Company on the completion of said new line of Road, will transact its passenger and freight business thereon.

Resolved That the President procure a survey of the said contemplated new route of Road to be submitted to this Board for its approval.

Resolved That the President and Messrs. Banks, Little, King and Pruyn be a Committee on the part of this Board, to confer with the said Committee appointed by the Common Council of the City of Albany, with full power to carry out and perfect the details of the foregoing proposition and to make such alterations in the terms thereof as they may deem proper, and that the President be authorized on the completion thereof to execute such agreements and Instruments in writing under the Seal of this Company as may in the judgment of the said Committee be necessary fully to carry out the views of the parties and also to execute under the Seal of this Company the said Bond and Mortgage on the Company's Road and property to the Mayor, Aldermen and Commonalty of the City of Albany, to secure the sum so to be borrowed by this Company from the said Corporation, with such clauses, covenants and conditions therein as to the said Committee may consider proper.

August 12th, another resolution was adopted further indemnifying Albany by the issue of stock as collateral security to be held in trust by members of the Board. Surveys were pushed and on October 5th, Mr. Craven, the engineer, submitted his report and the Board approved a written contract dated September 26th with Albany, and voted that when the same had been executed by Albany, it would proceed to the construction of the new road specified in the contract and that the Governor be requested to appoint commissioners to locate the route pursuant to the provisions of the Act of 1838.

The salient provisions of the very lengthy contract are that the Company would without unnecessary delay construct a new double track road, one track at least to be laid with heavy H rail, on the Patroon's Creek route in such manner as to avoid the inclined plane and use of stationary power. The new road to intersect the main line about five miles from the Hudson river and extend to the ferry at the foot of Maiden Lane. The city agreed to purchase a perfect title in fee to the necessary land for right of way within sixty days after the commissioners had located the route and also to land for depot buildings containing not less than 20,000 square feet, not less than 80 nor more than 110 feet wide, south of Lumber street and east of Broadway in the city, the precise location to be agreed upon, and to lease the lands and depot grounds to the railroad company for twenty years from January 1, 1844, at the rent of one cent per annum. That at or any time after the expiration of said term, the railroad company might purchase the said lands and premises at the original cost thereof without interest thereon. That after the expiration of said twenty years and until such purchase the railroad company should hold the lands and grounds on lease at a rent in perpetuity equivalent to five per cent on the original cash cost thereof without interest. The Company could also at any time during the said twenty years become the purchaser at the original cost without interest.

The city also agreed to loan to the Company $125,000 or so much thereof as might be necessary which should be expended in constructing the new route and the erection of suitable depot buildings. Any part of the $125,000 not necessary for these purposes to be expended in the laying of heavy H rails and the superstructure thereof on the new route and westwardly therefrom on the main line. The loan to be secured by bond and mortgage on the road payable January 1, 1864, with interest at 5 per cent per annum. The Company agreed it would not make any lease of its road or any agreement for the use, management or control of the same without the consent of the city.

There were further provisions for the issue of 3500 shares of capital stock of the Company to the nine directors of the Company, but in trust, as collateral security for the payment of the $125,000.

November 14, 1842, the city had consented to the construction of a new branch road connecting with the main line at any point west of the inclined plane and the use of streets for the purposes of such branch road.

December 16, 1843, proposals for the grading and masonry for that part of the new line lying outside the city were submitted to the Board and contracts were authorized as soon as the route was located by commissioners. One Adams was the engineer in charge. April 27, 1844, contracts for grading varying somewhat from the foregoing were approved and also a contract for fencing the entire new route. Commissioners had located the new line February 6, 1844.

Nothing has been found regarding the progress of the work during 1844, but September 30, 1844, the first train was run over the new line to the depot on Broadway in Albany and that route has since been in continuous use.

So ended the use of the inclined planes, stationary

power and horse power on the Mohawk and Hudson. The total cost of the new line on the present route through the Patroon's Creek valley and exclusive of the amount paid many years after by the Central to Albany for the land was $201,736.57.

October 29, 1845, the Company advertised for sale, forty-eight parcels of land on the old main line between the junction with the new line and South Pearl street and seven parcels between South Pearl street and the river, pursuant to a resolution adopted August 25th, authorizing the sale by a committee of "such of the Real Estate owned by the Company as in their judgment is not needed for the uses of the road and is not now occupied therefor." April 4, 1846, a committee was authorized to reconvey any property "on the old line of the Company's Road now abandoned, to the original owners without compensation if in their judgment the interests of the Company will be subserved thereby." Parcels have been sold since from time to time.

FREIGHT TRAFFIC

Unlike most of the railroads paralleling the Erie Canal, the Mohawk and Hudson was not restricted by its charter from carrying freight. It was given the power to fix the tolls and charges, "*Provided* that at no time during the existence of this corporation the tolls and charges thus fixed, regulated and received for transportation shall exceed the amount of tolls and duties, together with the charges of freight to which property is subjected, as the cost of transportation on the Erie Canal, at or before the passing of this act" (Section 12). This obscure provision seems to have received a somewhat peculiar construction from the Company, but with this we cannot deal since it was never, so far as known, criticized or objected to by the state or any individual.

In 1831 no freight was carried, no provision having been made for handling it, but in 1832, a demand for the transportation of property sprang up and was met to some extent. April 3, 1833, it received the attention of the directors to the extent of appointing a committee of three to examine into and report upon all the questions involved. Two of the committee ceased to be directors at the annual meeting in June following, and on July 20th Samuel Glover, a resident of New York City, the sole remaining member, made a report which though extremely optimistic affords us a clear view of the traffic at that time and of the anticipations for its future growth. Its findings may be summarized as follows:

1. Transportation of merchandise had already commenced in advance of expectation and of accommodation for its successful prosecution.

2. That there had already been carried during the season of 1833, 900 tons of merchandise and that it might be fairly presumed that the fall business would greatly augment, if not double, that amount.

3. That the toll or charge was ten shillings ($1.25) a ton (this it will be observed was very nearly 8 cents per ton mile). That the owner had been subjected to a further charge of from 4 to 6 shillings ($0.50 to $0.75) a ton for bringing and conveying the same to and from the road.

4. That the committee had returns from the Canal Board from which it appeared that in 1832, exclusive of cord wood and lumber, there had been carried from Schenectady to Albany 109,300 tons and from Albany west 46,479 tons, subject to charges on down freight at an average of over 60 cents per ton and west bound

of $1.40, giving an aggregate of $125,000 paid for freight and toll. The amount for 1833 is estimated at $150,000.

5. That in January, 1833, the engineer and superintendent, John B. Jervis, had submitted a report containing a detailed estimate of costs of transportation calculated on the basis of 270 tons per day and in the ratio of two tons down and one ton up, which showed a cost to the Company of 45⅓ cents per ton.

6. That the forwarding lines found the accommodations now afforded by the Company at Albany very inadequate.

7. That it had been found difficult to fix with precision the amount of Canal freight and tolls between Schenectady and Albany. That from the best information obtainable the committee stated it to have been from 6 to 7½ cents per hundred on down freight, and from 10 to 12½ cents per hundred on up freight.

8. It seems that at that time it was customary for shippers or their representatives to travel with their property and in the same boat. It was difficult to ascertain the annual number, but the committee had been informed by an agent of the forwarding lines residing in Albany that probably not less than 40,000 tons a year pass westwardly from Albany and this number was increasing. The committee thought such passengers riding on the freight wagons could well afford to pay from three shillings (37½ cents) to half a dollar for the transportation of themselves, and a reasonable quantity of baggage.

On the basis of these facts the committee indulges in a roseate view of the prospect of freight transportation culminating in dithyrambics in the following: "It seems to your committee upon a careful view of this subject that your Road possesses bountiful and multiplied resources (far beyond any similar work in this country) which if successfully developed must redound to the credit of this Board and bring a rich harvest to those we represent."

The Board during the three days previous to the presentation of this report had been holding daily meetings in Albany engaged in viewing the road and studying its requirements in detail, had passed the resolution authorizing the president to order the two locomotives subsequently named Mohawk and Hudson, had determined it wise to abandon the construction of the addition to the State street branch from Eagle street to the Albany Basin, and to continue the main line from Gansevoort street to State street or still further along Quay street. Obviously the freight situation as set forth in Glover's report had been fully and carefully canvassed, for the report was accepted on the 20th and deemed of sufficient importance to be ordered entered in the minutes. The hard headed Albany directors of whom Erastus Corning, then vice president of the Company, was one, and Isaiah Townsend another, concurred, and it was unanimously resolved to construct with the Company's workmen 30 freight wagons, 10 carriages for carrying property and passengers; to construct without delay a storehouse at the corner of Gansevoort and Quay streets in the town of Bethlehem (the terminus of the main line at the Hudson river); that the superintendent make alterations in the machinery at the head of the western inclined plane at a probable cost of $2,000, and that he erect a building suitable for an office building and such other conveniences as the business of the Company might require. Bright, indeed, seemed the prospects. The Saratoga and Schenectady road had opened the previous year. The Utica and Schenec-

tady Railroad Company had been chartered the previous April, the stock amounting to $2,000,000 had
all been subscribed for and $100,000 paid in thereon
ten days previously at a meeting of the commissioners
held in Albany, thus making sure a new and valuable
connection to the west. Things were looking up.

Events did not prove this optimism justified. Up
to December 31, 1839, the total number of tons of
freight carried was 144,897; the receipts for transportation amounted to $130,497.72 and the expenses
charged to the same amounted to $126,571.57, leaving
but the paltry sum of $3,926.15 as the net profit for
seven years of freight traffic.

The following table shows the results year by year,
and it is instructive to note the results in 1837 and
1838, which presumably followed as incident to the
great financial collapse in 1837.

Freight Statistics 1833–1839

Year	Tons from Albany	Tons from Schenectady	Receipts $	Expenses $	Net	Av. per ton $	Av. per ton mile cts.
1833	2,096	870	3,708.02	1,029.01	2,679.01	1.25	7.8
1834	5,282	11,313	12,733.77	13,693.23	— 959.46	.767	4.8
1835	10,522	19,762	26,287.73	23,227.56	3,060.17	.868	5.4
1836	12,866	18,577	28,185.67	23,993.26	4,192.41	.896	5.6
1837	6,331	10,373	14,429.06	19,996.34	—5,567.28	.864	5.4
1838	8,966	11,549	19,276.28	19,210.08	66.20	.940	5.8
1839	12,310	14,080	25,877.19	25,422.09	455.10	.981	6.1
Total	58,373	86,524	130,497.72	126,571.57	3,926.15	.90	5.6

A report from the superintendent dated January 29,
1840, from which the foregoing figures are taken contains the following: "The general rates for transportation of freight via railroad from Schenectady to Albany
have been as follows:

For freight received from Canal boats
    at that place..................... $0.62½ per ton
For freight forwarded by citizens of
    Schenectady .... 1.00   "   "
For freight coming from Saratoga Rail-
    road .... 1.25   "   "

Obviously discrimination was not regarded either
by the public or the Company in its present light.
Classification of freight does not seem to have obtained.

This report was made to the executive committee
in consequence of inquiries made by a large number
of stockholders and in response to those inquiries
the committee itself made a long and comprehensive
report in which the freight situation was exhaustively
considered.   Some of their observations are well worth
transcribing.

The rates of toll for transportation of freight received from
the canal, on this road, are only about one-half of the average
price per mile, of what is charged on all the railroads in the
United States; and considerably lower than on roads of a level
grade, which bear no comparison in expense with this, in the cost
of their operation respectively.

Since the report shows that freight from the canal
was carried 16 miles for 62½ cents per ton, or a little
less than 4 cents per ton mile, if this statement is correct, the average freight rate per ton mile throughout
the country was probably somewhere between 6 and 8
cents.

The expense, attendant upon the reception and delivery of
goods on a short route, are the same as on a long one, no matter
of what extent; and the responsibilities of handling and trans-
shipment, minuteness of detail in keeping of accounts, etc. are
alike—making it necessary in both cases, to have competent,
efficient, and consequently expensive agents, at both ends of the
route.

This shows that practical experience in 1840, had demonstrated clearly certain truths regarding long and short haul which have ever since been in controversy. The committee, in this connection, calls attention to the fact that the expenses of the freight storehouses in 1839, amounted to $9,225.97 out of a total freight expense of $25,422.09. The "expensive agents" were paid generally about $50 per month.

It also sternly recalls disappointed expectations as follows:

At the time when this company determined to engage in the carrying business, (1833–1834), it was confidently asserted by the friends of the measure, and believed, that an amount equal to 70,000 tons of property, and upwards, coming to and from the canal, would be transported on the road the year following, which amount would annually increase, in the ratio of business on the canal. The fact is, that from 1833 to 1840, the gross quantity carried on the Railroad is only 144,897 tons, being an average of 20,699 tons per annum, including local freight.

The whole report is pertinent, pungent and well worth consideration. It recommends abandonment of competition in prices with the canal, confining the Company's business chiefly to the transportation of passengers, as the most profitable branch of business, and such local freight as may accommodate citizens of Albany, Schenectady and Saratoga, and afford remunerative prices. It should be remembered that at this time the Utica and Schenectady Road was not allowed to carry freight. The Company had put several hundred thousand dollars into freight facilities since 1833 and had received a return thereon of less than $4,000. This was undoubtedly one of the principal factors which produced the gloomy and disheartening conditions of the Company during the next few years and which made difficult the obtaining of

funds to improve the road under the enabling act of
1838. To obtain an adequate tonnage of freight at
remunerative prices was probably impossible so long
as the Utica and Schenectady was forbidden to engage
in freight transportation. Not until 1847 was it possible to get freight from that road during the entire
year and then it was burdened with the payment
of canal tolls. A road but 16 miles in length, running
over a hill, with no local traffic, did not present an
alluring prospect for investors in the cold light of actual
experience despite the brilliant anticipations or dreams
of the committee of 1833. That the movement of
freight over this route has justified the hopes of that
committee we know, but it has been made a success
under conditions which did not prevail while the road
was a separate operating unit and throttled with
restrictions almost prohibitive.

FREE PASSES

The subject of free passes having been the subject
in later years of much popular discussion, and of drastic legislation, a brief statement of the manner in
which it was handled on the Mohawk and Hudson, so
far as it is now ascertainable will possess interest.

At the outset of operation, no passes seem to have
been granted, except upon resolution of the Board of
Directors. Whether this practice was maintained
inflexibly during the entire corporate existence of the
road can not be ascertained. There is some but slight
indication that it was not, which, however, is not sufficient to warrant the conclusion that authority to issue
was exercised by others than the Board. That body
at one time adopted a resolution calling for an investigation of the free list, but considering the rapid succession of new directors, and the frequent changes in

the personnel of the Board, this may have been but the expression of a desire on the part of new members to inform themselves as to what had been done, and what was going on. Nothing has been found to show that any action was taken under this resolution. A more significant action was taken by the Board, March 1, 1849, by the adoption of the following resolution:

Resolved: that this Company will cooperate with the Utica and Schenectady Railroad Company in petitioning to the legislature for the passage of a law prohibiting the issue of free tickets on their respective Roads.

What action of the Utica and Schenectady Railroad led to this can not be ascertained. The first free pass authorized is shown by the minutes of May 9, 1833: "Resolved: that his Honor, the Chancellor [Reuben H. Walworth] be permitted to pass over the road free of charge, and that the President be requested to communicate the substance of this resolution to him." The reasons for this are not disclosed, but it can not be considered other than a graceful courtesy and mark of respect. The next action of the kind was preceded by a whereas well worth transcribing.

Whereas, the interests of the Mohawk and Hudson, and the Saratoga and Schenectady Railroads are closely allied, and the directors of one road would in passing over the other have an interest in noting and suggesting matters connected with the welfare of the same, therefore, Resolved: that the directors of the Saratoga and Schenectady Railroad Company be permitted to pass over the Mohawk and Hudson Railroad free of charge.

Like privilege was extended to the directors of the Utica and Schenectady when it came into operation, and also to other roads both to the west and east including those of the Western Railroad of Massachusetts.

In June, 1834, the superintendent was authorized

to allow free passage over the road to the proprietors, officers or agents of the two boat lines, running between New York and Albany; to such members of the Canal Association as have or may become interested in the contract with this Company for the transportation of passengers and property whenever said persons shall have occasion to travel between Albany and Schenectady on the business contemplated by said contract, and also "That he be authorized to allow free passage over the Road to such other persons employed in public conveyances running to and from the Road, as in his discretion he may deem advantageous to the Company." Help to get us business and you shall have a free pass, is the free interpretation of this.

But on the same day they took a firm stand and drew the line on principle, as witness the following from the minutes:

The application of Edward C. Delavan and others, dated 19th March, 1834, soliciting the free passage over the Company's Road for the Rev'd. Mr. Davis, a City Missionary was laid before the Board, whereupon it was unanimously resolved, that in the view of this Board, such permission would be inconsistent with the principles, which ought to govern the administration of the Company's affairs, and that the Secretary communicate the same to the Rev'd. Mr. Davis.

The failure to specify more particularly the principles they allude to, leaves us free to conjecture just where the line was drawn, except that it excluded Mr. Davis.

The foregoing comprises all the action of the Mohawk and Hudson relating to free passes recorded in the minutes of the Board.

SUPERINTENDENTS OF CONSTRUCTION AND OPERATION

The practical work of construction and operation naturally demanded both experience and ability for

its direction and supervision. Experience could not
be had except such as had been gained in other business. Ability was sought and construction having
been resolved upon, on May 22, 1830, on motion of
John Jacob Astor, Churchill C. Cambreling, of New
York, then a member of Congress from that city, and
a close business associate of Mr. Astor, was appointed
commissioner of the Company, and Astor, Catlin and
Renwick were appointed a committee to confer with
him "with power to assign his duty and fix the terms of
his engagement." Mr. Cambreling was also a director
having been elected in 1829, to succeed Mr. Featherstonhaugh upon his resignation. July 29th, the committee reported that it had conferred with Mr. Cambreling "on the objects of his appointment, and have
assigned to him the duties of locating the road agreeably to the map and survey of Mr. Jervis, the engineer;
to make agreements and contracts for the purchase of
or obtaining the land which will be required for the
Road; to procure deeds and titles for the same; to ad-
vertise for and enter into contracts for grading and
forming the Road, and for the materials for the same;
to make arrangements with the Corporation of the
City of Albany to lay out a street to facilitate the construction of a lateral road to a central part of that
City for transporting passengers; to exercise a general
superintendence of the concerns of the Company, and
to recommend to the Board such measures as may
promote the interest of the Company, and expedite
the accomplishment of their object."

The committee had agreed to pay him for these
services and such other as might be assigned to him,
and which he might be able to execute before the meeting of Congress, $2,000. The committee was "im-
pressed with the belief that all the important agree-

ments, contracts and arrangements may be completed within that time."

The Board promptly and unanimously adopted a resolution recommended by the committee, "that a power of attorney be executed under the seal of the Company to C. C. Cambreling authorizing him at any time previous to the first day of January next, to make and sign contracts on behalf of the Mohawk and Hudson Railroad Company for grading, constructing and finishing a Railway from Albany to Schenectady, and for the necessary materials, and that the Secretary be directed to affix the seal of the Company thereto." The power of attorney had already been prepared and was at once executed.

Mr. Cambreling seems to have entered at once upon the performance of his duties but at some time, which can not be determined, he seems to have put details largely into the hands of John I. DeGraff of Schenectady, who was then also a director. Cambreling pushed grading work vigorously in the latter half of 1830, but apparently only for a single track, for April 21, 1831, the Board authorized the commissioner "to make contracts for the excavation and embankment preparatory to making a double track in such places as he may deem expedient."

On March 31, 1831, on motion of Mr. Astor, the Board appointed C. C. Cambreling "Commissioner of the Company with a compensation of two thousand dollars." No term of service was designated. He was re-elected a director in 1831, but on December 3rd of that year, presumably because of the necessity of attending to his congressional duties, he resigned as director, and it may be inferred, although there is no express record to that effect to be found, also resigned as commissioner at that time since in a report submitted to the Board, July 10, 1832, it is said "That in the management of the business of the Company hitherto in constructing their Railroad, it was deemed necessary and proper to appoint a Commissioner to whom full powers were given to superintend the concerns of the Company immediately connected with the construction of the road, to make contracts and to make all payments for lands, materials and labor and other expenses incurred at Albany and Schenectady. All the concerns of the Company immediately connected with the construction of the road have therefore been under the direction of the Commissioner, and in his absence and since his resignation, of John I. DeGraff, Esq."

On July 11th, the report of this committee was adopted, the office of commissioner abolished, a committee appointed to investigate and settle the accounts of DeGraff, all work and duties connected with the construction of the road committed to John B. Jervis, the chief engineer, and the office of agent of transportation created with general superintendence of all transportation operations with the advice and consent of the committee of supervision.

July 21st, John B. Jervis was appointed the agent for transportation, and acted in that capacity as well as chief engineer until April 10, 1833.

The committee to investigate and settle the accounts of Cambreling and DeGraff, as commissioners and acting commissioner, reported April 2, 1833, and found that their total disbursements were $500,297.18. This did not cover the entire cost of the road to that date, large sums having been paid by the Treasurer direct and not entering into the commissioners' accounts; nor did it include the compensation for services. Cambreling was paid $2,000 and May 8th, DeGraff presented a bill for $3,752.22, which was settled November 1st by the payment of $3,000.

The committee in its report take occasion to criticize sharply the manner in which the commissioners had kept their accounts, taking care, however, to disclaim even a shadow of doubt on the general character of the disbursements, large as they were, saying they had found a satisfactory voucher for every dollar expended, and believed the money was fairly paid to the parties entitled to receive it. They say, "The road has cost more, much more, than was expected, but if anything improper has been done to produce this result your Committee have discovered no clue to it."

Considering that this was one of the first cases of railroad accounting in this country on a considerable number of diverse transactions, it will be proper to transcribe in full the censure passed by the Committee.

Considering the high reputation of the Commissioner (Mr. Cambreling) as a commercial man, your Committee were much disappointed in the manner of keeping the accounts. Instead of regular books showing under appropriate heads the different branches of expenditure, nothing more was kept than a mere record of the daily payments, and if you wished to know, for instance, how much has been paid for "Land and Damages," "Excavation and Embankment," "Fencing" or any other particular division of the work, you would have to examine probably a large portion of the vouchers and perhaps every one of them.

It may be suggested without impropriety that possibly the directors may not have been wholly free from fault in failing to instruct their agent how they wanted the accounts kept, and were to some extent derelict in not knowing, as the work progressed, in what manner the payments were being recorded. The treasurer of the Company merely advanced to the commissioner from time to time upon his draft, large sums of money such as $10,000 and $25,000, and the use made of these sums was wholly under the control of the commissioner, and all records and vouchers relating to the same were kept by him. Doubtless it was another instance of no one knowing, due to lack of experience, just what should be done, and like everything else in rail-roading, had to be worked out from the necessities of the case.

At this meeting (April 3, 1833) Mr. Jervis stated that in his judgment, his services as engineer and superintendent would not be required after the 10th. His resignation was accepted and Asa Whitney was appointed superintendent and agent during the pleasure of the Board from and after April 10th, at a salary of $1,500 per annum, together with the use of the dwelling house and grounds occupied by him.

Whitney seems to have proved acceptable to the Board. June 18, 1834, it adopted a resolution con-cluding as follows, "and that they avail themselves of the present occasion to evince their satisfaction of the able and practical manner in which he had treated the various important subjects embraced in said reports, and to express at the same time their entire approba-tion of his general management of the Company's business." May 2, 1835, they gave a more practical appreciation of his services by increasing his salary to $2,500 annually with use of dwelling house, although they accompanied this with an expression of "having also full confidence in his ability to manage the Com-pany's business judiciously, and to their entire satis-faction."

On May 16, 1836, Whitney resigned to enter other business and the resignation was accepted, effective June 1, and again a very complimentary resolution was adopted.

Peter L. Parsons, who was a freight agent of the Company, was elected his successor with a salary of $2,000 and the use of house and grounds. Parsons resigned March 31, 1837, and one W. H. Talcott was employed temporarily on half time. Whitney's business venture apparently did not succeed, since the Board on April 8th invited him to return as superintendent at the same salary and on the same terms as when he resigned. He accepted and his new service commenced June 10th. Apparently he brought back with him his former vigor. February 28, 1839, he submitted a lengthy report on the condition of the affairs of the Company and the Board ordered 250 copies to be printed for the information of the stockholders. He advocated the elimination of the westerly plane and the extension of the easterly end up to some central point in Albany. He seems to have left the service of the Company October 31, 1839, but for what reason can not be discovered, but probably because the executive committee, which had October 24th been given full authority to revolutionize affairs insisted on reducing his salary. At all events, John Costigan was appointed superintendent by that committee. In a report to certain stockholders made in February, 1840, they say they had appointed Costigan and remark a "saving of eleven hundred dollars per annum, in the salary of this officer only, has been made by this appointment."

Costigan remained superintendent until June, 1843, when he was summarily discharged by the directors for conduct not specified. He brought a law suit against the Company in that year, but it related apparently to some land transaction connected with the extension to Ferry street.

Who succeeded him as superintendent does not appear, but John T. Clark, who was one of the resident engineers in constructing the road and was in 1853 elected state engineer, served as such for several years. Later on, one of the presidents, Norton, seems to have acted as superintendent.

Some Financial Results of Operation

It would be interesting, as well as important, if a complete showing of the financial results of the operations of the Mohawk and Hudson could be made. Unfortunately, due to absence of data in both the records of the Company now remaining and the files in the office of the Secretary of State at Albany, this is impossible. Even the year 1850 cannot be shown. The act of 1848 required railroad companies to report for calendar years, and accordingly the report for 1849 was for the calendar year. The railroad law of 1850 required reports to be made for a fiscal year ending September 30th. The report for 1850 accordingly begins with October 1, 1849, and ends September 30, 1850. The returns for the months of October, November and December, 1849, accordingly appear in both reports, not in detail but only in the yearly totals.

The figures for three separate periods are available. In the directors' minute book No. 1 at page 284, appears the following table which is self-explanatory and which will enable those interested to ascertain some general facts relative to the amount and character of the business done, as well as the receipts and expenditures.

| Year | Tons of Freight from | | Receipts for Transportation of | | Disbursements | |
	Albany	Schenectady	Passengers	Freight	Passengers	Freight
			$	$	$	$
1832	—	—	51,675.47	—	27,309.94	—
1833	2,096	870	69,300.38	3,708.02	35,623.29	1,029.01
1834	5,282	11,313	68,210.35	12,733.77	37,220.35	13,693.23
1835	10,522	19,762	84,776.95	26,287.73	42,943.68	23,227.56
1836	12,866	18,577	103,470.43	28,185.67	54,857.42	23,993.26
1837	6,331	10,373	97,767.82	14,429.06	63,102.71	19,996.34
1838	8,966	11,549	101,023.94	19,276.28	64,999.66	19,210.08
1839	12,310	14,080	116,664.26	25,877.19	59,019.38	25,422.09
Total	58,373	86,524	692,889.60	130,497.72	385,076.43	126,571.57

The reports to the Secretary of State for the five years 1843–1847, are summarized in the following table:

| Year Ending Dec. 31 | Operating Revenue | | | | Operating Expenses | Net Income | Operating Ratio |
	Passenger	Freight	Other	Total			
	$	$	$	$	$	$	%
1843	49,782.77	9,215.01	10,059.79	69,057.57	58,780.36	10,277.21	85.12
1844	66,293.81	10,059.79	4,228.64	80,582.24	34,040.69	46,541.55	42.24
1845	79,644.85	14,781.08	4,068.51	98,494.44	37,367.32	61,127.12	37.94
1846	92,194.67	18,321.59	3,340.82	113,857.08	41,776.84	72,080.24	36.69
1847	110,051.67	46,591.67	3,243.96	159,887.30	60,310.42	99,576.88	37.72
Total for 5 Years	397,967.77	98,969.14	24.941.72	521,878.63	232,275.63	289,603.00	44.51

It will be noted first, that the total income from operation in this table is $289,603. During the first four years of the period covered no dividends were paid. The fifth year, 1847, a dividend of $25,000 was paid, thus leaving for the five years net earnings to the amount of $264,603, which was applied to corporate purposes. In January, 1848, another dividend of

$25,000 was paid which must have been taken from 1847 earnings, reducing the above net to $239,603. During the period covered, $90,649.09 were used in paying debts incurred prior to 1843 and the interest on bonds issued for construction purposes. The remaining sum of $148,953.91 was used in paying for construction. It was in the years 1843, 1844 and 1845, that the new lines eliminating the inclined planes were constructed.

The following is a table of the reports for the fiscal years ended September 30, 1850, 1851 and 1852:

Year Ending Sept. 30th	Operating Revenue				Operating Expenses	Net Income	Operating Ratio
	Passenger	Freight	Other	Total			
	$	$	$	$	$	$	%
1850	132,207.69	70,242.69	6,134.50	208,584.88	91,171.98	117,412.90	43.71
1851	146,649.61	87,432.64	5,765.50	239,847.75	103,689.35	136,158.40	43.23
1852	171,752.74	117,859.94	6,500.00	296,112.68	131,664.87	164,447.81	44.46
Total for 3 Years	450,610.04	275,535.27	18,400.00	744,545.31	326,526.20	418,019.11	43.86

For these three years the net income was $418,-019.11 which may be compared with the total of $289,603 for five years in the first table. Another interesting comparison is of the total freight revenues for the two periods—$98,969 for the five years and $275,535.27 for the three years. We may also note the jump in freight revenues for 1852 to $117,859.94, the canal tolls having been abolished December 1, 1851 (see elsewhere the history of canal tolls). The difficulty of handling this rapidly expanding business between Buffalo and Albany by eight different organizations was one of the great factors leading to the consolidation of 1853.

Efforts for Operation with the Utica and Schenectady

The year 1836 brought into existence a new problem which the Company seems to have struggled with a long time and which must have contained for it elements of extreme difficulty, which judged by the experience of ninety years seem to be not difficulties at all. Up to the opening of the Utica and Schenectady August 1st of that year, excepting the Saratoga and Schenectady, the Mohawk and Hudson had no railroad connection. Its trains could be hauled only from one terminus to the other, a short distance of 16 miles; there was no change of cars, no waiting for connecting trains; no transfer of baggage from one road to the other; no division of rates; no passing of equipment into other custody and control.

The opening of the Utica and Schenectady speedily showed to the directors that this primitive condition of affairs was gone forever and that the convenience of travellers and the encouragement of traffic demanded new arrangements for which no precedents existed. The Mohawk and Hudson handled both freight and passengers; the Utica and Schenectady passengers only. The passenger station at Schenectady had been constructed at joint expense. The first point to be determined was the time schedule of trains. This was not taken up by the superintendents or executive officers, but by committees of the two Boards. That of the Utica and Schenectady submitted the following propositions:

1st. Trains to start from Albany at 8 A.M. and 2 P.M. and from Utica at 9 A.M. and 3 P.M.

2nd. Passengers to be transferred at Schenectady but baggage cars to be run through from Utica to Albany and vice versa without change, baggage car to be furnished by the Utica and Schenectady with baggage man.

3rd. Passengers from Utica to Albany to be permitted to pay fare at either end.

Due consideration was given by the Mohawk and Hudson committee to this elaborate proposal; and a meeting of the committee was held at which they in turn submitted their proposition in the following terms:

While the committee is disposed to forward any arrangement which will promote the mutual interest of both companies, it appears obvious to them that to leave Albany with the two principal daily trains at the usual hours for breakfast and dinner would occasion much inconvenience. It also appears that the adoption of the measure proposed on the part of the Utica Company without further action would fail to afford all the accommodation to the public, etc., etc.

If, however, an arrangement can be made for seating the passengers at Albany and Utica for the entire route without change and with as little delay as possible the committee think it very desirable to do so and suggest the following basis:

1st. Cars to run through the entire route and each company to furnish the proportion of carriages according to their respective mileage.

2nd. Trains from Albany to start at 8½ A.M. and 2½ P.M. or first train at 7 A.M. Cars to leave Utica at a corresponding time as near as may best suit the Utica Company.

3rd. On account of the minor interest of the Mohawk and Hudson in the collections and additional responsibility and trouble upon the collector at Albany the Utica Company to allow him $200 per annum.

Neither proposition was acceptable to both parties so it was agreed to adopt in a modified form the propositions of the Utica Company as a temporary arrangement to continue only for the then present season, and a formal minute to that effect was agreed to by both companies.

Certain propositions on the part of each Company were considered and after some time spent thereon the plan of uniting the two roads by running cars through from Albany to Utica (as proposed by the M. & H.) was deferred for the present; and it was agreed to modify the proposition of the U. & S. so as to fix the time of starting from Albany at 7½ A.M. and 1½ P.M. and to adopt the same as a temporary arrangement commencing Sept. 20, 1836, or as soon as the state of the Schenectady depot will permit. Said arrangement to terminate the ensuing winter.

This grave matter engaged the attention of seven men on two different occasions and resulted only in an agreement as to the time of starting two trains daily from each city and the running of a through baggage car to be furnished by the Utica and Schenectady. The reluctance of the Mohawk and Hudson committee to disturb unduly the breakfast and dinner hours of the Albanians can only be commended, but how starting the trains half an hour prior to each of those events helped the situation, is unfortunately left without any explanation. Why the Utica road was insistent upon passengers changing cars at Schenectady we are not informed.

General Review

The variegated and hectic experience of the Mohawk and Hudson has now been considered with reference to the principal matters connected therewith. A broader and more comprehensive view of the united whole, an exposition of what it accomplished and a review of its numerous and at times astonishing errors are all necessary to a fair and complete understanding of this pioneer road.

That it was conceived by George William Featherstonhaugh, in many ways a most remarkable man, at a time when the idea of railroads was floating in other

minds is unquestionable. John Stevens had endeavored in a somewhat futile way to interest the public
in a railroad in the Mohawk Valley in 1823, as he did
both before and after that in other localities. Railroads consisting of a track for the carrying of horse
drawn vehicles containing a load of heavy freight had
been in use to some extent in Great Britain for a considerable number of years. We have Featherstonhaugh's own evidence that he had seen and studied
much that had been printed about them and that on
his visit to England he found they had developed far
beyond what he had known. But nowhere until the
opening of the Stockton and Darlington in 1825 had
they been used for the accommodation of the general
public and with steam as the motive power. Even
that road did not seem to settle the practicability of the
use of steam locomotives, thus giving greater speed and
greater capacity, and the question was mooted until
the opening of the Liverpool and Manchester in 1829,
and the success of George Stephenson's Rocket then
proved that a new method of transportation capable
of tremendous expansion had come into being.

The merit of Featherstonhaugh is that he had the
genius to understand the possibilities and the force
and ability to induce others to put their money into
the experiment. That cruel misfortune took him from
the stage of action before a blow was struck in the actual
work of construction is true, but this does not detract
in the least from the credit which is due him for originating the scheme and pushing it by his unaided
efforts to a point where others had become so imbued
with his hopes and enthusiasm that they carried it into
practical operation. It is necessary to point out that
though Stephen Van Rensselaer was one of the two
incorporators of the Company, was its president until

uation forced the city of Albany into the adventure and compelled it to give the financial aid indispensable to carry the road through to success.

These troubles were attributable to a lack of knowledge on the part of the builders, of the power which could be developed in a steam locomotive, of the nature of the track required to carry the motive power and the traffic, of the tremendous amount of accessories to the mere track and power required to handle the traffic and of the proper location of the facilities to accommodate the public and meet competition. This lack of knowledge can not in the main be subject to just criticism, but no account of the Company can be complete or adequate without a just presentation of all these troubles and the causes from which they sprang.

As already explained the design was to connect the valleys of the Mohawk and of the Hudson. The event has more than justified the choice of location, but the situation involved, as already explained, carrying the road in a distance of 16 miles over a ridge 185 feet above the easterly terminus and 105 feet above the westerly. The topography forced this elevation to be overcome within a distance of five miles on the easterly end and less than two miles on the westerly. It was not believed that a steam locomotive with smooth driving wheels working on a smooth track would possess tractive power sufficient to haul a load over the grade. No one knew; no one could know until the experiment had been tried. There was no locomotive in existence in this country with which to make the trial. There was no railroad grade in England on which it could be made with the one or two crude locomotives which were all in existence there. So it was determined to operate over the stiff grades on inclined planes with stationary engines pulling up and letting down the cars with long ropes assisting the operation with loaded balance cars on the second track. Actual use for five or six years showed this to be entirely inadequate as well as expensive and as early as 1838, permission was obtained from the legislature to make a change of route which would do away with inclined planes, but the expense of such a change would be very great and the money was lacking. Not until September, 1844, were the necessary changes finished. Six long years were needed to get rid of this initial error after it was fully ascertained to be an error.

The next error was in the track. The track of today was unknown. Not an iron rail had been rolled in the country. English practice had led to the belief that a solid, inflexible foundation of stone was essential. Hence the track as already described was designed and constructed. It proved to be enormously expensive, the wooden superstructure was short lived. It was unsuited to traffic requirements. The strap rail proved inadequate and unsafe and within sixteen years, the entire track had to be reconstructed and iron rails substituted.

The next defect was in the original locomotive power. How this could have been avoided it is impossible to see. Approved locomotives in 1826–30 did not exist. They had to be designed and constructed as purely experimental. Of the two first put on the road, one was of English, the other of American manufacture. The latter proved that a steam locomotive was possible, but that it was not itself a practical success, and after two years it was retired and in 1835 scrapped. The English machine made by R. Stephenson & Co., then the best and most experienced manufacturers of locomotives in the world, had to be materially altered before it was a practical success and no later than 1837, was entirely rebuilt, only the boiler being retained in the reconstructed machine. In 1833, two new locomotives, the Mohawk and Hudson were ordered from England and were doubtless the best that could be made at that time, but we find that November 29, 1845, after only twelve years of service, the Board ordered the Hudson, which stood on the books of the Company at $7,000 to be sold at from $1,500 to $2,000. It and its mate had become obsolete and it was economy to replace them with the improved machines which practical use had developed. Such an experience as this, has lasted until our own day. Urgent demands of traffic have forced from time to time new locomotives of greater utility, the new machines have forced the construction of new track and new bridges and when the process will cease, no man can say. But what might happen in the future did not make less difficult and onerous the burdens of the thirties and forties of the last century.

Another perplexing problem which was troublesome at the very outset and continued a source of great annoyance until 1844, was the location of the eastern terminal at Albany. Over it, excited public meetings were held, written remonstrances were filed, public opinion was divided and the report of the commission which finally established the present route in January, 1844, shows that although both the Company and the city authorities of Albany were endeavoring to obtain the Patroon's creek route, private interests were still struggling for the road down either the Hudson avenue or the Fox ravine, the two ravines on either side of the ridge upon which the Capitol is situate, and the report recites that the personal knowledge of one of the commissioners (John B. Jervis) was one of the reasons inducing the commission to refrain from further surveys of those locations.

The failure to comprehend what would be required to make a complete operating railroad it must be admitted is somewhat astonishing. There has been given above an estimate of cost made by Featherstonhaugh on which or something like it we may assume the original capital stock of $300,000 was based. Yet the authorization in the charter to increase to $500,000 unquestionably was a precautionary measure based upon full appreciation of the uncertainty of any estimate which could be made. So there is shown above the cost estimate of the engineer Fleming who for a long time had been investigating the question and it is less than $300,000. Both estimates are more remarkable for what they do not contain than for what they do. And we can not be surprised that in January, 1832, the directors reported to the state that up to that time they had expended $483,215 and that to complete it $156,693 more would be required, a total of $639,948. Nor need we wonder that up to the time of the consolidation in 1853 over $1,800,000 had been expended on the road.

To obtain this additional $1,200,000 or thereabouts was a nerve racking task. From 1840 to September, 1847, no dividends were declared. Net earnings were put into improvements. Overdrafts at banks at times amounted to more than $100,000. Directors loaned to it their money and credit and guaranteed its bonds. Bonds were hawked around at times in as small lots as one bond at a time. Short time notes for materials and supplies were frequent. Money to eliminate the westerly inclined plane was obtained on bonds which were rendered marketable only by the guaranty of the city of Albany, which city had to lend the money necessary for the easterly elimination. But the Company turned, twisted and fought: in every bond issue but that to Albany there was a provision for convertibility into stock and after 1844 was passed, matters improved, nearly all the bonds outstanding except $125,000 to Albany had been converted prior to the consolidation in 1853, in 1848 annual dividends aggregating 7 per cent were reached which in 1852 were increased to 8 per cent, and in that year the stock was selling in the market at a premium.

The financial troubles thus briefly sketched probably explain some rather curious facts. During a corporate existence of 27 years with a maximum directorate of 9, the road had 70 different directors of whom 3 served less than one year, 17 one year, 13 two years, 11 three years and 9 four years. Of presidents there were no less than 11, of whom 10 served in the 21 years from 1832 to 1853. Length of service in both positions increased materially after 1844 when troubles were decreasing and prosperity increasing. At one time John T. Norton gave his entire time to his duties as president and superintendent, and the Board in gratitude voted him the munificent sum of $2,500 for the year, presumably $1,000 as president and $1,500 as superintendent.

In the year 1847, by act of the legislature the name of the Company was changed to The Albany and Schenectady Railroad Company and by that it will be designated subsequent to that date, although, as the pioneer road, it will for all time be known chiefly as the Mohawk and Hudson. The reason impelling this change can now be only conjectured, although it may yet be learned from some long forgotten record.

CHAPTER II

THE UTICA AND SCHENECTADY RAILROAD

THE Utica and Schenectady Railroad Company was incorporated April 29, 1833, by Chapter 294 of the laws of that year, with an authorized capital stock of $2,000,000, consisting of twenty thousand shares of a par value of $100. It was to extend from the city of Utica to the city of Schenectady, a distance of about seventy-eight miles, to continue for fifty years, and was to be managed by a Board of thirteen directors with at least one director from each county through which the road passed. It was provided in the charter that the Company might fix tolls and charges for the transportation of persons and baggage, but at no greater sum than four cents per mile for a passenger and his ordinary baggage. Owing to its paralleling the Erie Canal, the charter peremptorily declared, "no property of any description except the ordinary baggage of passengers shall be transported or carried on said road." Owing to assumed injury to the business of the Mohawk Turnpike Company, owning a turnpike road paralleling along the Mohawk river, the charter also provided the railroad company should pay $22.50 per share for the stock of the turnpike company before commencing the transportation of passengers.

No exclusive rights or privileges were conferred upon it as in the case of the Mohawk and Hudson, and it was thereby left open to the competition of any other railroad which could obtain a charter to build along the Mohawk valley. The prohibition upon the carrying of property led to the enactment of Chapter 12 of the laws of 1837, authorizing it to carry United States mails, and the limitation to ordinary baggage brought about Chapter 363 of the laws of 1837, authorizing it to carry extra baggage but without charge.

The prohibition upon carrying property other than baggage and its modification and final abolition will be discussed elsewhere.

The charter named twenty-one commissioners who should receive subscriptions to the stock of the Company, the sum of five dollars per share to be paid at the time of subscription. They were to assemble in the city of New York on the second Monday of July, or as soon thereafter as the whole capital stock should be taken, and distribute the capital stock among the subscribers, and this being done, to give notice of a time and place of a meeting of the stockholders to elect directors. Subscriptions were to be received in the cities of New York, Albany, Schenectady and Utica. The commissioners met at the City Hotel in New York, July 8, 1833. All the stock had been subscribed, and the $5 a share paid in in cash. It would seem that the stock had been oversubscribed, but to what extent does not appear for the final allotment was not completed until July 10th. The enthusiasm which existed for new railroads and the favorable location of this one along the Mohawk valley brought in subscriptions very largely other than merely local. The commissioners themselves were evidently large subscribers for their first determination was that there should be allotted to a commissioner not to exceed one hundred shares. They next determined to allot the stock to localities as follows: State list, 1,435 shares; Utica, 5,500; Schenec-

Erastus Corning

tady, 2,500; Albany, 5,000; New York, 5,565. Total, 20,000.

The first meeting of stockholders for the election of directors was appointed to be held at Congress Hall in the city of Albany on August 17th, and the first meeting of directors at the same place at 3 o'clock in the afternoon of the same day.

The stockholders meeting was held pursuant to appointment and resulted in the election of thirteen directors as follows:

Nicholas Devereux, Utica; Alfred Munson, Utica; Henry Seymour, Utica; Nathaniel S. Benton, Little Falls; Tobias A. Stoutenburgh, Johnstown; Alonzo C. Paige, Schenectady; John Townsend, Albany; Erastus Corning, Albany; Lewis Benedict, Albany; James Porter, Albany; James Mason, New York; Churchill C. Cambreling, New York; James Hooker, Poughkeepsie.

These directors then elected as officers Erastus Corning, president, Alfred Munson, vice president, James Porter, secretary and Gideon Hawley, treasurer. Erastus Corning was each year during the existence of the Company elected a director and the president, and served the whole period of twenty years without compensation, except that in recognition of his services the stockholders and directors in 1850 took action which may well be set out in full at this time.

At a meeting of the stockholders of the Company held in the city of New York on the 19th day of November, 1850, a letter which had been addressed to Nicholas Devereux by stockholders owning upwards of 1100 shares and residing in and near Boston was read to the meeting, requesting that, as a mark of esteem and respect, and in testimony of his faithful, judicious and long continued service as president without compensation, the company present him with a valuable service of plate. The meeting unanimously requested the directors to do this.

At the next meeting of the Board the foregoing was reported to and considered by it and a committee of five appointed to procure the service of plate as requested by the resolution and present the same to Mr. Corning, all of which was accordingly done at a cost of $6,074.10.

It has not been possible to ascertain who conceived, promoted and pushed through to completion the organization of this Company, but it may be conjectured with every probability of correctness that it was the work of men whose names appear on the first Board of Directors and that Erastus Corning was not the least of them. His election as the first president is strong, though not conclusive, evidence of this.

Some little delay occurred after August 17th in securing a chief engineer. Finally on October 1, 1833, at the fourth meeting of directors, William C. Young was appointed to that position with a salary of $2500 per annum and Gideon M. Davison was appointed commissioner with a salary of $2000. Messrs. Mason, Benton, Benedict, Seymour and Stoutenburgh constituted an executive committee. At the third meeting on September 4th, a resolution was adopted that red cedar timber should be used in construction and contracts were subsequently made for same, but for some reason the contractors largely failed to meet their agreement. A great deal of trouble was occasioned by this failure; some delay ensued; other timber of various kinds was largely used. Later on the contractors gave their notes for damages to the amount of $13,500 and when at the maturity of the first of the series appeal was made for a reduction in the amount, the Board summarily and sternly said no.

Unfortunately no exact description of the track construction has been found. It can be gathered from the records that in general it was of the strap rail type, the rail being carried on longitudinal stringers, fastened together by cross ties. The iron strap rail was somewhat heavier than that used on the Mohawk and Hudson, being ¾ inch in thickness and 2½ inches in width. Little real light has reached us as to the difficulties encountered in actual operation with strap rail, but an extract from a letter of the treasurer of the Auburn and Syracuse road is worth quoting as giving a little information. It appears that road had first ordered strap rail the same size as on the Utica and Schenectady, but afterwards in order to save $15,000 reduced the size somewhat, subject, however, to inquiry. In a letter dated February 9, 1837, the treasurer says:

I understand that Mr. Young, the engineer of the Utica and Schenectady, was formerly on the Mohawk and also the Saratoga R. R., where the 2¼ by ⅝ has been and now is in use and that with the experience derived from those roads he had selected the 2½ by ¾ for the Utica and Schenectady R. R. The objection made by our resident engineers to the 2¼ by ⅝ is that by the friction of the wheels the bar becomes elongated so as to cut off the head of the spike and the ends of the bars coming in contact are raised up, and they give that as probably one of the reasons why 2½ by ¾ was selected by the U. & S. R. R.

No reply to this letter has been found but the facts stated in the excerpt are illuminating. The stone foundation supporting the longitudinal sills used on the Mohawk and Hudson seems not to have been used.

The first work of engineer Young was to survey and locate the route. Although the road was necessarily confined to the narrow valley of the Mohawk, the surveys occupied a long time. There were different views on the Board as to the location in the cities of Utica and Schenectady. All the questions came up for determination in September, 1834. There were three routes considered in Schenectady. The one selected was adopted by a vote of 7 to 5. The route was finally adopted nearly a year after surveys were begun and on September 4, 1834, the executive committee was authorized to let contracts for grading, masonry and bridges on the entire line; to purchase the necessary lands, rail plates, spikes, carriages, engines and other necessary materials. The location in Utica and perhaps elsewhere was not then determined, for at a meeting on December 10th, we find the Board resolving, "that it is expedient that this Board locate the entire line of the said road during its present session" and at that session another struggle was had over the Utica location. The difficulties arising in ascertaining what contests were about nearly a hundred years ago are well shown by a resolution adopted in this case, "That the line of the said railroad be extended from Mrs. Bradstreet's to the termination on the square in Utica at the foot of Genesee street by the route which is termed the Water street route and which crosses the river at Nourse's and runs in the rear of Bogart's house." Two Utica directors voted against this.

The route as finally established extended from State street in Schenectady to Genesee street in Utica, a distance of 78 miles, and substantially upon the present line of the New York Central between those points. At that time Utica and Schenectady were little more than large villages, their population in 1835 being, Utica 10,183, Schenectady 6,272. In that year Albany had only 28,109 inhabitants.

1835, saw construction in active progress under the supervision of Commissioner Davison and Engineer

Young. Few meetings of the directors were had. January 21st, a delegation from Schenectady made objections to the route in that city, raising a legal question upon which the Board obtained the opinion of Greene C. Bronson, Attorney General, and Marcus T. Reynolds, two of the ablest lawyers of the day.

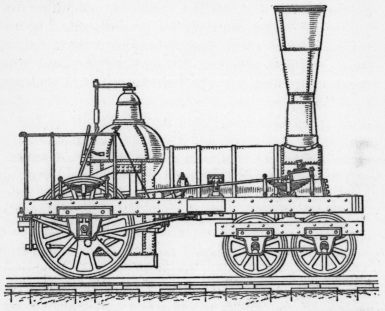

LOCOMOTIVE BUILT BY BALDWIN, ONE OF THE FIRST USED ON THE
U. & S.

The same day it signed a certificate showing line of road as prepared by the engineer, directed the executive committee to procure iron for rails, red cedar for longitudinal sills for sixty miles of road, to contract for locomotives, to enter into negotiations for purchase of Mohawk Turnpike pursuant to charter requirements, authorized the committee to order white pine, cedar or other suitable timber for longitudinal sills and southern pine rails, and audited the bill of W. Miller for one dozen curl maple chairs, $15. June 1st, a contract for iron rails was confirmed, also contract with M. W. Baldwin, founder of the Baldwin Locomotive Works, for six locomotive engines, and authority given to contract for sill timber of suitable quality to supply any deficiency in red cedar.

Some business of the Board transacted September 23rd, gives rise to a question which has not been fully solved, namely to what extent was the use of horses contemplated as motive power. It was engaged in fixing "stopping places or depots for receiving wood, water, passengers &c." and among other resolutions is the following:

Resolved, that accommodation places for barns or stables of horses with occasional watering of engines be established for the present at Hoffman's Ferry in the town of Glenville, at Spraker's Tavern in the town of Palatine, at a point in the village of St. Johnsville where the railroad intersects the public road leading from the turnpike to the Mohawk river and at such point between the village of Little Falls and Utica as the Commissioner and engineer shall select.

These locations were made on the express condition that "all ground required for barns or stables for the accommodation of horses and for the supply of water for engines" be granted to the Company gratuitously and "under an express stipulation that the Company shall at any time be at liberty to discontinue such occupation on surrendering up the said grounds so occupied to the several owners thereof." This looks like a provision against possible contingencies, but another resolution was adopted "that a place for stabling of horses and occasional watering of engines be established in the village of Herkimer, . . . and that the ground if any required for that purpose be purchased by them (the Commissioner and Engineer)." Certainly horse power was in mind as tentatively probable. The location of these barns or stables is significant. In round numbers Hoffman's Ferry is 9 miles west of Schenectady; Sprakers, 26 miles west of Hoffman's Ferry; St. Johnsville 11 miles west of Sprakers; Little Falls 10 miles west of St. Johnsville; Herkimer 7 miles west of Little Falls and 14 miles east of Utica. But beyond these resolutions nothing is known of the matter.

At this meeting of September 23rd, work was evidently being rushed. A very considerable number of important details regarding buildings at both Utica and Schenectady were disposed of, the contract for red cedar was modified, the commissioner was authorized to buy white cedar ties to lay down ten miles of road,

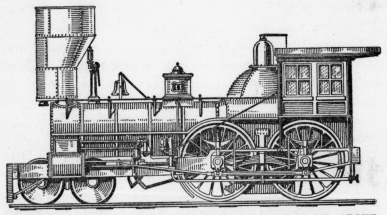

LOCOMOTIVE BUILT BY DAVID MATTHEW FOR THE U. & S. ABOUT 1840.

the executive committee was authorized to make contracts for railroad cars as many and of such plans as they deemed proper, the chief engineer was authorized to employ David Matthew (who ran the first engine on the Mohawk and Hudson) as chief locomotive engineer from and after January 1, 1836, at such "sallery" as may be agreed upon, and the commissioner was authorized to settle with Andrew A. Fink of Manheim for damages to his tavern building and his tavern business occasioned by blasting by paying $500, the amount of his claim "if a settlement can not be made with him for a less sum." Probably the commissioner did not show his authority for settling to Mr. Fink.

November 18, 1835, a large amount of business was dispatched by the Board. It appeared from the report of a committee to examine the accounts of the treasurer that moneys "received and passed" by him since the 30th day of May amounted to $480,055.02, and with but $36,215.71 remaining on hand, a very considerable sum for those days, and indicating that the work had been driven at full speed. Two additional locomotives were directed, ten railroad coaches "calculated for winter use," also ten additional coaches, character not specified, the purchase of not exceeding one million feet board measure for road sills "said timber to be either hemlock, white pine or chestnut (due to failure to get red cedar), five hundred thousand feet of Georgia pine at $28 per thousand of the dimensions of from 18 to 40 feet in length and 5 by 6 inches in size." It is only from such data that a clear idea of the construction can be obtained. The commissioner was also authorized to send some suitable person to Canada to attend to the purchase of red cedar, and "the procuring of such timber as will be suitable for cross ties, sills and rails." This is, of course, to be taken in connection with the authorization to purchase and discloses the difficulties in that early day attendant upon securing even timber for construction. Sellers were not in the field soliciting. They had to be searched for.

No further directors' meeting of importance was held until August 1, 1836. At that time Commissioner

Davison resigned, effective October 1st. Chief Engineer Young was elected Superintendent and Engineer, at a salary of $3,000 per year, he to devote his time exclusively to his railroad duties. It is proper to note here that he held these positions until August, 1849, when he resigned to become chief engineer of the Hudson River Railroad then building. In 1837 his salary was raised to $5,000 a year in consideration of his contracting to remain with the Company five years, the directors reserving the right to remove him at pleasure.

The letter of resignation was laid before the Board at its next meeting after August—January 10, 1850—whereupon it resolved "That the members of this Board do hereby express their high appreciation of the energy, skill and faithfulness of Mr. Young during the long period of his official connection with this company as the Superintendent and Engineer of its road and works, and their best wishes for his success and prosperity in his future professional career and especially in the important and laborious post which he has accepted." A most valuable man. The great success of the Utica and Schenectady must be largely attributed to the energy and wisdom of those managing its affairs and of these, William C. Young stands in the foremost rank.

We have now reached the period of time when the road was opened for operation. That event occurred August 1, 1836. On that day a large party left Albany by the Mohawk and Hudson and on reaching Schenectady, they took their seats in two trains of ten cars each and were taken to Utica which was not reached until half past two in the afternoon. That town was found to be overflowing with people. It was Utica's great day. The party remained in Utica until the next day, leaving at 8 o'clock in the morning in a train with about 300 passengers that being the first regular trip over the road on which fare was taken. The train did not arrive at Schenectady until half past two, six and a half hours to make seventy-eight miles. But the road was new, the equipment was untried and the load was heavy. Twelve miles an hour, governed as the movement was by the modern maxim, safety first, was not so bad and passengers were confident that it could be made in less than four hours—say 20 miles or more an hour. One representative of the press proudly chronicles the fact that having left Utica at 8 A.M. Tuesday, he arrived at New York (by boat from Albany) at 5:30 A.M., Wednesday, 21½ hours for the whole trip. The distance is now covered by the Empire State Express in 4 hours and 52 minutes.

It is said in a newspaper account that the receipts of August 2nd were nearly $4,000. If this be correct as it probably is, it is indicative of the number of people who were desirous of a first ride on the first day of a new railroad.

The third annual report of G. M. Davison, the commissioner in charge of construction, was dated June 6, 1836, about two months prior to the opening of the road, but it gives a very clear and comprehensive account of what had been done, of the existing state of things and indulges in calculations as to future prospects of great value in judging how a man of intelligence looked at the future of transportation at that time. It is a document well worth preserving but can be printed here only in part.

To the President and Directors of the Utica and Schenectady Railroad Company.

GENTLEMEN:—I herewith submit the following report of disbursements in constructing the road of this company, its present condition and future prospects.

1. *Of Disbursements.*

The total amount of monies expended by me at the
last annual meeting of the board was $266,435.11
Since then, up to the period of my last settlement
with the treasurer, on the 30th ult., I had dis-
bursed 698,126.13

Making a total of $964,561.24

Of this sum there has been paid, For preliminary surveys	$16,730.83	
Engineering	35,297.57	
Lots purchased and appraised in the city of Schenectady, and the expenses of procuring titles	39,382.87	
do. do ....at Little Falls	34,381.34	
do. do ....at Utica	15,237.45	
Other lands, fencing,* damages and procuring to titles	182,734.71	
Grading, including alteration of turn-pike	324,141.87	
Masonry	62,790.73	
Slope or river wall	17,924.41	
Bridges	61,003.61	
Red Cedar Timber	40,619.54	
Timber, other than red cedar, and exclusive of that used for bridges	48,143.77	
Superstructure of road, including transportation of materials	34,160.14	
Coaches and wagons	18,390.32	
Carriage houses, barns, shops and other depot buildings	23,039.82	
Printing, stationery and advertising...	716.06	
Fuel for locomotive engines	2,539.69	
Miscellaneous expenditures, including salary of Comm'r	7,236.51	964,561.24
From which is to be deducted one half the cost of the depot grounds at Schenectady, to be refunded by the Mohawk & Hudson Railroad Company	6,375.00	
The monies advanced on the appraisal of the depot grounds at Utica, which are to be refunded by individuals owning real estate in that city	8,840.00	

* The fencing in a great proportion of cases is to be perpetuated by the
owners of adjoining lands,—a covenant having been inserted in their conveyances to that effect, and an extra compensation allowed therefor.

Brought forward................	$15,215.00	
Fuel purchased for locomotive engines, chargeable to the transportation account..........................	2,539.69	
And monies advanced for red cedar for the second track.................	5,000.00	$22,754.69
Leaving.....................		$941,806.55
The Treasurer has also advanced on account of Iron..................	150,084.62	
Southern pine rails.................	35,667.54	
Locomotive engines................	25,705.00	
And for miscellaneous purposes.......	10,089.61	221,546.77
Making a total of...........		$1,163,353.32

With the monies thus expended, all the necessary lands, with a slight exception, have been purchased—the fencing, grading, masonry, and bridges nearly completed—the iron plates procured—nearly two-thirds of the timber and superstructure for a single track paid for—and an important advance made towards engines, carriages and depot buildings.

2.   *Of the Present Condition of the Road.*

With a few unimportant exceptions, the road is graded for a double track from State street in Schenectady to the terminating point at Utica, and about two-thirds of the superstructure of a single track completed. Had the Oswego and Seneca canals been open as early as usual, and the navigation of the latter remained uninterrupted so that the timber under contract could have been received within the time originally contemplated, the road would have been put in operation as early as the 15th or 20th of July. But the delays incident to this interruption will prevent the running of carriages until about the middle of August; when it is believed the whole line will be in readiness for the conveyance of passengers. Preparatory to this, five of the eight locomotive engines ordered last year will be placed on the road, and the remaining three delivered soon thereafter—Added to which, fifty pleasure carriages, carrying 24 passengers each, and fifty wagons for the accommodation of emigrants, are nearly completed. Arrangements are also making to construct, without delay, an additional track of from 12 to 15 miles long, equidistant from Utica and Schenectady—so that until the second track shall have been finished, a convenient passing place of sufficient extent may be afforded, to prevent any delay in the transmission of passengers. But with a business of such magnitude as already exists on the line of this road, and which must be greatly augmented whenever it is opened it will undoubtedly be found important to complete the second track at as early a day as may be practicable. That the period of such completion should not be extended beyond another season, I believe will be admitted by all who are conversant with the amount of travel through the valley of the Mohawk.

From the unusual depth of snow which fell during the last winter, it had been anticipated that on the breaking up of the Mohawk and its tributary streams, the railroad would receive serious injury, and much pains had been taken to open the ditches and culverts in exposed localities, and guard the bridges with stone and other burthens. But the result has shown that even these precautions were unnecessary. No injury whatever was experienced; but on the contrary, the gratifying evidence furnished that the road will always be beyond the reach of the ordinary annual freshets, and probably beyond any that will ever occur.

3. *Of the Cost of the Road.*

The amount already expended, on account of construction as heretofore stated has been...... $1,163,353.32

The estimated cost of completing the single track and putting the road in operation, is as follows:

On the first division, extending from Utica, to the Nose, so called, in Palatine, about 46 miles, agreeably to the estimates of Mr. Higham, the resident engineer................ $70,850.00

On the second division extending from the Nose to the Ballston Road in Glenville, about 30 miles, agreeably to the estimates of Mr. Lee, the resident engineer................... 33,150.00

On the third division extending from Ballston road to State street in Schenectady, agreeable to the estimates of Mr. Lake, the resident engineer....................... 38,707.15

Balance for engines and putting them in order, about................. 31,000.00

Brought forward...............$173,707.15
Do.   for carriages and wagons 37,281.00
Do.   for timber, including the cen-
tral branch of fifteen miles, about..   20,000.00
Do.   for Iron, about.............   5,000.00
Engineering......................   8,000.00
Horses..........................   5,000.00
Harness.........................   1,000.00
Miscellaneous, estimated at.........   5,000.00
                                                    $254,988.15

To which must be added the purchase
of the Mohawk turnpike, required
by the charter of this company....   62,000.00
                Total..................... $1,480,351.47

Calls to the amount of $1,500,000 having been made of the capital stock, no further payments from the stockholders will be necessary during the present year.   The laying of a second track and an increase of engines and carriages to correspond with an increase of business, will probably require an expenditure of the residue of the capital.   I have, therefore, in the estimates which follow, assumed as a basis that the road, when completed, will cost $2,000,000.   That it will not exceed that amount, I think is evident from the expenditures and progress already made in the work.

This report is taken from the *American Railway Journal* of July 16, 1836, page 437.   Checked with the books of the Company it is found that an item of $90 for horse keeping and charged to construction is omitted.

Little or nothing of interest has been found in the operations of the road for several years subsequent to the opening for business.   The financial results of the investment were apparently good; the volume of business did not materially increase.   There was nothing to add to the traffic until connections bringing additions to through traffic from points farther west and east were constructed.   Such connections were slowly appearing, but not until 1843, did the road form one link in the long hoped for central line from the Hudson to Lake Erie.

June 20, 1844, Superintendent Young advised the Board that the double track, evidently meaning the second track, needed repairs and advised taking it up and the Board seemed to be unwilling to face the responsibility of decision and stepped aside from it by authorizing the superintendent to do as he might deem best. In September of the same year it began to manifest more courage and requested the superintendent to report the cost of laying heavy iron rail and in November it resolved to apply to the legislature at its ensuing session for an increase of stock or power to borrow money to lay heavy iron rail. This subject will be more fully treated in the chapter devoted to the change of track to iron rails.

The importance of western connections and general railroad development was early appreciated and one of the first proofs of this is found in a somewhat amusing resolution adopted January 28, 1845, concerning which the minutes say, "The Superintendent was authorized to contribute Fifty Dollars (provided the entire line to Buffalo will contribute in the same proportion) to be paid to ———— Miller towards improving the road between Chicago and Peoria in view of the benefit to be derived from the southern travel to New York by the interior route."

TELEGRAPH

It will be remembered that the first demonstration of the practicability of the electric telegraph was had May 24, 1844, on a line constructed from Washington to Baltimore. The enormous importance of this invention in railroading one would suppose would have been so apparent as to have attracted instant attention and have caused railroad managers to take prompt steps to secure its advantages. On the contrary the Utica and Schenectady seems to have remained calmly indifferent, for it was not until June, 1845, that any consideration was given to it. The minutes of June 2nd contain the first mention of this revolutionary factor in operation; "A communication was read from John Butterfield dated 30th day of May last asking permission to construct a line of Morse's magnetic telegraph on the line of the Company's road in such a manner as not to obstruct the business of the Company, under the direction of the Superintendent. Referred to Ex. Com. with power." Either Mr. Butterfield or the executive committee felt no great need of haste, for it was not until more than six months later that preliminary negotiations resulted in an agreement. December 17th, the proposed agreement was reported to the Board and when certain modifications, not specified, were made it was approved and its execution by the president directed.

Free Passes

The subject of free passes became a matter of concern as early as 1846. On April 10th, on motion of Mr. Benedict of Albany the Board adopted drastic measures to abate the evil in the following resolutions.

Resolved, that from and after the 16th day of April instant, no person except the officers and agents of this Company be allowed to pass free over the Utica and Schenectady Railroad.

Resolved, that the Secretary send a copy of this resolution to the President of each railroad Company between Hudson's River and Buffalo and that the same be published.

How long the rule thus established was maintained can not be ascertained. That it fell into disuse is certain. Its adoption was coincident with a radical change in passenger fares.

PASSENGER FARES

The Company's charter authorized a rate of four cents a mile. The distance from Utica to Schenectady was 78 miles which at the lawful rate per mile would have made a charge of $3.12. The regular charge had been $3, but probably in view of the known prosperity of the road and without consideration of the expense involved in reconstructing the track many people considered this excessive and brought severe pressure in many ways to force a reduction. The Board recognizing this complaint, on the 10th of April, 1846, adopted a resolution reducing the fare from $3 to $2 from and after April 16th. The resolution abolishing free passes being adopted at the same meeting was doubtless an attempt to avoid too drastic a cut in the operating revenues.

This reduction of fare continued in force a little more than a year and its results proved unsatisfactory to the Board. May 25, 1847, it adopted the following preambles and resolutions;

Whereas this Company on the 16th day of April 1846, reduced the fare on their road from Three Dollars to Two Dollars in the expectation that the roads west of Utica would reduce their fare in proportion and thus create an increase in travel sufficient to compensate in part for the reduction;

And, whereas, none of the roads west have reduced their fare and the receipts from passengers on this road have diminished and this Company are required under an act of the legislature passed on the 12th day of May instant to proceed without delay to relay their road with the heavy iron rail and erect a new superstructure therefor which will render necessary an additional outlay before the same is fully completed of full one million dollars, therefore;

Resolved, that the fare on the Company's road be increased to Three Dollars from and after the first day of June next.

Resolved, further, that this Board will at any time reduce its fare to Two Dollars whenever the roads west of Utica will make a proportionate reduction in their fare.

Upon these resolutions the Board was not unanimous, nine directors voting in the affirmative, two in the negative and two not voting.

SALARIES AND WAGES

The subject of wages and salaries paid has received great attention, but accounts were kept in such a way that a complete statement is impossible. Occasionally they were fixed by a resolution of the directors, but apparently in many cases by the executive committee or superintendent and all record of such action, if any were made, has disappeared. July 23, 1846, the Board took action in quite a number of cases which is here transcribed. The office collectors were what are now known as station agents. The rate given is that per month.

Office Collector at Utica.................	$60.
Office Collector at Schenectady...........	50.
Traveling Collector on the two main trains..	60.
Traveling Collector on other trains........	50.
Supt. of engines and work shops...........	60.
Asst. Supt. roadway repairs Montgomery Co.	55.
Asst. Supt. roadway repairs Oneida & Herkimer Cos...............................	65.
Asst. Supt. roadway repairs Schenectady Co.	40.

May 25, 1847, the salary of the collector at Schenectady was increased to $60 and that of Vibbard, the company's bookkeeper to $1200 per annum. On the resignation of Young, the superintendent, in 1849, Chauncey Vibbard was appointed superintendent and was in 1853 made the first superintendent of the Central which position he held for many years.

Sunday Trains

The running of trains on Sunday for the carrying of passengers and the mail was commenced at an early date not now determinable, but it seems to have been the subject of criticism and strong objection, as must have been anticipated in view of the ideas prevailing at that day regarding Sunday observance. This was, however, a subject upon which other roads and the Postmaster General had, in the judgment of the Board, to be consulted. The agitation in 1843, was sufficiently great to induce the passage of the following resolution on November 29th:

Resolved, that this Company is willing and desirous to discontinue the Sunday trains on their road and will do so as soon as the proper arrangements for that purpose can be entered into by the several railroad Companies between Hudson's river and the Post Office Department and that a copy of this resolution be forwarded by the Secretary to the Postmaster General and to the Presidents of the said Companies.

Proper arrangements for some reason did not materialize and nearly three years later the directors' minutes for July 24, 1846, show that the Auburn and Rochester proposed to discontinue Sunday runs if the Utica and Schenectady would do so. Letters on the same subject from individuals were also presented and considered. All this resulted in another resolution.

Resolved, that a copy of the resolution passed by this Company on the 29th day of November, 1843, on the subject of Sunday runs on their road be forwarded to the several Rail Road companies on the route between Hudson's river and Buffalo and also to the Postmaster General.

No record has been found that Sunday runs were discontinued.

Some Financial Results

Much interest is usually manifested concerning the financial results of the first years of operation of a new railroad. Clearly no general rule has ever prevailed. If a road is built in an old and developed region where traffic exists and is clamoring for service, one result may be looked for. If a road is built in an unsettled and undeveloped country with the hope and expectation of developing the region by affording transportation facilities needed for that end, another and different result must follow. The Utica and Schenectady was built in a settled and productive region, and on a line of through travel from the western part of the state to Albany and Hudson river points. Consequently a good financial showing was undoubtedly expected by the stockholders and they were not disappointed.

On the 5th of February, 1841, the Assembly of the New York legislature asked for a report by the Company on a large variety of details, possibly with an eye to taking over the road by the state at the proper time, but this is mere conjecture. At all events no legislative action is known to have resulted, although a bill was introduced to reduce passenger fares and to compel the Company to carry freight. It should be kept in mind that the Company was during the period in question restricted to passenger traffic only. The following details are condensed from the report which was dated February 5, 1841:

Cost of construction to Dec. 31, 1840	$1,901,785.21
Authorized capital stock	2,000,000.00
Amount paid in on stock	1,800,000.00
No. of calls on subscriptions	19

Amount called by years

1833..............	$100,000	
1834..............	60,000	
1835..............	640,000	
1836..............	700,000	
1837..............	200,000	
1838..............	100,000	$1,800,000

Dividends declared

1837 Feb. 1.......	$5.25 a share	
Aug. 1.......	5.60 " "	
1838 Feb. 1.......	5.00 " "	
Aug. 1.......	5.00 " "	
1839 Feb. 1.......	5.00 " "	
Aug. 1.......	5.00 " "	
1840 Feb. 1.......	5.00 " "	
Aug. 1.......	5.00 " "	

The road commenced operations Aug. 2, 1836.

Whole amount received for carrying passengers from Aug. 2, 1836 to Dec. 31, 1840

4 years and 5 months........................	$1,497,640.78
Expenses of operation.......................	551,958.23

By years	1836	5 Mos.	$ 33,498.42
	1837		122,738.46
	1838		126,632.10
	1839		131,584.03
	1840		137,505.22

No. of passengers carried

	1836	5 Mos.	45,391
	1837		79,095
	1838		82,459
	1839		95,776
	1840		86,823

Corresponding 5 months in each year compared with

1836	45,391
1837	40,371
1838	44,958
1839	49,811
1840	44,234

An illuminating statement in this report as to the service life of wooden rails is found in the following paragraph.

During the fourth and fifth years' past use of the road there have been expended for timber and labor on renewals of wood work about $40,000. It may be assumed that with the tenth year's use of the road all the wooden parts will have been renewed, excepting the red cedar ties, and will require, as per account of past expenditures,

For 100 miles superstructure..........	$300,000
20,000 rods of fence..............	20,000
Wooden bridge structures.........	70,000
Temporary buildings.............	10,000
Total......................	$400,000
Deduct amount expended for the fourth and fifth years, as above......	40,000
Balance......................	$360,000

The following table is a summary compiled from the reports to the Secretary of State for the years 1843–1847. No reports previous to 1843 are to be found in that office.

Year Ending Dec. 31	Operating Revenues				Operating Expenses	Net Income	Operating Ratio
	Passenger	Freight	Other	Total			
	$	$	$	$	$	$	%
1843	277,163.81	(Not	40,243.62	317,407.43	128,850.09	188,557.34	40.59
1844	306,278.75	Author-	29,580.15	335,858.90	132,838.41	203,020.49	39.55
1845	358,810.11	ized)	15,489.58	374,299.69	147,557.87	226,741.82	39.40
1846	347,535.51	65,296.57	15,563.90	428,395.98	167,820.82	260,575.16	39.17
1847	509,782.26	153,101.79	35,830.81	698,714.86	234,243.10	464,471.76	33.52
Total for 5 Years	1,799,570.44	218,398.36	136,708.06	2,154,676.86	811,310.29	1,343,366.57	37.65

The following table is compiled from the reports to the state engineer for the years 1850, 1851, 1852, and shows the financial results for those years.

Year Ending Sept. 30	Operating Revenues				Operating Expenses	Net Income	Operating Ratio
	Passenger	Freight	Other	Total			
	$	$	$	$	$	$	%
1850	595,472.27	255,668.47	72,285.25	923,425.99	308,173.86	615,252.13	33.37
1851	560,523.94	251,599.68	45,495.68	857,619.30	281,303.41	576,315.89	32.80
1852	619,903.72	361,656.81	48,214.25	1,029,774.78	305,004.05	724,770.73	29.61
Total for 3 Years	1,775,899.93	868,924.96	165,995.18	2,810,820.07	894,481.32	1,916,338.75	31.82

Attention should be given to the operating ratios shown in this and the preceding table. This road was perhaps the most prosperous of the group. When we consider that the operating ratio for the 5 years 1843–47 was 37.65, and for the 3 years 1850–52 was 31.82, there is nothing to discuss as to the real source of that prosperity. We may also observe that the ratio constantly declines as the volume of traffic increases until in 1852, it was less than 30. The difference between railroad financial results today and those of seventy-five years ago may be largely explained by one sentence—rates have decreased, operating ratios have increased.

OPERATING RULES

It is almost the universal habit to preserve no record of ordinary, every day transactions. Men know at the time how they are carried on. That is enough. They do not reflect that a hundred years later the methods of their day will usually have become matters of intense interest to their descendants and successors. It follows that it is a matter of great difficulty to ascertain just how operations were carried on by the earliest roads, to what rules and regulations the employees were subjected, what measures were taken to prevent accidents, the extent of the duties of each employee and the like. These are matters of deep interest to us and particularly to those who are now engaged in railroad operation. Diligent search has been made for information along these lines but with very little success except in the case of the Utica and Schenectady. The information obtainable for that road is not earlier than 1848, at which time the road had been in operation a dozen years. Fortunately there has been preserved by the merest chance a series of printed regulations issued by the superintendents and also certain regulations governing the operation of through trains from Albany to Buffalo adopted by all the roads on the line.

In most matters the other roads seem to have followed the lead of the Utica and Schenectady and we may reasonably assume their working rules, if not precisely the same as its, were at least very similar.

Some printed regulations which have been found are herewith printed and throw much light upon the methods of operation.

UTICA & SCHENECTADY RAILROAD

INSTRUCTIONS to be strictly observed by persons employed upon trains or at stations

SCHENECTADY, Dec. 17, 1849.

FIRST. All trains going west, will run upon the north track, and all trains coming east will run upon the south track, according to time table.

SECOND. Conductors of trains, and engineers, must compare their watches daily, with the office time at Schenectady, which shall be the standard time.

THIRD. No train must arrive at a regular station in advance of the time specified in time table; and freight and working trains must give a clear track to passenger trains on the road and at stations. Freight trains must not be run over fifteen miles per hour, nor must they leave a station less than twenty minutes in advance of the time of arrival of a passenger train. Trains leaving behind time, shall not be run at a greater speed than allowed by time table—(that is, no time shall be made up, unless lost upon this road).

FOURTH. If a train breaks down, or stops between stations, a man must be sent back immediately, at least eighty rods, with a flag in the day time, and a lamp in the night time, to warn approaching trains.

FIFTH. Whenever an extra train, or engine, is following another, in the day time, a flag must be carried upon the forward engine; and in the night time, a red lamp must be carried upon the forward engine. The train or engine following, must be kept at least ten minutes behind, and run with great care.

SIXTH. Engineers, in approaching stations, switches or cross roads, must see that the way is clear, and the switch is right. The bell must be rung, eighty rods before approaching a cross road or station, and rung until passed.

SEVENTH. Red lamps must be exhibited at night on the rear car of all trains.

EIGHTH. Brakemen on passenger trains, must be at their posts, on the forward platform of the rear car, and apply the brakes on the proper signal of the engineer. One puff of the whistle, signifies that the brake must be tightened; two puffs, to be loosed again; and a continuous sound, approaching a station. Conductors will be particular to know that baggage and brakemen attend to their duty, and will be held responsible therefor.

NINTH. The conductors of freight trains will see that the brakemen attend to their duty, and keep the doors of freight cars closed. The brakemen must be stationed on the rear of the train.

TENTH. All working parties upon the track must give notice of any obstruction by their work, by exhibiting a flag at least eighty rods.

ELEVENTH. Engineers will not allow any person to ride upon the engine, without express authority.

TWELFTH.   All persons employed on passenger and freight trains, or at stations, must wear the badge prescribed by law.

THIRTEENTH.   Conductors will not pass any person free, without a ticket from a proper officer of the company.

FOURTEENTH.   Any person in the employ of the company, who refuses or neglects to observe the above instructions will be promptly discharged.

C. VIBBARD, Sup't.

UTICA & SCHENECTADY R. R.

REGULATIONS

STATION AGENTS MUST LODGE AND BOARD IMMEDIATELY ADJOINING their respective railroad stations, and be present at all times excepting when necessarily and reasonably absent; and then, a substitute must be provided by the station agent absenting himself.

They will keep record of all transactions worthy of note; irregular passing of trains, &c.

They will be ready to receive and give advice, in regard to all extra trains passing, and of the time between the passing of trains following each other, at their respective stations.

Station agents may advise at all times with conductors, and in cases of glaring necessity, will be responsible for not advising; but such advice shall not relieve the conductors from the full responsibility of their station.

Freight agents are the station attendants, and will superintend (under a general supervision of the superintendent of roadway construction and repairs,) all the business at their respective stations, relating to freight, passengers, wood and water.

The badge prescribed by law, will be worn by each person at the stations, authorized to assist in receiving and delivering passengers, baggage and freight.

WM. C. YOUNG,
Sup't. & Eng'r.

May 15, 1848.

SIGNALS

UTICA & SCHENECTADY

RAILROAD

A WHITE FLAG OR HANDKERCHIEF—All is right.
A BLUE FLAG—Great Caution.
A RED FLAG OR HAND LANTERN—

1. When shown on the line of road, or at stations—A full stop.
2. When carried on an engine—A train following close.
3. When held from the side of a train—Stop at next station.
4. When violently waved—Stop immediately.
5. When held above the head to an engineer on an engine standing—Back the engine.
6. When waved to an engineer on an engine standing— Go ahead.

FROM AN ENGINE—

One sound of bell, whistle or steam valve—Down brake.
Two sounds   do.   do.   do.   Up brake.
Several sounds do.   do.   do.   Approaching
stations, cross roads, or obstacles on the track.

WM. C. YOUNG,
Superintendent.

May 15, 1848.

RAIL ROADS BETWEEN THE HUDSON RIVER AND BUFFALO.

The following Resolutions were passed at a meeting of Delegates from all the Rail Road Companies between the Hudson River and Lake Erie, on the Central Line of Railway held at Albany, 6th March, 1850:—

Resolved, that this line of Rail Road, being limited in the amount of freight which may be transported by the State Tolls, which are required to be paid, cannot reduce the fare of Passengers to the same rates that other lines are able to fix, where tolls are not required.

Resolved, that there should be a difference in the fare between the Express Trains and those which are run at a lower rate of speed.

Resolved, that in order to meet the expectations of the public as far as practicable, having proper reference to the principles set forth in the foregoing resolutions, that the first class through fare on all other than the Express Trains, be fixed as near as may be at two and a half cents per mile for the whole distance between Buffalo and Albany.

Resolved, that hereafter each Road regulate its arrivals and departures by the local time at its extremities.

Whereas, it is indispensably necessary in order to make the Day Express trains perform uniformly, their trips in the time allowed—12 hours — and in order to preserve uniformity and perfect concert of action, without which it will be impossible to depend on each other for promptness on this line.

Resolved, that the Day Express Trains shall stop on the several roads, at the following and no other places, for wooding, watering, and change of cars, namely: Schenectady, Fonda, Little Falls, Utica, Oneida, Syracuse, Auburn, Geneva, Canandaigua, Rochester, Batavia and Attica.

Resolved, that in the event of the tolls being taken off from freight, transported on this line of Rail Road, between Buffalo and Albany, the charge for transportation will be reduced at least equal to the amount of the tolls, and the fare for first class passengers, on all except the Express Trains, in the judgment of this Convention, may be reduced to two cents per mile.

Resolved, that no other persons than those employed by the Rail Road Companies, at the several stations, shall be allowed to take any charge of Baggage, or of the Checks, except by direction of the owner of such Baggage.

Resolved, that it is hereby recommended to the Companies at the termination of the Line to adopt a system similar to that practiced at Philadelphia on the arrival of the trains from the south, where a responsible person goes through the trains before the arrival at the terminus, taking the checks of passengers and delivering the Baggage as directed by the owner.

Resolved, that it shall be the duty of every Company on this line of Rail Road to keep a book in which shall be carefully entered a description of all Baggage or Freight lost or miscarried that shall come to the knowledge of the Superintendent of such

Company, and all Baggage remaining uncalled for, for two weeks, shall be sent to Syracuse on the 1st and 15th of each month, with a description of the time and circumstances under which it was received, and that a printed description of the Baggage shall be sent to each office from Syracuse, quarter yearly.

Resolved, that a Committee be appointed to mature a plan in regard to free passengers, and communicate the same to each company here represented, and to solicit their action thereon, and an interchange of their conclusions, in regard to the plan presented; and that the same committee prepare a circular on the subject of free passengers, and communicate the same to the various Rail Road Companies in the Union. Messrs. Wilkinson, Corning, Whittlesey and How, were appointed this Committee.

THOMAS Y. HOW, JR.,
Sec'y of the Convention.

FREIGHT TARIFFS

But little has been found showing the freight rates on this road; in fact nothing but two handbills issued by Superintendent Vibbard late in 1849, which are herewith given. It should be remembered that the rates given included the canal tolls required to be paid to the state, but how much those tolls were cannot be determined.

The peculiar situation of freight transportation on this road owing to the existence of the Erie Canal is so interwoven with the situation on the other roads that it can be more clearly treated in a separate chapter.

UTICA & SCHENECTADY RAILROAD.

TARIFF OF PRICES

per car load for transporting Cattle, Sheep, Hogs, Lumber, &c., from Utica and Way Stations to Schenectady, Albany and Troy, including Canal Tolls.

Stations	To Schenectady			To Albany or Troy		
	Lumber &c.	Cattle & Hogs	Sheep	Lumber &c.	Cattle & Hogs	Sheep
Utica.........	$20	$25	$20	$25	$30	$25
Herkimer......	16	19	16	20	25	20
Little Falls....	14	18	14	18	23	18
St. Johnsville..	12	15	12	16	20	16
Fort Plain.....	10	13	10	14	18	14
Palatine Bridge	9	12	9	13	17	13
Fonda.........	7	9	7	11	14	11
Amsterdam....	5	7	5	10	12	10

N. B. Not more than eight tons shall be loaded in a Car, and Live Stock entirely at the owner's risk, so far as injury may arise from Suffocation, Crowding, Trampling, &c.

C. VIBBARD, Sup't.

Schenectady, Dec. 24, 1849.

UTICA & SCHENECTADY
RAILROAD.

PRICES OF CAR LOADS OF CATTLE, SHEEP and Hogs, from the following places to Albany or Troy:—

From Herkimer, Cattle,	$31	Sheep and Hogs	$26
" Little Falls, "	28	" "	24
" Fort Plain, "	20	" "	18
" Palatine Bridge,	20	" "	18
" Fonda, "	16	" "	15
" Amsterdam, "	15	" "	14

C. VIBBARD, Supt.

Schenectady, Nov. 20, 1849.

CHAPTER III

THE SYRACUSE AND UTICA RAILROAD

THE Syracuse and Utica Railroad Company was incorporated May 11, 1836, by Chapter 292 of the laws of that year, with an authorized capital of $800,000, consisting of 16,000 shares of a par value of $50 each. It was authorized to carry both persons and property being allowed to charge not exceeding four cents per mile for a passenger and his ordinary baggage. Although unrestricted as to transporting property, it was required to pay tolls upon that carried by it during the navigation season on the Erie Canal.

The minute books being lost or destroyed, we know but little of the time and manner of organization or of its officers. John Wilkinson was the first and only president and seems to have been a very active and efficient man. The engineers were O. H. Lee and C. B. Stuart. From a newspaper publication we learn that books of subscription for the stock were opened the 19th, 20th and 21st days of July, 1836, at Syracuse, Canastota, Utica, Albany and at the Farmers' Loan and Trust Company in New York City. Upon the same authority it is said that there was subscribed at Albany, $250,000; at Syracuse $400,000; and at Utica over $600,000. How much was subscribed at other places is not known. Syracuse at that time was but a village and the amount said to have been subscribed there, if the statement can be relied upon, is certainly very generous for a village in those days of limited capital.

The road was to be constructed from Syracuse to Utica and was laid out not on the most direct line, that now substantially taken by the West Shore railroad, but at Oneida ran in a northeasterly direction to the Mohawk valley at Rome and thence down that valley to Utica. The reason for selecting the longer route can only be conjectured. Probably the difference in grades was a controlling factor. Total length of road 53 miles.

The consent of the village of Syracuse that the road might be constructed the full length of Washington street was given on July 1, 1837, and the westerly terminus of the road was at the site of the present passenger station in Syracuse; the easterly termination in Utica at the westerly end of the Utica and Schenectady at Genesee street. The original passenger station in Syracuse was by the unanimous vote of the public meeting of the taxable inhabitants of the village constructed in Washington street, that street being widened four feet on each side to afford proper accommodations for the building and also to allow public travel on both sides.

The road was completed and thrown open for public travel on the 3rd day of July, 1839. Its completion was the occasion of a public dinner and celebration. An account of these functions published in the *American Railway Journal* gives a glowing picture of the light in which new railroad facilities were regarded in those days and is interesting enough to reprint in its entirety.

The Directors of the Syracuse and Utica Railroad Company having invited those who had taken an interest in the construction of their Road to pass over it, and participate with them in a public dinner in honor of its completion, at Syracuse on Wednesday the 10th inst., a large party of guests from this city, including the members and officers of the Common Council,

Messrs. Bloodgood and Townsend, former Mayors, General Solomon Van Rensselaer, the veteran Revolutionary officer, Judge Buel, Lt. Matthew Gregory and Adjt. Gen. King, Messrs. Hawley and Benedict, Directors in the U. and S. Railroad Company, left here on Tuesday afternoon in a train handsomely tendered by Messrs. Whitney and Young, the agents of the M. and H. and U. and S. Railroads, for their accommodation.

The party having been met at Utica by the President of the Syracuse and Utica Railroad Company, left that place on Wednesday morning, with a large accession of guests, including the fine martial Citizens' Corps, of Utica, with its excellent Band and were whirled off to Syracuse, on a Railroad running mainly through a dense forest and over morasses and swamps, which consumed but little more than a year in its construction!

At half past eight o'clock yesterday morning we were at Syracuse, where a cordial reception from a committee of citizens was tendered. The Citizens' Corps was received and escorted in the village by a fine company of Artillery.

At two o'clock from four to five hundred sat down to a superb dinner prepared by Mr. Rust of the Syracuse House, Gen. E. W. Leavenworth, President of the village presided. As a full account of the celebration is to appear in the Syracuse papers, we will not attempt to anticipate them.

The Utica and Syracuse Railroad has been pushed vigorously forward. It has been constructed by the stockholders without either the aid of the State or a resort to loans. The capital is $800,000 of which eighty-seven and a half per cent has been called. It is fifty-three miles in length, and has, as will be seen, been made for twelve and a half per cent less than its capital. It is worthy of remark, that this Road has been completed within the time fixed, and has cost less than the sum estimated. For all this the public and the stockholders are indebted to the intelligent, enterprising and efficient services of Messrs. Wilkinson and Lee the president and engineer of the Company. We rejoice to find this link in one of "the three great lines of Railroads" thus auspiciously supplied. Syracuse, already a large enterprising, enlightened village, is destined to become a great inland city. It possesses in its soil and its mines the potentiality for acquiring wealth "beyond the dreams of avarice." These advantages will all be improved by an indomitable yeomanry. Syracuse is now within nine hours (150 miles) of Albany, and

within nineteen hours (300 miles) of New York. The rapidity
with which we pass between these two places is amazing. We
left Albany at half-past two P.M. on Tuesday, went to Utica in
the afternoon, where we remained until five o'clock next morning.
Was at Syracuse at half-past eight o'clock yesterday morning,
remained until four o'clock and was at home this morning,
breakfasting on a salmon taken from Lake Ontario night before
last, having travelled 300 miles, passing a night at Utica, nearly
a whole day at Syracuse, and being absent only forty-two hours.

THE TRACK

The track construction was of the flat rail supported
upon longitudinal stringers type. A considerable part
of the road was located through swamps or a swampy
region and there the track was laid upon and supported
by piles. The average depth of the muck was said to
have been 15 or 16 feet, but in many places piles were
driven by a steam pile driver so constructed as to drive
two piles at one operation. When driven, cast iron
rollers were placed on their heads and the machine by
means of an inverted rail, moved on to the next place.
The heads of the piles sawed off to the proper level were
found sufficient to supply the furnace with fuel. The
piles were of various timbers, white, yellow or pitch
pine, white elm, cedar, black ash, tamarack and hemlock, measured at the butt end not less than 12 nor
more than 17 inches in diameter, were driven 4.98 feet
from center to center transversely and 5 feet from center
to center longitudinally, were charred to increase their
durability and an auger hole bored in their heads was
filled with salt and securely plugged up.

Upon the tops of the piles were placed cross ties
of white cedar, 8 feet in length, sawed square edged 12
inches by 4 inches in section, one over each pair of piles.
They were neatly fitted upon the piles and an auger
hole $1\frac{7}{8}$ inch in diameter bored through the tie and 12

inches deep into the head of the pile. Into this hole a
white oak pin 16 inches long, 2 inches in diameter and
octagonal in section was driven. When within 3 inches
of the hole, the head of the pin was split, a wedge
inserted and then it was driven home.

The longitudinal wood rails were sawed precisely
eight inches square from white and yellow pine, were
laid longitudinally on the cross ties and directly over
the center of the piles beneath and were accurately
spaced 4.65 feet apart. At each intersection of the rail
and cross tie, two cast iron knees were spiked in the
angles so as firmly to secure the rail upon the cross tie.
The rails were joined by simply bringing their square
ends in contact and holding them in position by a
double knee of larger dimensions than the intermediate
ones. Near the ends of each rail, auger holes were
bored, filled with salt and securely plugged up.

Directly over the center of the rails was laid a sawed
white oak ribbon, 3 by 1¼ inches in section and of
lengths varying from 15 to 30 feet, so laid as to break
joints with the rails beneath them. Upon these wooden
ribbons was laid an iron plate 2½ by ¾ inches in
section, in lengths of 15 feet and weighing 30 tons to the
mile, so placed that the inner edge corresponded with
the inner edge of the ribbon and, so placed as to make a
distance of 4 feet 8¾ inches between the parallel rails.
No joint of the iron plates was allowed within 5 feet of
the joints of the ribbons or rails underneath. At each
joint of the iron plates end plates of wrought iron 2½
inches broad, 6 inches long and ¼ inch thick fitted
with a hole in each end corresponding with the holes
in the iron plates, were fitted into the oak ribbon so as
to bring their surfaces even. When the iron plates,
end plates and oak ribbons were carefully adjusted,
they were firmly fastened to the rails with pressed

spikes 6 inches and ¾ inch square, one in every 18 inches.

The total length of that part of the road constructed in this manner was 19–26/100 miles. The remainder of the road was graded in the usual manner. We have an exact description of the track superstructure which is here given as showing the best type of track construction then in use. The stone foundations used on the Mohawk and Hudson had been abandoned.

A trench was excavated of the proper size and the sills were firmly bedded in it. Where the sills abutted end to end they were supported by a piece of wood of the same section laid beneath them. At right angles to and upon the upper surfaces of the sills were spiked the cross ties and again at right angles to the cross ties and immediately over the sills were laid the longitudinal rails. The center of the rail and the sill were in the same vertical plane. Upon the longitudinal rails the oak ribbons and the iron plates were firmly spiked, the detail of the rails, ribbons and plates being in all respects as described for the pile road.

The two way method of computing grading quantities was used and in a reliable work it is said the average price for earth excavation was 11–75/100 cents per cubic yard and for embankment 11–55/100 cents, making a total average on the one way method of 23–30/100 cents per cubic yard.

In a letter dated October 7, 1839, treating of the pile construction, C. B. Stuart, the resident engineer in charge of the piled part of the road says:

The average number of 15 feet piles, driven in 10 or 12 feet muck, by a well managed machine, will be about 100 per day, including the sawing off of the tops to receive the rails. Piles, 25 feet long, driven in 20 feet muck, averaged 80 per day for 60 days, although 120 piles, of this size, were driven by the same machine in 14 hours—and by another machine, 220 piles of 12 feet in length, were driven in the Mohawk river flats in the short space of 13 hours.

The average length of the piles, on the Syracuse and Utica railroad, (in 19½ miles of piled road) was 18 feet. The cost of timber 2½ cents per lineal foot, delivered and the expense of driving, about $285 per mile, including the sawing off to the proper level of the road. If sawed off within two or three feet above the surface of the ground, no danger need be apprehended from lateral motion.

Too great care cannot be taken to have a competent and trusty foreman to take charge of these machines, it being very important for the safety of the road, to have the piles, in every instance, driven till they reach the hard, or solid bottom, thereby preventing any liability to settle, when passed over by the heavy locomotives.

In several instances, on the road alluded to, the substratum was found from 50 to 60 feet below the surface, and was reached by driving piles 30 feet in length, one upon another, and connecting them by a suitable pin at the joint. In every instance, when the bottom was found, not the slightest settling has been perceptible and the experiment, so confidently made by the enterprising company, has more than realized their highest expectations.

John Weale, an English engineer, published in 1843, a careful and authoritative work on the construction of this road which is elaborately described both in letter press and cuts. He gives an estimate of cost of super-structure for one mile of pile road based on an average of the prices for which the work in question was executed. It is undoubtedly accurate and is given here as a matter of curiosity, since this type of construction had the approval of some of the best engineers of the day, was highly recommended by Weale for use in Great Britain, and lasted in actual use less than 10 years.

Amount		Price	$
56,320	feet board measure, white and yellow pine, rails delivered	$14.12 per M.B.M.	795.24
1056	white cedar cross ties, delivered at	41 cts. each	432.96
3300	feet, white oak ribbons, delivered at	$25. per M.B.M.	82.50
30	Tons, iron plates, delivered at	$75. per ton	2250.00
720	lbs. of end plates, delivered at	9 cts. each	64.80
6758	lbs. of cast iron knees, delivered at	5½ cts per lb.	371.69
1500	lbs. of pressed spikes to fasten on rail plates, delivered at	9 cts. per lb.	135.00
1089	lbs. of pressed spikes to fasten knees to rails and cross ties, delivered at	9 cts per lb.	98.01
2112	white oak trenails to fasten cross ties to piles, delivered at	1 ct. each	21.12
	salting and charring piles		50.
	workmanship, putting timber together and spikes on iron plate		350.
	add for contingencies		50.
	Total for one mile of superstructure		4701.32
	Average cost of piling timber and for driving the same per mile		1864.48
	Grand total per mile		6565.80

The cheapness of such a superstructure is evident. Experience demonstrated with equal clearness its unsuitability for a railroad track. As elsewhere shown this timber and flat rail track was entirely removed in 1845–49 and replaced by a double track laid with heavy iron rail. The reports of the Company for those years show the following expenditures for this new track with gravel ballast:

1845, $25,629.78; 1846, $38,241.12; 1847, $248,115.66;
1848, $302,313.76; 1849, $341,687.99; Total, $955,988.31
—an average per mile for double track of $18,038.51.

Like most of the new roads the business at the very
outset yielded flattering returns and the operating
expenses were relatively small. January 1, 1840,
when the road had been in operation six months, the
directors published a statement of cost of road up to the
opening, receipts and expenses for the first six months
operation, which follows. The revenue figures do not
agree precisely with those found in official reports later
but the discrepancies are not substantial.

*Statement of the Directors relative to the Syracuse and
Utica Railroad to January 1, 1840.*

This road was commenced in 1838 and put in operation, the
3rd of July, 1839, at the following outlay of capital. The distance is 53½ miles.

For Land damages..........................	$ 71,245.42
Grading, fences and bridges...............	322,552.67
Superstructure...........................	411,751.92
Buildings, coach, engine, wood and water houses..................................	30,445.65
Engine and shop tools, snow plough, etc......	1,250.50
18 Freight cars..........................	4,979.93
Engineering, including preliminary surveys...	35,294.38
Commissioners department, and incidental expenses................................	36,868.95
	$914,389.42
Deduct to show cost of road, this sum for iron and stock on hand, included in above......	20,500.00
	$893,889.42

Net income for first 6 months, is as follows:—

Receipts—July 3, 1839 to Jan. 1, 1840
    48,483 through passengers
    34,053 way passengers

82,536 Passengers..........	$121,972.55	
Freight..............	850.00	
U. S. Mail..........	2,801.08	
		$125,623.63

Expenses of transportation:

Superintending, collecting and clerk hire............................	$ 2,177.38	
Services of engineers, firemen, brakemen and stations..............	5,394.40	
Fuel for locomotives..............	10,525.93	
Oil...............................	454.22	
Repairs and alterations of engines...	2,308.96	
Repairs of coaches and oil for same..	1,307.69	
Taxes assessed on road............	1,777.64	
Incidental to transportation.......	1,973.87	
Repairs of roadway, watching track, clearing away snow, and sundry work on road.................	7,037.06	
Incidental expense, cattle killed, repairs on Depot in Utica and two-fifths interest on cost of depot....	1,810.96	34,768.11
Net receipts in 6 months on outlay of $893,889.42.................		$90,855.52

An operating ratio of 27.6 per cent is something more than extraordinary; it is astounding. Doubtless the stockholders were filled with delight at 10 per cent net earnings in the first six months of operation, and railroad construction generally was greatly encouraged. The saddening effects of later experience were yet to come.

The passenger traffic of this road was, for the times, quite heavy and was the principal business. The following compiled from reports to the state shows the number of passengers carried each year, 1839 being for only six months and 1853 for only 10 months. The years are calendar years, except beginning with 1850, the year covered ends September 30. Hence the number carried for the months of October, November and December, 1849, appear in both 1849 and 1850.

1839..............	82,536	1844..............	121,746
1840..............	122,141	1845..............	123,534
1841..............	132,677	1846:.............	155,279
1842..............	119,728	1847..............	198,512
1843..............	114,843	1848..............	216,810

1849.............	294,416	1852.............	570,051
1850.............	340,945	1853.............	456,197
1851.............	449,870		

No data exist for showing the density of passenger travel except for the years 1850, 1851, 1852 and 1853. In those years, it was as follows:

1850.............	265,914
1851.............	347,036
1852.............	443,500
1853.............	331,198—10 months only.

Informative freight statistics for everything except receipts and canal tolls paid are lacking for all years prior to 1850.

The following table showing operating revenues, operating expenses, net income and operating ratio has been compiled from the reports of the Company on file in the office of the Secretary of State, for the years 1840–47.

Year ending Dec. 31	Operating Revenues				Operating Expenses	Net Income	Operating Ratio
	Passenger	Freight	Other	Total			
	$	$	$	$	$	$	%
1840	178,509.57	1,636.29	14,726.63	194,872.49	66,526.65	128,345.84	34.14
1841	190,829.32	2,341.16	6,343.25	199,513.73	66,696.22	132,817.51	33.43
1842	155,224.95	1,620.01	12,590.31	169,435.27	59,970.50	109,464.77	35.39
1843	147,353.00	2,119.82	14,227.86	163,700.68	66,796.44	96,904.24	40.80
1844	176,342.15	3,457.09	9,427.89	189,227.13	71,068.81	118,158.32	37.56
1845	182,484.78	12,946.50	8,858.85	204,290.13	82,378.67	121,911.46	40.32
1846	229,708.56	19,623.50	8,305.16	257,637.22	106,389.90	151,247.32	41.29
1847	285,941.61	52,494.46	11,743.84	350,179.91	124,631.96	225,547.95	35.59
Total for 8 Years	1,546,393.94	96,238.83	86,223.79	1,728,856.56	644,459.15	1,084,397.41	37.28
Total for 5 years 1843 to 1847	1,021,830.10	90,641.37	52,563.60	1,165,035.07	451,265.78	713,769.29	38.73

The following table has been compiled from reports to the State Engineer, for the years 1850–52.

Year ending Sept. 30	Operating Revenues				Operating Expenses	Net Income	Operating Ratio
	Passenger	Freight	Other	Total			
	$	$	$	$	$	$	%
1850	366,077.07	90,878.97	15,819.73	472,775.77	202,728.14	270,047.63	42.88
1851	371,935.86	111,090.15	15,221.90	498.247.91	212,009.43	286,238.48	42.55
1852	409,308.19	192,744.23	14,865.69	616,918.11	240,893.15	376,024.96	39.05
Total for 3 Years	1,147,321.12	394,713.35	45,907.32	1,587,941.79	655,630.72	932,311.07	41.29

As in the case of the Utica and Schenectady, attention is called to the operating ratio, the meagerness of the early freight business owing to the canal situation elsewhere discussed and the great increase in freight revenues in 1852, owing to the abolition of canal tolls.

John Wilkinson, the president, believed in making his annual reports to state something more than a mere collection of statistics, and accordingly he freed his mind by pungent statements on various topics which were of interest to him and which he correctly thought should be of interest to others and especially to the legislature. In the report for 1848, he devoted much attention to the presence of cattle on the track, enlarging upon the theme, "there is great hazard in attempting a high rate of speed on account of cattle and other domestic animals which are allowed by their owners to run at large: they *will* stray on to the railroad, if so allowed, though the greatest care may be exercised by the company to prevent it. . . . The hazard of injury to passengers from this cause is greater than from any other; and it will be increased in proportion to the speed if the owners of domestic animals are not required to restrain their going at large." It was many years before the legislature was induced to see this danger and take measures to restrict it.

Mr. Wilkinson's stand on free passes was very emphatic and the result of large experience. In his annual report for 1849, he says:

> The number of persons who pass free upon the railroads in this State is very large and is increasing. This company has endeavored to restrict the number within some reasonable limit, but has not been as successful as could be desired, by reason of the fact, that other companies pass them, and when the same thing is declined on this road, it leads to controversy, and often induces an undeserved hostility which is exhibited in various ways. So far as we are informed, the number of free passengers is very much greater in this State than in other states, while in foreign countries, as we are advised, they are not allowed at all. We constantly pass great numbers free because of inability to pay. This is all proper, but beyond this class of persons it is very questionable whether any should be passed free.
>
> As the railroad is made to carry passengers for pay, the rate should be uniform, and it is unfair to those who do pay, to pass any considerable number of persons without pay. It is also unfair to the stockholders, and is with them a subject of just and somewhat general complaint.
>
> It would be proper and important, to keep a record of the number of persons passed free, and the reasons for the same stated, and reported in classes, with the annual reports of the railroad companies.

He had earlier kept such a record for nearly a year and a half in 1845–6 in which full details are given day by day. In it there is just one lonesome entry for March 10, 1846, "Not a single dead head to-day." November 9, 1845, we are told, "It snowed like fury all day." Mr. Wilkinson's statement that the road constantly passed great numbers free because of inability to pay is abundantly verified by this record. "One poor blind man and boy"; "A poor woman in emigrant car and had a small infant"; "A very poor man"; "A poor family"; "two exiles"; "poor man and woman by request of Judge Beacher"; "A poor crazy man"; "two mutes"; "one lame man"; "poor colored man," are typical entries occurring nearly every day. The banner days for free rides for the poor and unfortunate were September 2, 1845, when we find in the poor column the following: "2 deaf and dumb boys"; "six blind girls"; "five mutes, two blind boys," fifteen in all, and July 22, 1845, when apparently an excursion was given from Utica to Syracuse to 36 blind persons.

In the forties the state militia was of some importance and the names of militia captains who were willing to ask free rides occur with frequency and occasionally the name of a general appears. One judge and his family were fond of traveling and a judge of the United States District Court was content to pass free.

The hearts of the officers of the Company were sympathetic in cases where poverty was not involved. November 24, 1845, the record reads, "Aaron Burt's Daughter & wedding party (4 seats) Syracuse to Utica." Nor did they scorn the lowliest. May 19, 1846, one entry reads, "Very poor, King Alcohol, Syracuse to Rome, his headquarters." To counterbalance this, Syracuse editors were not denied free rides.

The first week this record was kept, the posting of the free list is as follows:

1845, July 13, Sunday	21
14, Monday	34
15, Tuesday	22
16, Wednesday	24
17, Thursday	28
18, Friday	32
19, Saturday	35
	196

In the report for 1850, he again airs the subject of free passes with an unsparing hand. He says, "The whole system was by this company changed on the first of July last, since which time the only persons allowed to pass free are the officers and men in the service of the company. Before the rule adopted by this company was put in force the number of free passengers had become so large as to become burdensome. This is the necessary tendency of the system. . . . The system runs into favoritism. It is corrupting, it is not business-like, and ought not to be tolerated."

His words on this topic were energetic but vainly spoken. For many years the evil grew precisely as he declared it would and finally required the action of congress and legislature to abate it.

He also in the same report wrote at length upon the carelessness of individuals as a fruitful cause of unnecessary accidents. "The rules of the company," he says, "forbid any person standing on the platform or getting on or off the cars while the trains are in motion. Notwithstanding this passengers will violate these rules so necessary for their safety. If they would keep their seats personal injury would rarely occur to them. . . . Another kind of accident happens to those who walk on the track. This is a very great evil often resulting in the most serious accidents and always in impeding the trains."

He again recurs to the subject of cattle allowed to run at large, getting on the tracks, and this at considerable length. One statement he makes is interesting and undoubtedly correct. "The ground is assumed by the owners of the cattle that their animals have as good right to occupy the public highway at a railroad crossing at the same moment when a train of passengers are passing them that they have." Another illustration of how the ordinary man is more prone to insist upon supposed rights than to regard ordinary duties.

He has a blast for those who attempt to defraud the Company of fare showing how the efforts of the Company to avoid being defrauded result in regulations which are frequently irksome to the honest passenger. He notes a state of mind as prevailing then which possibly has not wholly disappeared seventy-five years later. "Those only who are entirely familiar with this business can be aware of the extent of the sentiment that it is not quite as wrong to get the advantage of a railroad company as of an individual. To place this branch of business upon a proper basis and to advance the comfort of passengers those who do attempt to cheat, should be made liable to some penalty."

In the report for 1851, he notes, "The rates of charge on the transportation of property after the first of December have been so fixed in all instances, to save to the owner an amount equal to the state tolls, which had been required up to that day." The tolls were always really paid by the owner of the property transported. "This has been done to meet the pledge given that such a reduction would be made as soon as the tolls were taken off."

Thus it is made to appear that some if not many believed that the tolls were paid by the railroad and not by the public whose property was carried. Economic fallacies, are not the exclusive possession of the present day.

In the report for 1850, he speaks with characteristic clarity on depreciation, a subject generally overlooked for many years thereafter, and even now a matter of great debate.

The cost of the construction and the operation of railroads has yet been very imperfectly ascertained and while we have learned little of their ultimate capacity, we know quite as little of their true cost of maintenance and repair. What is the actual depreciation and therefore what will be the cost to keep them up to a proper standard are as yet not well known. It is already quite certain that everything about them goes rapidly to decay arising from exposure and the severe wear to which most of the works are subjected. We have already found that the iron rail gives way quite fast. The whole wear both of machinery and structure is very much in proportion to the speed. The public constantly demand more rapid rates of travel, &c.

A very liberal allowance beyond the ordinary current expenses must therefore be made to provide for depreciation.

A plain spoken, forthright man, John Wilkinson. It is such glimpses as he gives us that enable us to draw a correct picture of railroading in the forties of the last century. Had more railroad managers been possessed of his spirit our knowledge of their trials and burdens would be infinitely increased. But doubtless in his day many regarded him as a common scold.

EARLY LOCOMOTIVE ENGINES

It is not within the scheme of this work to trace in detail the growth and development of steam locomotive engines. Information of that character is available to those interested in several technical publications. Here the attempt is to show so far as practicable just what locomotives were used on the roads we are considering. The first locomotives on the Syracuse and Utica were built by Rogers & Co. The only description of them which has been found is contained in Weale's book above mentioned from which the following is excerpted:

The following are the dimensions of several of the best engines on the road:

Engines having six wheels—two drivers, 4 feet 6 inches in diameter: the other four being 33 inches and connected to what is termed a truck or pilot frame, forming a separate carriage, which carries the front part of the engine and vibrates on a center pin allowing the engine to go round the curves with great ease; cylinders—18 inches in diameter, stroke 11 inches; number of tubes in the boiler one hundred and eleven, 8 feet long, $1\frac{7}{8}$ inch in diameter; area of fire box 40 square feet; area of fire grate 7.84 feet.   Gross weight of the engine, 22,215 lbs.; weight on driving wheel 14,325 lbs.   These engines are used for light trains and their average speed is 20 to 25 miles per hour.

The engines used for the heavy trains are of the following dimensions:

Engine—eight wheels—4 drivers, two in front of the furnace and two at the back, of 4 feet six inches in diameter, the four drivers being coupled on the outside; the other four wheels are on a pilot or truck frame, as described above, moving on a center pin.   Cylinder 18 inches in diameter, stroke 12 inches; number of tubes, one hundred and thirty-seven, 8 feet long, $1\frac{3}{4}$ inch diameter; surface of fire box 42 square feet.   Total weight of engine 22,351 lbs.; weight on the four drivers 15,833 lbs.; the connection between the drivers and truck frame being very ingeniously arranged to throw either more or less weight on the principal driving wheels.   These engines are calculated to draw very heavy loads, their average speed being 15 to 18 miles per hour.   The price of these engines is $8000.

CHAPTER IV

THE AUBURN AND SYRACUSE RAILROAD

THE Auburn and Syracuse Railroad Company was incorporated May 1, 1834, by Chapter 228 of the laws of that year, to construct a railroad from the village of Auburn to the village of Syracuse, a distance, as the road was located, of about twenty-six miles. The record books of the Company are not available but other sources of information show that the stock which was authorized to the amount of $400,000 was all subscribed in December, 1834, and that soon thereafter, on January 20, 1835, organization was completed by the election of Elijah Miller, Nathaniel Garrow, Asaph D. Leonard, Geo. B. Throop, John M. Sherwood, Edward E. Marvin, Richard Steel, John Seymour, Allen Warden, S. Van Anden, Henry Raynor, V. W. Smith, and A. Fitch, as directors; Elijah Miller, as president, Nathaniel Garrow, vice president, Asaph D. Leonard, as secretary, and George B. Throop, as treasurer. The service of Throop as treasurer was brief. January 1, 1837, Thomas Y. How, Jr., succeeded to that position and continued therein for some years, but just how long has not been ascertained. During the severe struggles of the Company for existence through the panic of 1837, and its aftermath, he seems to have been in great part the driving force which kept within it a breath of life, and finally brought the work to completion. Not one of these first officers and directors appeared on the directorate of the Rochester and

Syracuse Railroad Company at the consolidation of 1853, into which company the Auburn and Syracuse was consolidated in 1850. Edwin F. Johnson was appointed chief engineer and remained such during the construction of the road. It is believed that all the stock was subscribed by residents of Auburn and Syracuse, and of the intermediate and surrounding country, but large blocks soon fell into hands of New York city parties. As in the case of most, if not all, of the new railroads, after the successful opening of the Mohawk and Hudson, local enthusiasm was very great, and glowing anticipations of the future were not in any respect tinged by moderation, if we may judge by articles in the press. The *American Rail Road Journal* of September 5, 1835, reflects this feeling in the following language, based, of course, upon local information:

> This road in addition to being a part of the line of the great thoroughfare will have the advantage not only of carrying goods and produce as part of the great western trade but also of the local transportation from Auburn and its vicinity and intermediate country to the canal at Syracuse. The amount of the business is almost incalculable. It embraces the merchandise and country produce which is bought and sold at Auburn; the produce of the inexhaustible stone quarries and lime at Auburn; the raw materials and manufactures at the State Prison which employ constantly 700 hands; the trade through Owasco lake from Homer and its surrounding country; the trade from Skaneateles, Camillus, Marcellus, &c., and also the great manufacturing power of the village. To these sources of revenue which must make it one of the most profitable railroads in the state, may be added the great travel which the business between the two places must necessarily create.

Rosy, indeed, is the story, but noticeable for the absence of any cold, hard figures of tonnage and anticipated daily number of passengers.

At all events the directors struck out vigorously,

relying for money upon calls of installments upon the stock. It was, according to a private letter, dated May 5, 1835, "designed to have the road complete for cars as soon as the Utica and Schenectady road is completed," which event occurred August 1, 1836. The engineer went actively to work and by May, 1835, was able to make a preliminary report of his examination. He found that Auburn's elevation above Syracuse was 274 feet, making an average inclination to be overcome of $10\frac{1}{3}$ feet to the mile. The heaviest inclination was 30 feet per mile for a distance of $1\frac{3}{4}$ miles. Surveys were pushed and reached such a point that August 22nd, the engineer advertised for sealed proposals for grading, masonry and bridges. Plans for structures were to be ready October 1st and proposals would be received until October 15th.

Early the following April, the engineer reported that in December and January excavation had been commenced on a few of the more expensive sections with a view of advancing the work upon them and to avoid thereby any delay in the opening of the road. He had learned that deep snows and severe cold were features of a winter in central New York and his anticipations had been somewhat blighted thereby. Contracts had been made for the superstructure timber in quantity sufficient to construct a single track.

White cedar and Norway pine were to be used, the rail timber to be exclusively of the pine. The track construction and track gauge were to be the same as those of the Utica and Schenectady. He deemed a greater gauge desirable and his reason for adopting one not wholly to his liking is noticeable as being one of the items of evidence showing what was anticipated from the first as to the ultimate result of building the series of roads called the central line.

A greater width was deemed desirable but as the Auburn and Syracuse road is to be a link in the same chain with the roads mentioned it was concluded to adopt the standard which had been established on those roads.

A more accurate survey had established the elevation of Auburn above Syracuse to be 271 feet, making an average descent of 10.54 feet to the mile. Sixty-two per cent of the road was straight line. The report concludes as follows:

The road will be completed and may be put in operation, it is confidently believed, if no unexpected difficulties occur, previous to the month of September next year in time for the fall business.

The unexpected difficulties did occur, or rather difficulty. The financial panic of 1837 struck the country. Considerable of the stock had been transferred to persons in New York City where the blow of the panic was first felt. Expenses continued but stockholders could not pay their assessments, contractors could not, unless paid, pay workmen and for material. General ruin for a time seemed imminent. And now came the time of tribulation for Treasurer How. A letter copy book, which has in some inexplicable manner survived the frequent removals in which other records of the Company have disappeared, gives a faithful picture of the agony which this early panic caused and of the trials of building a railroad if adequate financial means are not forthcoming. John Delafield, cashier of the Phoenix Bank in New York City, was the registrar of stock and seems to have been the managing representative of a considerable block of stock in that city. An assessment had been levied in November, 1836, which was still unpaid in January, 1837. Mr. How visited the city in January and supposed he had got everything in good shape, but the money didn't come. January 28th, he drew on Delafield two sight drafts, one for \$11,991.53, and the other for \$11,570, and wrote a long letter of explanation concluding, "The crisis of our affairs has come, and if we can not have money now we shall be obliged to let go after having reached the shore."

It appears that the 9th installment on stock was due January 18th; the 10th would be due February 6th, and the 11th March 6th, each being 4 per cent. The two drafts were for unpaid balances on previous installments due from New York stockholders. The drafts above mentioned were paid but considerable correspondence ensued showing that the Company was greatly embarrassed by failures to pay installments. March 7th, How drew again on Delafield for \$10,600, saying in his letter of advice the same day;

The cashier of the Cayuga County Bank has declined to make us any further advances for the reason that he has it not in his power to do so and unless this draft is honored and I am advised that it is paid, it will be necessary for us to say to the contractors whose estimates for the month of February are now due and unpaid that we can not pay them. The consequence of such a result will be equivalent to a declaration of our insolvency. The work will be abandoned.

This draft was apparently paid, but March 25th, How felt compelled to draw for another \$10,000 through a Buffalo bank, the Cayuga County Bank refusing to cash it. He advises Delafield at great length of the unsuccessful efforts which had been made to induce the grading contractors to retrench or delay their work; of moneys due for a large amount of timber contracted for and delivered, etc., etc.

If we should suspend our operations until next fall we could not finish the road and put it in operation until the latter part of August, 1838. In the meantime a large quantity of plaster belonging to the company worth from 30 to 40 thousand dollars would be almost entirely destroyed from exposure to a second winter. If by the failure of the stockholders in your city to pay the installments called and due we are compelled to declare ourselves unable to meet our engagements we must be sued and not only what we have expended lost entirely but the road itself, the soil and fixtures sold on execution and the company in fact dissolved.

We have this morning had a meeting of our Board and your last letter was read; and we came to the conclusion from an examination of all the facts that unless relieved by the payment of the calls now made and due or by a loan of 60 to 70 thousand dollars to help us along until the calls can be paid, say for 6, 9 and 12 months, we must go to ruin without hope of redemption. This is a sorrowful aspect of things but a true one. The distress you speak of has, I assure you, been felt here but so far as our road is concerned, it is not new. We have felt it for 8 months past.

Notwithstanding this moving tale the $10,000 draft was protested for non-acceptance.

May 6th, he writes that the time for payment of the April estimates has arrived; that the $10,000 draft at the Commercial Bank of Buffalo which was protested must be arranged,—"We have used the money and it will be the grossest injustice for us to stop with the debt to the Bank here and at Buffalo unpaid. The Honor of every stockholder is pledged to the payment of these debts for they command a preference over every other species of indebtedness. If the city stockholders would only display half the energy that the country stockholders are now shewing in their payments upon their stock we should be able to pay our debts and stop with honor to ourselves."

In a letter to stockholders in New York, dated May 11th, he says that there are $102,009 due and unpaid on regular calls on the stock: that the pressing indebtedness amounts to about $46,600: that the local stockholders are making arrangements to pay one-half their dues and give their notes for the balance. "The period between this and the 22nd determines the fate of the road. If we can pay our pressing debts we can make arrangements with some of our creditors and pass on uninjured: if not, we sink the whole." May 22nd he writes Delafield, "Our contractors will all be ruined unless relief comes speedily. We had promised them payment as soon as we heard from you and they were waiting on all sides when your letter came. We have put them off for a week longer in hopes that something may yet be effected in their behalf." And he sends a man to New York to drum up the defaulting stockholders. The Company had issued some notes, not to banks, but had peddled them out, "and they are pretty well received by the public."

And so matters went on month after month, but in some manner work was kept going, crises were surmounted and September 19th, How writes, "The road is going steadily on, not so fast as it would if we could command more cash. I have no doubt that 23 of the 26 miles will be ready for the cars from the 1st to the 15th of October next provided always that the arrangements made for money do not fail."

October 25th, another crisis had arrived and the cry for help was as urgent as in the spring previous. The succession of expedients suggested and the measures taken to obtain relief are too tedious for narration, but somehow the road managed to pull along, though constantly harassed by debt and lack of money. It seems that the Auburn and Rochester was in like straits and in November proposed both roads should go to the legislature for relief and on the 23rd of that month, How wrote its president that his Board con-

curred in the plan.   The result of this move was that
by Chap. 293 of the Laws of 1838, passed April 18th,
the legislature authorized a loan of state stock to the
Company to the amount of $100,000 whenever it should
have expended $300,000 in construction and purchase
of land.   And there was also authorized upon further
conditions of construction and payment additional
loans of state stock until there should have been issued
not exceeding in the aggregate the sum of $200,000.
The act was carefully drawn and elaborate in its
provisions for securing the debt and this is the proper
time to say the principal and interest were all promptly
and duly paid.

The financial situation of the Company was so
precarious that April 26, 1839 (Chap. 257, laws of 1839),
the Company was authorized to charge five cents per
mile passenger fare for three years.

January 4, 1838, How writes to a stockholder a
gloomy letter relative to his financial troubles but also
sets down information as follows:

Before proceeding to that, however, (financial difficulties) I
am much pleased to be able to state that 22½ miles of the road
is so far finished that we have made a contract with J. M. Sherwood, the mail contractor, to run that part of the road which
is ready for use with horse power until the first day of July next,
he giving us ½ of the receipts from passengers, one half of the
receipts from freight.   Inasmuch as 3 miles of the road are not
yet graded and will not be finished until May or June next, we
deemed it for our best interests to contract out the use of the
road upon liberal terms to the stage proprietors so as to dispose
of any competition with them and turn the travel entirely over
the road.   On Monday next the stockholders are to take a ride
over that part of the road which is finished and survey the result
of our labours.

In the same letter, after detailing his woes, he
continues, "I am almost in despair but my whole soul

being given to the object I must have hope. Is there no sale for the stock? The regular trips upon the road commence on Monday and we expect nothing less than $60 per day for our share of the income of the road unfinished as it is." It further appears from the same letter that notwithstanding horse operations were to commence the next Monday, the road had made no contract for rail, "for the reason that it was deemed best by our directors not to contract for the iron until we had our capital stock increased or until the legislature should afford us relief."

Every one must judge himself how operations were carried on with that situation existing. Incidentally he remarks (this in January, 1838), "The country is now suffering with unabated severity what you experienced in the city long ago. Money is not to be had."

Sherwood did carry on transportation with horse power and the financial results to the Company were realized at the end of each month, not only for the six months specified in the contract, but for at least thirteen additional months, until about July 1, 1839. They were as follows:

1838

January	$ 427.71	November	$ 823.76
February	275.73	December	728.49
March	426.51	*1839*	
April	694.78	January	462.85
May	590.03	February	
June	741.88	March	} 877.06
July	985.29	April	1,374.02
August	1,036.78	May	1,069.11
September	1,170.80	June	2,793.82
October	1,148.15	July	1,308.50

The total thus received from Sherwood for horse operation by him down to sometime in July, 1839, was $16,935.27.

Steam operation seems to have been commenced on a small scale at sometime in June, 1839; at least Lewis, the agent in charge of the road, or, as we would say, superintendent, on June 29th, paid to the treasurer $159.07 "way money for June." July 31st, the treasurer charges himself with:

Way money received................	$ 267.88
Rec'd at Syracuse office.............	3,355.53
Rec'd at Auburn office..............	1,398.21
Total......................	$5,021.62
Adding to this the amount received from Sherwood...................	1,308.50
Total receipts for July are.....	$6,330.12

These receipts indicate that for a short time there was mixed horse and steam power operation, but the precise date when one ended or the other commenced it has been impossible to ascertain.

Unfortunately Mr. How's letter book stops before the road commenced steam operations and we are deprived of the illumination which he might have afforded us during the early years of that operation.

A concise history of the issuing of the notes of the Company and a detail of receipts and expenditures to the 11th day of December, 1837, are given in a report filed in the office of the Secretary of State in December, 1837. An account of the issuing of notes by a railroad company in sums not less than $5 is well worth preserving in any story of railroad financing and hence it is here given in full.

On the 5th day of June, 1837, owing to the general derangement of business of the country, and the difficulty of enforcing the payment of installments upon the stock, preferring to proceed with the work rather than to abandon it after the expenditure of so much money, if the credit of the Company would enable them to do so, and upon the request of many of the creditors of the Company and particularly the contractors who urged the same as a measure absolutely necessary to preserve them from ruin, by a Resolution entered in their minutes on that day, the Board of Directors authorized the Treasurer to issue the Notes of the Company at 6 months bearing interest, in sums not less than $5.00 and to an amount not exceeding $100,000. for the purpose only of paying the debts of the Company. The number of contractors employed and the men engaged under them, who relied upon the Company for their pay, requiring the issue of the Notes in sums suited to the debts due to the contractors and workmen.

At the same time an arrangement was made with the greater part of the stockholders to execute their Notes to the Treasurer for installments, which Notes were collateral to the stock and were considered an additional security for the payment of the Notes issued by the Company.

Under this Resolution, to the 11th December 1837—$72,325. of these notes have been issued for the payment of the debts of the Company, and $13,230. redeemed, so that there are at this date outstanding of these notes $59,095. and they are daily paid as they fall due. The Company have also been able to extend their credit for one and two years to the amount of about $35,000.

The annexed statement shows the Receipts and Expenditures to the 11th day of December, 1837. The grading of 3 miles of the road is not yet completed, and a large portion of the Expenditures to be made upon the Superstructure and Transportation accounts do not appear in the statement. A large force is now employed in finishing the grading and superstructure.

Statement

1835 From Jan.	Cash paid by Treas. and charged as follows:		1834 Dec. 11	By 10% pd. on subscription		$40,000.00
	Commissioners Exps. $	335.32		Interest on same		1,501.47
28 to	Office Expenses	580.22	1835			
	Engineer Dept.	12,186.83	From	By Installments		
	Land Expenses	37,595.01		paid on Stock		139,322.00
	Grading Contracts	140,783.00	June	Interest on same		117.52
	Timber "	4,455.00	10 to Jan. 6			
	To Paid protested Drafts of Secy.		1837			
	and charges	13,963.00	1836 Oct.	Pd. by A. Whitney		
1836				Estate for Depo.		1,079.00
Jan. 7	Discounted Notes	14,300.70				

Statement—Continued

	Brought forward	$224,199.08		Brought forward	$182,019.99
1837			July	Avails of Discounted Nov.	
Jan. 6	" "			Notes	28,684.28
	(L. Lewis, Agt)	1,011.70		Avails of Draft of	
From				Secy. on I. Delafield and H. Bun	13,960.00
Jan.	Grading Contracts	81,501.97	Dec.		
6	Timber "	12,561.05	31	Cash returned by	
to	Superstructure Acct.	6,828.72	1837	L. Lewis, Agt.	800.00
	Office Expenses	1,958.31	From	By Installments	
	Engineering Dept.	8,959.22		paid on Stock	147,733.71
	Land Expenses	24,912.68	Jan. 6	Interest on same	994.19
	Transportation Acct.	190.00	to	By avails of discounted note and	
	Interest "	1,994.59		cash borrowed	22,322.29
	Bills Issued	13,230.00	Dec.	By avails of Draft	
	To Pd. Discounted Notes, cash borrowed and protested Drafts	18,865.71	11	of Treasurer on Phoenix Bank, N. Y.	10,000.00
Dec.					
11	Bal. in Treas. hands	10,301.43			
		$406,514.46			$406,514.46

A large amount of money is paid out by railroads annually in the settlement of claims. The method of dealing with them has not always given satisfaction to the claimant. Anything which will enlighten us as to the early practice is of interest. The only light on that point which researches for this work have developed is a letter written by Mr. How in 1847. It is so characteristic of the man it is well worth printing in full:

Auburn, Aug. 26, 1847.

B. Davis Noxon, Esq., Syracuse.

Dr. Sr. I am in the receipt of your letter of the 24th instant in which, as the legal friend of the Rt. Rev. Dr. Potter, Bishop of Pa. and by his direction you ask The A. & S. R. R. Co., to reimburse, to the ch. fund of that state to assist clergymen of straightened means, the sum of $12. taken from it on account of an accident happening on the above named R. R. on the 12th inst. in consequence of which, as alleged, the distinguished prelate named was subjected to additional expenses in the discharge of his duties.

Having a high respect for the Rt. Rev. Gentleman and being a churchman I respond to this call, by recourse to my own pocket, upon the understanding that the remarks herein written may be submitted to Dr. Potter in connexion with the money. You will please find herein a Drft. for $12.

As a member of the Board of Directors of the R. R. Co. I question the right of Dr. Potter to claim remuneration in this case for the following reasons.

Negligence or misconduct on the part of the Co. is not to be assumed and should not be charged to this a/c without some evidence to sustain it. It is a well known fact that accidents and detentions occur in all the various modes of conveyance of persons and property in this country and indeed in the world both upon land and water—accidents and detentions which no human prudence or management could foresee or prevent. It would be neither reasonable nor conscientious to ask remuneration for damages occurring in the management of temporal affairs because an all wise Providence has not given us sufficient foresight or power to prevent them, any more than it would be to claim damages of spiritual guides because after their most elaborate watchfulness and care some of them over whom they are set to watch become cast away.

The accident which detained Dr. Potter at Syracuse was of a kind which occurs sometimes upon the best conducted rail-roads in the world, and which does not bring reproach upon human judgment or management, and the Dr. doubtless knows that works of art give as palpable evidence of the inferiority of human judgment, and preach as forcible a lesson against the pride of human skill and confidence, as any of the workings of the passions do against the waywardness of the heart.

Dr. Potter under the circumstances, and in view of the knowledge he must have had of the reasons why the engagements alluded to were not fulfilled errs in complaining as much as he would have done if a storm had arisen upon the Seneca Lake and detained him there, and he had claimed to hold the Steam boat company as his guarantors against the violence of the wind. This is so or else he assumes upon loose evidence or no evidence at all that we were to blame.

The accident might have happened, as it has in other instances, from latent defects in machinery which to all appearance was perfect. The Dr. knows the kind of structure of which our rail road, with the rest of the line was composed, and the accidents and detentions sometimes and unavoidably, met with on it being matters of public notoriety, could not have been unknown.

I have been thus tedious because as a member of the company I wish to send along with my individual response to this claim a distinct protest against that view of the legal or moral obligations of R.R. Co.'s or other common carriers which requires them to become guarantors against events which Providence has not endowed them with power or ability to prevent.

With much respect,

I am your most obt. sv.

THOMAS Y. HOW, JR.

Auburn, Aug. 26, 1847.

B. D. NOXON, Esq.

DR. SR.

Within is my answer to yours of the 24th. In the hope that the moral instructions contained in it may compensate you for any labor you may have bestowed in the case.

I remain, Very truly your obt. sv.

THOMAS Y. HOW, JR.

RESULTS OF EARLY OPERATION

Much labor has been expended to ascertain the early operating results of this road. No reports covering this subject can be found prior to that for 1843. A solitary treasurer's journal has survived but the accounting used in it is not according to modern standards in all respects and may not be understood as to every transaction noted. Thus in 1839 there was charged to transportation some $11,108.64 purchase price of locomotive engines, which, of course, did not belong in that account which should have covered only operating receipts and disbursements. In subsequent years the same thing was done to some extent. As Mr. How, who was responsible for these entries, was a careful and methodical man of good business capacity, he must have had in mind some theory which justified to him his practice. It may be deemed as practically certain that he regarded the cost of locomotives, for instance, as being properly chargeable to the same account as cost of fuel; that both would be consumed in the operation of the road, the only difference being that the fuel would be consumed more quickly than the locomotive. It is certain that early theories of railroad accounting were in certain respects greatly different from those which have been worked out through long years of study and experience. For this reason it may be at times wholly unsafe to treat as properly comparable accounts kept and reports made eighty or ninety years ago and those kept today under the rules established by the Interstate Commerce Commission, without close and intelligent scrutiny of the older accounts. It is obvious in the case of the Auburn and Syracuse that items at least of equipment were not charged to the cost of road, nor made a capital account. Owing to the want of the account books, it is impossible to say how the accounting of this road was carried out in detail, but certainly this matter should not be overlooked in considering the reports made by it in later years. And this is true of the tabulated results which are herewith given.

In the years prior to 1843, so far as could be determined from the lonely journal, all such matters have been eliminated from costs of operation, but in the years 1843 and subsequently the operating expenses shown are totals from the report to the Secretary of State and may include items which do not properly belong to that account.

The following table shows the results of steam operation from July 1, 1839.

Year ending Dec. 31	Operating Revenue				Operating Expenses	Net Income	Operating Ratio
	Passenger	Freight	Other	Total			
	$	$	$	$	$	$	%
1839	34,600.02	353.57	13.25	34,966.84	10,696.63	24,270.21	30.59
1840	53,899.40	4,652.88	4,920.24	63,472.52	39,796.28	23,676.24	62.70
1841	67,909.59	11,672.98	3,476.07	83,058.64	36,911.10	46,147.54	44.44
1842	65,592.98	10,965.26	5,650.03	82,208.27	37,514.74	44,693.53	45.63
Total for 3½ Years	222,001.99	27,644.69	14,059.59	263,706.27	124,918.75	138,787.52	47.37

The following table is a compilation from reports in the office of the Secretary of State for the years 1843–47:

Year ending Dec. 31	Operating Revenue				Operating Expenses	Net Income	Operating Ratio
	Passenger	Freight	Other	Total			
	$	$	$	$	$	$	%
1843	67,651.29	14,590.09	4,050.00	86,291.38	38,531.23	47,760.15	44.65
1844	80,553.17	12,809.71	3,375.00	96,737.88	44,193.76	52,544.12	45.68
1845	79,500.29	15,577.53	4,725.00	99,802.82	44,325.96	55,476.86	44.41
1846	98,051.71	16,886.32	4,100.00	119,038.03	46,164.08	72,873.95	38.78
1847	123,848.04	28,794.24	4,466.87	157,109.15	61,209.17	95,899.98	38.96
Total for 5 Years	449,604.50	88,657.89	20,716.87	558,979.26	234,424.20	324,555.06	41.94

It may be noted from this and the preceding table that the Act of 1844 authorizing the Utica and Schenectady to carry freight during the suspension of canal navigation does not seem to have affected the freight receipts materially and we are left to infer that the freight business remained practically local until 1847.

This road having been consolidated into the Rochester and Syracuse in 1850, no indication can be given of the amount of its business subsequent to 1849.

CHAPTER V

THE AUBURN AND ROCHESTER RAILROAD

THE Auburn and Rochester Railroad Company was incorporated May 13, 1836, by Chapter 349 of the laws of that year. In one respect at least, its charter differed from most other special acts of incorporation. The usual practice was to designate the cities or villages in which the termini of the road were to be located and allow the directors of the Company to determine the precise location of those termini and also the most eligible route between them. In the case of this road, the act provided that it should be constructed between the village of Auburn and the city of Rochester, "commencing in the village of Auburn at the termination of the Auburn and Syracuse Railroad and running thence through the village of Seneca Falls and the town of Waterloo; the village of Geneva and the village of Vienna and the town of Manchester; the village of Canandaigua and thence through the town of Victor by the most eligible route to the city of Rochester where it may terminate at and connect with the Tonawanda railroad."

It is quite certain that prior to the passage of the act no preliminary surveys had been made and hence this location was fixed upon with no precise knowledge of the cuts and fills and curves necessary to be made other than such as might be afforded by a general familiarity with the contour of the country to be traversed. The naming of the principal towns and villages in the country between Auburn and Rochester as places to be reached indicates that the project was largely a local enterprise, designed to benefit the localities named and to ensure financial participation by the men of means of those towns.

The terminus of the road in Rochester was fixed by the directors just west of the Genesee river and at Mill street where the original passenger station was built and maintained for many years. This was not the terminus of the Tonawanda which was situate further to the west. That road was in operation before the Auburn road was located and why the latter did not avail itself of its right to connect with it was probably some local difficulty for which no explanation has been found. The gap between the two roads remained until after the passage March 19, 1844, of Chap. 50 of the laws of that year which authorized the Tonawanda to connect with the Auburn road at its termination upon such route as three commissioners named in the act, none of whom was a resident of Rochester, should determine and direct. Section 5 of this act may hint that some controversy with the city had hitherto prevented the joining of the two roads, it providing, "The Common Council of the city of Rochester shall have no power to change or alter the route or grade of any railroad track which may be constructed under the provisions of this act, or to prohibit the using of the same when made, or to prohibit the reasonable and proper use of railroad cars upon the same." So drastic and unusual a provision is unlikely to have been inserted in the act without a background of past experience.

The charter contained a rather curiously drawn provision with reference to the ever present canal problem. The right was conferred to transport property as well as passengers, but there was a limiting provision in the following words; "but the corporation hereby created shall not take and transport merchandise in such a manner as to lessen the income on the Erie Canal during the time when the canal is navigable." No penalty is fixed for a violation nor does the act provide any machinery to enforce the inhibition. Just what act would have been a violation and in what form of procedure and in what court the state could have enforced the act would have made a very pretty question in its day. But this was all changed by the tolls law of 1844 elsewhere discussed.

Passenger fare per mile for one person and ordinary baggage was restricted to three cents, but sufficient pressure was brought upon the legislature of 1837 to induce it to change that rate to a maximum of four cents (Chap. 11). The reason for this was most likely the impossibility of enlisting the aid of sufficient capital with the three cent limitation, other roads being granted better terms.

The capital stock was fixed at $2,000,000 to consist of 20,000 shares of $100 par value and it was provided that this must all be subscribed and ten per cent upon each subscription paid to commissioners named in the act prior to organization and election of directors. Subscription books were opened August 2, 1836, and at various other dates prior to December 31st, but it was found impossible to obtain the required amount. Accordingly early in January, 1837, application was made to the legislature for relief and this resulted in an act (Chap. 11 passed January 26th), authorizing the election of directors and the completion of the organization whenever there should have been subscribed $1,025,000. This sum, the supporters of the enterprise claimed, would be sufficient to construct the road, which claim was based upon a rather superficial reconnaissance and no detailed estimates of grading costs so far as can be learned. Perhaps a potent reason for fixing the amount at the sum named was found in its identity with the subscriptions already obtained.

Fortunately the stock book of the Company has been preserved and a study and analysis of the subscriptions confirms what the location of the road by the charter indicates, that the enterprise was inaugurated and pushed by the villages and towns along the line. At the time of the organization and election of 13 directors in March, 1837, there were five hundred and forty-one subscribers to the stock. The residence of three hundred of these is shown of whom only ten were from Auburn and sixteen from Rochester. Auburn was at that time having its troubles with taking care of its road to Syracuse during the panic of 1837 and a great part of its subscriptions was later forfeited for non-payment of installments. The subscribers had difficulty enough to meet installments on the road to Syracuse as may be seen in the account of that road.

Canandaigua was the moving spirit. It headed the list with eighty-five subscribers for 1921 shares. Seneca Falls followed with sixty-two subscribers and 813 shares; Victor with thirty-four subscribers and 263 shares; Geneva with thirty-three subscribers and 930 shares; Manchester with ten subscribers and 128 shares; Phelps with seven and 65 shares and some seventeen other villages and towns with lesser amounts. New York City was represented by 20 shares taken by one subscriber, John T. Ferguson.

The main office was located and maintained at Canandaigua and it would seem that James D. Bemis of that place was president for a time and Henry Dwight, treasurer, but quite early, Henry B. Gibson, cashier of the Ontario Bank was elected president, and Charles Seymour, secretary and treasurer. These two Canandaiguan men held these positions during the remaining corporate life of the road and seem to have been the controlling minds. When the Company was consolidated in 1850 into the Rochester and Syracuse, they were chosen to like positions in that Company and held them until that Company was in turn merged into the New York Central.

The minute book of the directors has not been found. Minute books being the primary source of information regarding the history of a road, it becomes impossible to follow in detail without them much of the early and interesting transactions. It is not possible to state the names of the first directors, but it is known they organized in March, 1837, and soon after selected Robert Higham as engineer and commissioner. Higham had been a resident engineer on the Utica and Schenectady and when his service there was terminated by the opening of the road in August, 1836, the directors passed a resolution highly appreciative of his skill and faithfulness. He constructed the Auburn and Rochester and was for some years its superintendent, and went from this road to the Hudson River railroad. His first duty was to locate the route. He pushed his surveys during the spring and summer and October 3rd submitted to the Board a preliminary report of his operations, much of which is well worth inserting at this place, revealing as it does, the point of view of an engineer of practical experience and recognized ability.

To the President and Directors of the Auburn and Rochester Railroad Company:

Gentlemen:—

We shall be able to pass the whole distance, between Auburn and Rochester, without having any grade to exceed twenty-eight feet ascent or descent, per mile, and that without any very deep cuttings on the summits, or high embankments in the valleys. The curves generally will be of a large radius only one being as low as 1000 feet.

The work throughout, will be of a plain and easy character, without any heavy rock excavation, or expensive river walling, and with as little perishable structure as perhaps any Road of the same extent in the United States. The superstructure of bridges over the Erie and Seneca canals, the Seneca and Genesee rivers, and some others of minor importance, (the cost of the whole amounting to $19,190) in fact, constituting the only perishable part of the road; and allowing that this will require an expenditure equal to ten per cent per annum, on its cost, to renew and keep it in repair, will amount to $1,919—a mere nominal sum for repairs, on so great a work. This permanency in the character of the work, will unquestionably be a consideration of great importance, with those who wish to have their money invested in stocks that will yield them an annual return of profits instead of having it consumed in continual repairs.

The grading for that portion of the route which lies between the village of Auburn and Seneca Falls, is through gravel and clay soils; for the remainder of the distance it is generally through loam, sand and gravel, and at three several points some slight lime-rock cuttings, but not more than will furnish the necessary quantity of stone to be used for culverts and bridge abutments, in their vicinity.

The character of the masonry, I have estimated to be of plain, rough, hammer dressed stone work, laid in quick lime mortar.

The following estimates are made for grading and masonry for a double track—the first track to be laid immediately, the second track as soon after as requisite. Considering this as one of the links in the great chain of Western Railroads, from Boston to Buffalo and the "far West," the estimates are made on a scale of corresponding character and magnitude to accommodate the business of this great and increasing thoroughfare; and nothing short of a double track will, in my opinion, be adequate for any great period. This is indicated by the fact, that the travel on the Utica and Schenectady Railroad, (which forms another link in this same chain) already requires the second track, to do the business of carrying passengers only; and the fact, that the

Tonawanda Railroad, (from Rochester to Batavia) with its present accommodations, having only a single track, is inadequate to the business, although trains of cars run day and night.

The subject of wooden superstructure, from its importance, has occupied much attention. From the experience of the present day, there can be no question, that a combination of timber and iron makes, under all circumstances, the preferable road for this climate. The greatest objection to roads of this character, is the large amount of perishable materials used in their construction, as all the different kinds of timber that can be procured in sufficient size and quantities for rails, are not of a durable nature; and from their exposed situation near the surface of the ground they must decay very rapidly. It is found, that in ordinary cases, the common timber of the country will require replacing, on an average, every six or seven years.

The following plan for a durable structure, is suggested for your consideration, as a better and cheaper road, than the common modes: The sills to be 4 by 12 inches, well bedded; the top surface four inches below the grade of the road; on the sills are spiked cross-ties of red cedar, three inches thick, of any width not less than 4 inches, and two feet from centre to centre. Between the cross-ties are red cedar blocks, 3 by 6 inches, and one foot long, leaving spaces between the ties and blocks, not exceeding 8 inches. Upon the blocks and ties, and under the rail plates, is a locust ribbon, one inch thick and three inches wide, to raise the iron rail, and clear the flanges of the wheels from the ties. Upon the locust ribbon is placed the rail plate, one inch thick, 2¼ inches wide on the bottom, and two inches wide on the top. The spikes to pass through the iron plate, the locust ribbon and the ties, into the sills, confining the whole together.

The locust and cedar being durable beyond any experience, may be considered, practically, as permanent as the iron. The sills may be of any timber of the country; being bedded in the earth, and remaining moist and free from the action of the atmosphere they will last for a great length of time. The bearing between the ties and blocks being so small, the plate and ribbon will be abundantly strong for any weight that can at any time be brought upon them. Their spikes being one foot from centre to centre, and passing into the ties and sills, would have an equal or greater hold to keep the rail in its place, than in the common wooden rails. It is believed that the increased size of the rail plate will be materially important in giving stability to the road, and will be more than sufficient to compensate for the large wooden rails, in keeping the road firm and in place.

The accompanying estimates show that at the same prices for materials, a permanent road, after this plan, can be constructed for less money than the ordinary road and will not require more repairs than an iron and stone road.

The following tabular estimates give an aggregate,

For excavation and embankment, (3,398,014 cubic yards)...................................	$373,272.27
" masonry in culverts and bridges (6,192 cubic yards)...................................	35,213.00
" superstructure in bridges (1,865 linear feet)...	19,190.00
" grubbing and clearing......................	7,365.00
" lands, damages for removing buildings, &c....	50,990.00
" road crossings and cattle guards...........	6,885.00
Making a total for grading, masonry, &c. of......	$492,915.27
For 156 miles of fencing......................	37,440.00
" 78½ miles superstructure for a single track, at $1,369.70 per mile.....................	343,021.45
Total amount for grading, fencing and superstructure................................	$873,376.72

Depots Buildings and Machinery.

Depot in the village of Auburn	$ 10,000.00
Depot in the villages of Cayuga Lake, Seneca Falls, Waterloo, Geneva, Vienna, Manchester, Canandaigua and Victor....................	32,000.00
Depot in the city of Rochester...............	10,000.00
	$52,000.00

8 Locomotive Engines at $7,000.............	$ 56,000.00
50 Passenger Cars at $1,000................	50,000.00
100 Freight Cars at $250....................	25,000.00
	$ 131,000.00
Engineering and Superintendence.............	45,000.00
Making a total for 78½ miles of..............	$1,101,376.72
or $14,030.27 per mile, graded for a double track, and a single track laid; or $18,399.97 per mile for a double track complete and a total of..	$1,444,398.17

Ten years later in 1848, the cost of the road had amounted to $2,644,520.35 as against his estimate of $1,444,398.17, the total receipts were $454,721.87 for the year 1848 of which only $83,136.85 were from freight as against his estimate of $72,879 from the same source, while passenger revenues were $358,471.30 as against his estimate of $268,638.50. This comparison is not to discredit his estimates which were undoubtedly made with great research and care but to show how little the best of men could forecast the development of traffic at the outset of railroad transportation. And perhaps it is unnecessary to confine the remark to any period of time.

Attention is called to the recommendation of Engineer Higham relative to track construction. The novelty in this consists in placing cross ties upon the sills at a distance of two feet from center to center with blocks, the thickness of the ties, resting upon the sills. The ties and these blocks support the rails which consist merely of locust ribbon one inch thick and three inches wide carrying the iron rail one inch thick and two and one-fourth inches wide at the bottom and two inches at the top, and wooden ribbon and iron rail to be securely spiked to the ties and supporting longitudinal sill. It has been impossible to learn whether this precise type of track or that in use upon the roads east was used. At all events the strap rail supported in some manner was used, but its dimensions have not been learned.

It is a tradition that these strap iron rails would become loosened at the end and by the action of the wheels the free end would be thrust upward through the car floor with resulting injury to passengers from the so-called snake head. The only authentic report of such an occurrence upon any of the roads constituting the Central line which has been found is contained in the annual report of the Auburn and Rochester for 1848, and is as follows:

June 10. A loose bar of the old plate rail structure entered one of the cars and inflicted flesh wounds on the foot and leg of one of the female passengers.

Since accidents were not required to be reported to the state prior to 1848, and in that year the plate rail was very largely replaced by iron rail on all the roads, we have nothing to confirm or contradict the tradition for the previous years.

Occasional criticism has been made upon the location of this road, the critics seeming to think it should have been constructed upon what is now the main line of the New York Central from Rochester to Syracuse which line was in fact constructed in 1851 and 1852. A little attention to the facts of the case in this as in other instances would have been useful. Mistakes in plenty were made in early railroad construction through lack of experience, but this was not a mistake. The country which this road traversed was in the thirties of the last century one of the most fertile and prosperous sections of the state of New York. The inhabitants of the section were greatly desirous of local railroad facilities which had been brought to their attention by the construction of the Mohawk and Hudson. The feeling for the project was intense in the counties of Monroe, Ontario, Seneca and Cayuga. Between January 8 and March 3, 1835, there was presented to the lower house of the legislature no less than forty petitions numerously signed by residents of those counties, asking for the incorporation of a company to construct a railroad from Auburn to Rochester by way of Waterloo, Geneva and

Canandaigua, and in some of these petitions residents of Wayne county joined. A bill for that purpose was introduced into the Assembly by its railroad committee, February 25th, and it received consideration from time to time until May 5th, when it failed of passage, the vote being 66 ayes and 40 noes, the journal of the Assembly recording, "there not being two-thirds of all the members elected to this House voting in favor thereof." Upon what grounds the opposition was based does not appear.

In the year 1836, the application for a charter was renewed with a favorable result and as already stated capital obtained from stock furnished the means for constructing the road with the exception of that procured by state aid. The panic of 1837 and the business depression which followed produced a situation which made it impracticable to complete the road with the avails of stock subscriptions and accordingly application was made to the legislature for state aid which resulted in the enactment of Chapter 195 of the laws of 1840, passed April 29th.

Under this act, $200,000 of the state stock was issued to the treasurer and further account thereof is given in another part of this work dealing with like issues to other roads. The first installment was all sold not later than in September. About December 1st, the second installment of $100,000 was issued, but in a letter of the treasurer dated March 26, 1841, it appears that the state stock could not be sold. The Company was still holding this stock December 27th of the same year: the same situation existed June 25, 1842. August 13, 1842, the treasurer sent this stock to an Albany bank, asking that it be disposed of to the best advantage in the City of New York. The letter of transmittal advised that it would be necessary for the cashier to go to New York in person to handle the matter and contains the following; "Please call on cashier Withers from whom we have a letter under date of the 8th instant in which he says, 'I believe $100,000 could be worked off at from 82 to 83 and it is possible something better might be done.'"

This stock bore interest at the rate of $5\frac{1}{2}$ per cent and that stock of the state of New York bearing interest at this rate could not be sold at more than 82 or 83 more than a year and a half after issuance is a peculiar light on financial conditions at that time.

The stock had been hypothecated to the Ontario Bank as security for loans and the avails of any sale were to be transmitted to that bank. It was actually sold in September, 1842, $50,000 for 82 plus accrued interest from January 1, 1841, to July 1, 1842, $11,000 for $84\frac{1}{2}$; $26,000 for 84; and $13,000 for $83\frac{1}{2}$. How the discount of $17,010 was handled can not be learned.

But little is known regarding the progress of construction work. The road was opened for operation by sections; from Rochester to Canandaigua, September 19, 1840; to Seneca Falls, June 9, 1841; to Cayuga, September 18, 1841; and through to Auburn November 4, 1841.

Concerning the promptness and efficiency of the service given, there seems at times to have been the usual differences of opinion. This is clearly disclosed by an article in the Canandaigua *Republican* in May, 1847. It says:

This road having been made the special object of attack by the Buffalo *Express* it has been promptly vindicated by the Rochester papers. The *Express* had charged that it was the worst managed road on the line and the mail failures west were mainly attributable to it. The Rochester *Democrat* furnishes a table of the time of departure and arrivals of trains between

Auburn and that place for 9 days from which it appears that the train has started from Auburn but once at the regular hour and then it arrived at Rochester on time. Twice it left at 15 minutes behind time and arrived in time. In all other cases it has been obliged to wait from 1 to 4 hours for the arrival of the eastern trains. The average time is 5 hours 31 minutes notwithstanding it has been obliged to lose time at meeting places, being, in consequence of the delay, an irregular train. The trains from Rochester to this place (Canandaigua) run with such precision that some of our citizens set their clocks by it and so far from being a badly managed road we doubt if there is a better one in the country. The agents and engineers are not only men of much experience and understand their business perfectly but are also gentlemanly and accommodating to a degree that attracts general attention.

This brief article shows that the average time for the 9 days was at the rate of about 14 miles per hour, which as elsewhere shown was about the schedule time for the through express trains. It discloses also the difficulty of fastening the responsibility for unreasonable delays upon the guilty party on a line 300 miles in length operated by eight independent companies. It also shows by the great delays in the arrival of trains at Auburn there was serious fault somewhere east of that point, but where and who was responsible does not appear. Such operation was not a success. How to get rid of it was a problem requiring six more years to solve.

The slow running time, as elsewhere shown, was attributable to the character of the wooden track which was inadequate to carry great speed.

On January 1, 1842, nine dollars per share was paid to the stockholders as interest on the money paid in by them on calls for stock installments. This is the first instance which has been noted of recognition of the principle of interest during construction, although it is impossible to say it may not have earlier been done by other roads.

The first attempt which has come to notice, to bring about the running of a through train from Albany to Rochester is found in a letter sent out by Gibson and Seymour under date of May 31, 1842:

Erastus Corning:

Pres. Utica and Schenectady R. R. Co.:

Sir: The undersigned on behalf of the several Rail Road companies between Rochester and Utica desire to present to you for your consideration and co-operation the following suggestions with a view to produce uniformity of arrangement and fare upon the Rail Road line west of Albany.

First. That passengers be allowed at the principal office on the line to pay their fare as far as they please.

Second. That they be allowed to put their baggage in for such place as they please and that they be furnished with a metal ticket therefor, a duplicate of which shall be attached to the baggage.

Third. That arrangement be made for running upon the Rail Road from Albany to Rochester (and ultimately to Buffalo) a daily line of cars of a plain but substantial character, the speed of which shall be slower than the other line and the fare upon which shall be considerably below the rate allowed by the Charters of the respective Companies; or, instead thereof, that a uniform rate of through fare be adopted that shall be as near 3 cents a mile as is consistent with ordinary currency.

In regard to the first two suggestions we are of opinion that if adopted they will add to the convenience of travelers and will save the Companies much trouble and responsibility as to baggage.

The last proposition is made to bring the matter up for discussion, without tenacity on our part, but under the impression that sound policy requires the Directors of the several Rail Road Companies deliberately to consider it.

An arrangement was consummated to sell through tickets from Rochester to Albany and such sale commenced July 22, 1842. The Auburn and Rochester received for its part $3 for the 78 miles of its road first class, and 87½ cents for second class.

A letter of the secretary dated June 6, 1842, shows that the Board of Directors had fixed salaries as follows: engineer and superintendent, $3,000 per annum; monthly salaries, receiver at Rochester $50, at Auburn $25; traveling collectors $50 (which term is used for conductors); general clerk at Canandaigua $50; freight agent $40; baggage men $25; locomotive engineers, per day, $2, except one who was given $2.25.

Another letter dated June 13, 1842, to Robert Higham, the superintendent, shows that Pomeroy & Co. were carrying on an express business over the road but the full terms of the arrangement with them have not been ascertained. Part of them are shown in the letter, "We have agreed with Pomeroy & Co. that their express men shall be allowed to take and carry with them over our road at their risk, free of charge, two trunks not to exceed 3 feet by 18 inches and two boxes of specie not to contain over $1,000 each; or three trunks of the above size and no specie: in case of excess for the whole distance or for part of the way only to be charged for the excess to specie say at the rate of one seat for every 4 boxes of $1,000 each; for trunks, etc. the same as you would charge any other person."

In August the salary of the receiver at Rochester was increased to $800 per annum in consideration of his increased labors due to the sale of through tickets to Albany, and in the same month second class fare was increased from 87½ cents to $1.50.

In December, 1842, a distinct unpleasantness arose with the Auburn and Syracuse which is well worth recording as evidence of situations arising from a multiplicity of roads on the line. Benjamin Folsom was put in charge of the business of the Company at Auburn, the clerk of the Auburn and Syracuse having hitherto handled it. In a letter to Mr. How of that road announcing the change, Mr. Seymour urbanely remarks:

Our President, Mr. Gibson, says he is about as sick of co-partnership as you would seem to be by the unceremonious manner in which you discontinued our recent connection for running our cars to Syracuse. He adds that if you had called and stated the difficulties or objections you had to continuing the arrangement they would have in all probability been obviated by us, but as it is we will hereafter do business on our own hook and leave you to the enjoyment of the same course, or any other you may deem expedient to adopt.

It seems that the Auburn and Syracuse had adopted a rule to deliver no freight to the Auburn and Rochester until its charges were paid. This, of course, made a rift in the harmonious feeling and the same day Mr. Seymour sent the foregoing letter to Mr. How, he sent another to Higham, his superintendent, directing him to pay all such charges on delivery of the freight and that thereafter no freight be delivered to the Auburn and Syracuse, "until our charges and the advances we have made are paid in full and that in no instance must this rule be departed from."

What the outcome was of these friendly interchanges has not been learned. Doubtless the feeling engendered was softened by time and negotiation and harmonious operating relations again prevailed.

Operating Statistics

The following for 1840 and 1841 have been summarized from a journal of the Company:

Year Ending Dec. 31	Operating Revenue				Operating Expenses	Net Income	Operating Ratio
	Passenger	Freight	Other	Total			
	$	$	$	$	$	$	%
From Sept. 19 1840	9,578.31	291.78	—	9,870.09	4,218.93	5,651.16	42.74
1841	79,987.76	1,110.05	113.00	81,210.81	22,627.63	58,583.18	27.86

The following have been taken from the annual reports filed in the office of the Secretary of State at Albany:

Year Ending Dec. 31	Operating Revenue				Operating Expenses	Net Income	Operating Ratio
	Passenger	Freight	Other	Total			
	$	$	$	$	$	$	%
1842	152,264.35	5,949.87	21,335.46	179,549.68	52,970.61	126,579.07	29.51
1843	170,412.93	4,434.10	14,846.03	189,693.06	100,201.12	89,491.94	52.82
1844	215,246.95	7,808.40	14,612.03	237,667.38	85,660.12	152,007.26	36.04
1845	214,143.29	17,127.98	7,788.60	239,059.87	96,984.70	142,075.17	40.57
1846	253,073.21	20,201.76	16,895.58	290,170.55	110,353.24	179,817.31	38,03
1847	334,710.81	47,471.13	13,585.82	395,767.76	154,613.97	241,153.79	39,07
Total for 6 Years	1,339,851.54	102,993.24	89,063.52	1,531,908.30	600,783.76	931,124.54	39.22

The following have been taken from the annual reports filed in the office of the State Engineer and Surveyor:

Year Ending Dec. 31	Operating Revenue				Operating Expenses	Net Income	Operating Ratio
	Passenger	Freight	Other	Total			
	$	$	$	$	$	$	%
1848	358,471.30	83,136.85	13,113.72	454,721.87	188,027.76	266,694.11	41.35
1849	408,424.90	111,579.72	7,859.21	527,863.83	201,842.40	326,021.43	38.24
Total for 2 Years	766,896.20	194,716.57	20,972.93	982,585.70	389,870.16	592,715.54	39.68
Total for 8 Years	2,106,747.74	297,709.81	110,036.45	2,514,494.00	990,653.92	1,523,840.08	39.40

CHAPTER VI

THE ROCHESTER AND SYRACUSE RAILROAD

THE Rochester and Syracuse Railroad Company was incorporated August 1, 1850, pursuant to Chap. 239, of the laws of that year, authorizing the consolidation of the Auburn and Syracuse, and Auburn and Rochester Railroad Companies, by filing the consolidation agreement in the office of the Secretary of State. The history of the two consolidating companies up to the date of consolidation is hereinbefore given. The new Company thus formed constructed the direct line from Syracuse to Rochester, now forming a part of the main line of the New York Central, and to the making of the consolidation agreement and the construction of the new road, this chapter will be directed.

Evidently the consolidation act was the result of previous consultation and agreement between the two companies. Outside parties would not have framed and secured the passage of such an act. They proceeded with great promptitude to avail themselves of its terms. The articles of association agreed upon by the directors were not required to be submitted to the stockholders for approval, but there were provisions requiring the new Company to buy the stock of those shareholders who dissented from the arrangement entered into. A meeting of the two Boards was called for July 17th, at Syracuse, and the consolidation agreement was made and signed that day.

The capital stock was fixed at \$4,200,000, divided into shares of \$100 each. One share of the stock of the new Company was to be issued for one share of the stock of an old company and adding thereto fifteen per cent of stock in the new Company. The then issued and paid up stock of the consolidating companies was,

Auburn and Rochester........................	\$2,196,765
Auburn and Syracuse........................	624,000
Total issued.................................	\$2,820,765
Fifteen per cent additional....................	422,114
Total to be issued............................	\$3,242,879

The consolidation agreement states that, "The said fifteen per cent is to compensate the stockholders for the amount paid toward the cost of construction of the two Rail Roads beyond the stock issued."

Fixing the amount of the capital stock in excess of the sum of that of the consolidating companies was expressly authorized by the consolidation act in the following words,—

They shall form articles of association in which shall be set forth . . . the amount of the capital stock of the company, which shall not be less than the aggregate amount of the capital stock of the two companies so uniting . . . and the terms upon which the two companies are united in one corporation.

The consolidation act also contemplated the acquisition by the new Company of all the rights and property of the direct railway between Syracuse and Rochester and the construction of that road as a part of the consolidated road. This necessitated a capital stock greater than that of the two consolidating companies. The actual cost of the new road up to June 1, 1853, was \$2,001,339.95, with work incomplete estimated to cost \$25,000. The capital stock of \$4,200,000 was therefore inadequate by over $1,000,000 to take care of the old stock and the new construction.

The old roads were turned over to the new Company for operation August 1, 1850.

Our attention may now be directed to the direct line between Syracuse and Rochester. Why a railroad over this route had not been built earlier is unknown. The probable explanation is that the early roads were projected to meet local needs and not primarily for through traffic. We have learned that the Auburn and Syracuse was constructed to bring Auburn into close connection with the canal and that the Auburn and Rochester was located so as to serve the local needs of the villages along the route prescribed by its charter. It would seem that the villages along the line of the canal between Rochester and Syracuse felt satisfied with the transportation facilities afforded by it and did not feel like investing local capital in the untried speculation of an experimental railroad. Circumstances and time wholly changed this feeling, if it existed. The change was gradual and a new road was long talked of before any active measures were taken to obtain one. This talk culminated in calling a convention at Lyons in Wayne county August 18, 1847, at which 108 regularly appointed delegates were present from fourteen villages and towns along the route and a few from other places. The meeting was organized and transacted its affairs in a highly business-like manner through carefully appointed committees. Various moderate and yet emphatic resolutions favoring the construction of a railroad along the canal route were adopted. One was that a committee be appointed to draw up a statement in relation to the propriety, the advantages and the value as an investment of the proposed railroad and that the same be published and presented to the legislature with the proceedings of the convention. An executive committee of five from each of four counties was appointed to take charge of an application for a charter. The statement drawn by the committee was exceedingly persuasive. Attention was directed to every material question involved. It was pointed out that the Auburn route was 104 miles long, whereas the proposed road would be only about 80; that the grades on the Auburn route were in places quite long and heavy, the proposed route was practically level. But the chief emphasis was placed upon the great through business which it was affirmed was sure to come. The document is a powerful plea for what soon after became an established fact and it is therefore unnecessary to quote it even in part.

The result of this movement was that the Direct Railway between Syracuse and Rochester was incorporated June 18, 1848. It did not, for some reason, materialize into action very successfully. Only 834 shares appear to have been subscribed, upon which there was paid in $8,340. No route was located, although one was surveyed. But it remained a menace to the Auburn roads, which they were desirous to control, and accordingly, the consolidation act authorized the consolidated company to purchase all the property and rights of the Direct Company and to proceed with the construction of the road. Apparently the whole procedure had been mapped out before the drafting of the act, for on August 1, 1850, the very day on which the Rochester and Syracuse came into legal existence, the proper officers of the two roads were at Canandaigua in the office of the Auburn and Rochester and executed the paper transferring all the rights and property of the Direct road as provided by the statute. The Rochester and Syracuse agreed to pay therefor to each of the stockholders of the Direct, an amount of stock equal to the amount held by them respectively in the Direct upon their paying to the Rochester and Syracuse ninety per cent thereon (they had already paid ten per cent on their Direct stock) or at their option to pay them the amount they had paid in in cash. The Direct stockholders elected to take the cash.

The Rochester and Syracuse also agreed to construct the direct line and in one year from the date of the agreement to expend on the same at least $200,000: the road to be in all respects a first class railroad with iron superstructure and to be completed and operated within the time allowed by the consolidation act, namely, within three years from August 1, 1850. The line which had been surveyed by the Direct was in the main the one to be followed.

The Company proceeded promptly with the work of construction. Mr. James Hall was engaged as chief engineer and agent. The winter of 1850–51 was employed in surveying the route; its location was fixed by the directors, May 2, 1851. Grading was commenced shortly after and the whole road was put into operation about June 1, 1853. Some portion of it had been operated prior to that date sufficiently to yield gross earnings amounting to $2,796.40, according to Mr. Hall's last report. The total cost, according to Mr. Hall, including some unfinished work he estimated would require $25,000 to complete, was $2,026,339.95, being an average per mile of $25,110.64, without rolling stock, except gravel cars used in construction.

The second and third annual reports of Mr. Hall have survived. He was an engineer who clearly understood that reports to be valuable must give proper details, and we gain from his a great deal of information of value which gives a pretty clear idea of unit costs and construction troubles in 1851–52. Some of the more important unit prices were: Iron rails, per ton, $43; spikes, per ton, $70; wrought iron chairs for rails, 4.75 cents per pound delivered in Syracuse. There were three hundred and twelve tons of these. Ties, cedar, 38 cents each; oak, 42 cents; chestnut, 38 cents; pine, 40 cents. These tie prices he declares high owing to the demand on the Rochester, Lockport and Niagara Falls, which was then building. Excavation prices varied according to character of material. One paragraph reads, "On section sixty, William Barker, contractor, the excavation proved so much harder than was anticipated, that we took the work off his hands and relet it to Messrs. Candee & Co. at fifty-five cents per yard rather than submit to paying Mr. Barker sixty-five cents, the original contract price being forty cents." He does not, other than this, state the contract prices, but his estimate prices were for earth, 16.8 cents, loose rock, 35.8 cents, solid rock, 70 cents, per cubic yard. First class bridge masonry he estimated at $6.47 per yard, arch masonry $8.26, fencing $1.10 per rod, truss bridging $28 per lineal foot. Gravel for ballasting cost about ⅓ more than earth excavation due to long haul. Ballasting after commencing operation he strongly opposes and thinks it would increase the cost at least 33 per cent.

Grading and masonry did not proceed as rapidly as required by contract and his explanation is well worth considering at the present day.

The greatest cause for the detention of the grading and masonry, has been the uncommon unfavorableness of the weather during the past season, for doing work located as this is well known to be, through a section of country in which a very large proportion of the excavations are to be made in a loamy and common clay soil, and in most instances, indurated clay sub-soil. In sandy and gravelly soils, work can be forwarded with much less detention than in those first mentioned, to say nothing of the difference in working them, for the reason that in working clayey soils, contractors are in many cases, after heavy or even comparatively light rains, obliged to suspend their work, for from one to four and five days, in consequence of the quantity and depth of mud. During this time they are unable to work teams, except at a great expense. In sandy soil this is not the case, as, after rains, however heavy, their work can again be resumed without detention.

A large portion of the road bed has been made from earth taken from side ditches, and borrowing pits taken in the most convenient places. Many of the swamps and intervals upon the line were partially covered with water for a large portion of the season. But a very small part of the grading was commenced until late in June. October, November and December, the months in which very many of the sections were to have been completed, proved to be very unfavorable for contractors to forward their work. There were but eight days in the month of November, in which men or horses could possibly be worked.

The road, as has been said, was put into operation about June 1, 1853; it was turned over to the New York Central, August 1 of the same year.

CHAPTER VII

THE TONAWANDA RAILROAD

THE Tonawanda Railroad Company was incorporated April 24, 1832, by Chapter 241 of the laws of that year, to construct a railroad with a single or double track "commencing at any eligible point within the village of Rochester in the County of Monroe and extending on the most direct and eligible route through the valley of the Tonawanda to Attica in the County of Genesee." Notwithstanding the furore which was then sweeping the country for railroad construction, some opposition developed to this road. At least three remonstrances from citizens of the counties of Genesee, Orleans and Monroe were filed with the Legislature while the bill was under consideration and sixteen members of the Assembly voted against it. Just why Tonawanda was selected as the name is wholly unexplained and at this time most likely unexplainable. The Company itself regretted the name as early as 1837, but took no steps to have it changed. For the benefit of those curious in such matters it may be noted that this name in 1832, was spelled in the Assembly journal and elsewhere "Tonnewanta." The Tonawanda is a creek in Genesee county, flowing from Attica to Batavia in a northerly direction, and thence westerly to the Niagara river at Tonawanda. The road did not enter the valley until it reached Batavia and its entire length in that valley was only about 11 miles from Batavia to Attica, while the distance from Batavia to

Rochester was 31½ miles. The road from Batavia to Attica was deemed of so little importance that it was not constructed until 1842 and then only because it would form a connection with the Attica and Buffalo, which was not incorporated until four years subsequent to the Tonawanda.

The capital stock was fixed at $500,000 with shares of $100 each. Commissioners were named in the act to receive subscriptions to the stock and whenever the same was fully subscribed and $5 a share paid in, they were directed to call a meeting of the stockholders to elect thirteen directors, who were thereafter to be elected annually. The commissioners were directed to publish notice of time and place of receiving subscriptions within six months of the passage of the act, but they did not for some reason move with great alacrity, the books not being opened until August 14, 1833, nearly a year and a half after obtaining the charter. On that day the whole amount of stock was subscribed.

No record remains of the first election of directors and officers, nor has it been possible to learn their names prior to August, 1837, at which time the directors were David E. Evans, Trumbull Cary, George W. Lay, Abraham M. Schermerhorn, Frederick Bushnell, Thomas Kempshall, David Scott, James Brisban, Daniel M. Chandler, Jonathan Child, Frederick Whittlesey and Joshua Lathrop. At that time the officers were David E. Evans, president, Jonathan Child, vice-president, Abraham M. Schermerhorn, treasurer, Frederick Whittlesey, secretary, and David Scott, superintendent. The stockholders at that time were sixty in number.

Nothing is known of the early operations of the Company other than what is stated in a report of a committee of the directors made to the Board June 16, 1837. This report shows that the road was completed from Rochester to Batavia in May, 1837. It is so full of interesting information that it is here given in part:

Report &c. to the Board of Directors of the Tonawanda Railroad Company

The books for subscription to the capital stock of this company, were opened by the commissioners appointed under the charter, on the fourteenth day of August, 1833; and, on that day, the whole of the capital stock was taken by ninety-six subscribers. No effort was made to procure subscriptions to the capital stock, from abroad. Individuals residing in the section of country in which it was contemplated the road would be located, knowing the importance and feeling confident of the success of the enterprise, determined to take the whole hazard of the experiment upon themselves. They justly thought that they could furnish no better evidence to distant capitalists, whose aid they might want, of the value of the stocks than by such manifestations of their own confidence in it; and it is worthy of remark, that this whole stock was readily taken in a single day and under a very short notice by persons who had the best opportunities of knowing its value, from a residence in the immediate vicinity of the work.

Immediately after the distribution of the stock and the election of the first Board of Directors, engineers of skill and experience were employed to survey and report upon the most eligible route upon which the track of the company's road should be constructed. As the line of the road was not described in the charter, with any particularity, a wide and ample field was left open for the selection of the most advantageous route. This gave rise to the necessity of several surveys and estimates, and furnished ground for some differences of opinion, as to the proper route; but after the reports and estimates of the different engineers were carefully examined by the Board, the line of the route was finally settled and arrangements made at once for the acquisition of title to the necessary lands for the construction of the track of the road; and this having been accomplished, the construction was commenced late in the year 1834, and vigorously prosecuted during the two following years and finally opened to Batavia in May of the present year. Elisha Johnson, Esq., of Rochester was selected as the chief engineer, to direct the construction of the road in that capacity; the track of the road was made on a plan believed to be heretofore untried, which was invented by Mr. Johnson and adopted by the Board of Directors. His plan consists in making a framework of heavy timber to sustain the grade of the road and support the embankments, upon which framework the earth for filling the grade was transported. Large posts of twenty-four or thirty inches in diameter were placed upon each side of the track, opposite to each other, so as to sustain the side timbers of the track. These posts were permitted to enter the earth so as to stand firm upon the hard ground, and were squared at the top. Each of these sets of posts was about ten feet apart. Upon the top of these posts, were laid transversely sticks of timber twelve or fifteen inches in diameter, morticed on the upper side, near each end, so as to receive the longitudinal timbers. The longitudinal timbers—being from sixteen to twenty inches in diameter, smoothed only upon the upper sides, and intended for the support of each of the rails—were let into the mortices of the transverse timbers and supported by them and the posts. This, where an embankment was to be made, presented a substantial framework of the proper grade. Upon the top of the longitudinal timbers, proper wooden ribands, as a substitute for iron rails, were laid. Railroad cars were provided to carry earth, with four different boxes each, turning upon hinges attached to the car frame so as to discharge the earth between the rails and over the outside of each rail. These cars were loaded with earth at places, where excavations were necessary, and transported by horses upon the railroad track and emptied without any delay, to make the embankment. The same framework of timber, with the exception of the posts, was laid where excavations were to be made. When the earth was finally prepared for operation, pine scantling, of the usual dimensions, was laid upon the longitudinal timbers, and the iron-plate rail upon the scantling, and all securely nailed together by heavy spikes seven inches long.

We have reason, from experience, to be very much gratified with this plan of construction, as simple, economical, and durable; and we cannot but feel very much indebted to Mr. Johnson, the engineer, for the ingenuity manifested in its successful application. In a country like ours abounding with timber, it seems peculiarly applicable. The removing of the earth upon the railroad itself, was a great saving in the expense of teams; and the facility and ease with which it could be thus transported considerable distances, caused the excavations and embankments both to be made with an expense very little enhanced from what either would have cost, if made in the usual mode. The whole timber work, with the exception of the pine scantlings, is covered with earth, which will prevent it from speedily going to decay; and as the framework and embankments mutually support each other, it must add materially to the strength of the road. Much of this road has stood the test of two winters and has exhibited the effects of frost much less than the common wood roads; and we are satisfied, from this experience, that the plan adopted is preferable to that of any road not made of more durable materials. The same experience has enabled us to pronounce, with great confidence, that the yearly expense of repairs will be much less than upon other roads, while the danger arising from cars running off the track, is much diminished, by the fact that it will, in such case, have a smooth road of earth to run upon, unobstructed by any cross timbers above ground.

Seventy dollars per share have been paid in upon the stock, making in the whole the sum of three hundred and fifty thousand dollars. There have been expended by the company, nearly three hundred and seventy-five thousand dollars. In addition to the expenditures upon the road itself, the company have purchased lands in Rochester and Batavia for the necessary purposes of the road, to the amount of about twenty thousand dollars. They have erected an engine house, machine shop, car houses, shops for making cars, and other buildings in Rochester. They have a warehouse upon lands purchased by them and also occupy another warehouse hired by them. They have two locomotive engines, ten passenger cars, and a large number of freight cars. Since the opening of the road, the locomotives make two trips daily between Rochester and Batavia each way, with passengers and freight. The passenger and freight cars were made in the company's shops. In their shops are also now manufactured wheels, springs and other articles for furnishing railroads; and it is not improbable that this company will hereafter manufacture all such articles for railroads west of us.

From calculations drawn from all these facts, and after making deductions for emigrants who will continue to travel in a great measure upon the canal, we think we are not too sanguine in assuming that, after the railroad shall be completed to Buffalo, from four to five hundred persons will pass over the railroad from Rochester to Buffalo daily, during the travelling season of the year. The price of passage from Rochester to Batavia is $1.50; from Rochester to Buffalo it will be $3.00. As the whole road will be run it is contemplated, under a single arrangement with one set of cars and locomotives, the expense of running cannot be very considerable, not greater certainly than that of the Utica and Schenectady road, while the yearly expenses of repairs to the road itself, we are also satisfied by experience, will be greatly less than is common upon wooden roads. The cost of constructing the entire road and finishing it fully, with cars, locomotives, depots, &c., cannot exceed the sum of $700,000. A slight calculation from the above data will show how great must be the income, even after making every allowance for expenses. If we suppose the receipts to be $1,000 per day (which is less than the above estimate would warrant) for two hundred and forty days, it would give for receipts $240,000. If we suppose the expenses to be $200 per day for the same time, (which is much greater than our present expenses would justify) it would give for our expenses, $48,000, and the balance or profit would be nearly $200,000 which upon capital of $700,000 would be nearly 30 per cent.

The construction of the track from Batavia upon the Tonawanda creek to Attica twelve miles, will cost about $100,000, and will, of course, add that amount to the capital. As this extends into the fertile country south of Batavia, it may be fairly considered that this part of the road will at least support itself. But if it should yield nothing, the income from the main track, will be, by the above calculation, about 25 per cent upon a capital of $800,000 and this for passengers alone.

There is no better way of bringing to mind the hopes and expectations of the public generally over the opening of the first railroad into a community than is afforded by contemporaneous writings. In the case of the Tonawanda there has been preserved a copy of a

letter written from Batavia the day the first locomotive
engine arrived in that village which gives a fairly
representative picture of such an occasion, not over
colored by excitement or exuberant enthusiasm.   Genesee county at that time was largely devoted to the
growing of winter wheat.   After the opening of the
Erie Canal, this wheat was hauled by teams to Buffalo

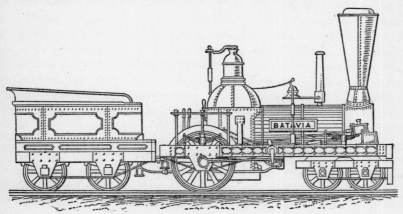

LOCOMOTIVE BUILT BY BALDWIN FOR THE TONAWANDA, 1836.

or Rochester or points westerly from Rochester on the
canal to ship to various markets or milling places.
What the farmers of the county needed was more and
cheaper facilities for marketing.   But to the letter,
which is, perhaps, its own best commentary:

BATAVIA (GENESEE CO.), May 5, 1837.

DEAR SIR:—The appearance here this morning of the first
locomotive engine, with its train of cars, created quite an excitement among us, and for a while dispelled the gloom of "Hard
times" and re-animated the spirits of our citizens.   The railroad,
34 miles in length, connects the flourishing city of Rochester with
this village, and brings the two places within two hours ride of
each other, at the same time opening a new avenue for the discharge of our surplus produce directly into the Erie canal.   In an
agricultural point of view, perhaps no portion of western New

York, is richer in all the great elements of wealth, than the section immediately around us; and, aided by this road, we must contribute greatly to the advancement of the commercial interests of Rochester to say nothing of the advantages to the country generally. As a point for the purchase of wheat, I think I hazard nothing in saying that no place affords greater advantages than this. It being the point where the Holland Land Company originally located their principal office, and where their business has always been done, the roads, which intersect the farming territory in every direction, have been made directly to this village, making it, necessarily, the natural place for a market. Suitable warehouses are now in progress of building, and we have nothing to ask but easy times for money and good crops, to keep half the flouring mills of the State in constant operation. The railroad itself passes through a very rich and interesting section, and is spoken of as among the most permanent and best constructed in the country, offering to persons travelling in this quarter an agreeable change, either from the canal at Rochester or from the usually travelled route by stage from Buffalo eastward. It cost for a single track, with suitable turnouts, three locomotive engines, passenger and freight cars, &c, &c., about $10,000 per mile, which has been furnished entirely by the individual means (with two or three exceptions) of persons resident in one or other of the two places it connects, and speaks well for the enterprising spirit. After this week the trips of the locomotives will be regular, and should anything bring you this way, allow me to hope you will make it convenient to pass over the Rochester and Tonawanda Railroad.

A florid and very bubbling description of the opening was given in the Rochester *Daily Democrat* for May 12, 1837, which contains enough of interest to justify its insertion here:

The Rail Road Celebration

Upon no occasion have we participated in a more pleasant excursion than that enjoyed yesterday upon the event of the completion of the Rochester and Batavia Rail Road. The morning was delightful, and the hour designated for the departure of the cars, they were thronged with our citizens desirous of participating in the celebration of an event so important to the interests of our city.

When we reached the Depot the engine was snorting like an impatient war horse; and at a given signal, it sped forward "like a thing of life." Hearty cheers from the multitude scattered along the line of road greeted its magic progress, and gave a thrilling animation to the scene.

In 40 minutes we were at Churchville. Its inhabitants gave us a cordial welcome. As we bade adieu to their kind gratulations, the waving of the 'kerchiefs showed us that the ladies also participated in the hilarity of the scene, and appreciated the important influence which the Road would have upon the prosperity of their pleasant village. Twelve minutes carried us over the three miles and one half that intervened between Churchville and Bergen. Here, too, we were most heartily received. The inhabitants for miles around had congregated to witness and participate in the joyful festivities of the day.

In a very few minutes we were at Byron and our reception was peculiarly pleasant. Friend Allis—whose spirited liberality even pressure cannot check—had a rich treat for his friends. They only wait for an occasion to reciprocate the kindness. Passing through one of the most delightful parts of the country the eye ever beheld, we were soon at Batavia. Here was animation. The Road, for a mile, was lined with citizens. The cheers were long and loud, and the thunderings of the cannon, called into requisition on this occasion, responded to the "three times hoorah" which was elicited from the cars by this grand reception.

At the place of landing the company were reviewed by the corporation and a Committee of citizens of Batavia; and escorted to the Eagle, where, in due time, a most sumptuous dinner was served up by "mine host" Mr. Smith. To gratify the palates of his guests, and to add to his own good name, he seemed to have monopolised the choicest delicacies of earth, air, and water. Fresh salmon, white fish and shad—wild ducks, snipe and pheasants—new radishes, sallad and cucumbers—were among the luxuries of the table. The mutual gratulations of the citizens of Rochester and Batavia, thus assembled to celebrate the completion of a work so important to the interests of both towns—were most cordial. Our neighbors felt that with them it was especially a proud day—and warmly and appropriately did they evince their joy.

After a few hours tarry at Batavia—passed in a pleasant inter-change of good wishes—the party returned, delighted with the excursion, and pleased with themselves. The Road may be ranked among the best in the United States. Their cars are the *very* best. Their Engineers—Messrs. Hayden and Smith—have not their superiors in the Union, while the Superintendent, Mr. Scott, and the agents, Messrs. Welbasky, Lyman, Fitch and Demerry, are intelligent, industrious and polite.

It appears from entries in the scattering books of account, that Thomas H. Rochester was commissioner in charge, Elisha Johnson was chief engineer. John B. Jervis was called into consultation on engineering in January, 1834, and paid $125.

For some reason not disclosed, work on the road from Batavia to Attica was not undertaken for some years. Apparently it was not considered a profitable part of the road unless the Attica and Buffalo were constructed to meet it.

In the spring of 1840, the Company had obtained state aid in state stock to the amount of $100,000 for the construction of its road (Chap. 200, passed May 1) and this could only have been required for construction from Batavia to Attica. The same year (Chap. 116, passed April 12) it obtained an extension of time for the completion of this part of its road. In 1841 and 1842, it did construct that part, completing the same about December, 1842, presumably using the money obtained from the state stock of $100,000.

Chapter 17 of the laws of 1844, passed February 17, authorized an increase in the capital stock to the amount of $250,000. The only reason which has been found for this increase is that given in a remonstrance submitted to the legislature in March, 1845, by the presidents of seven of the roads, of whom Heman J. Redfield, president of the Tonawanda, was one, against a proposed reduction of the rate of passenger fare on their roads. They say,

In the case of the Tonawanda railroad company the structure had become so decayed and the track poor that under the then embarrassed state of the company it could not be renewed, without further means derived from additional capital or loan. A law was passed at the last session providing for such increased means and fixing a fare of four cents a mile.

This statement of fact signed by the president of the Tonawanda was undoubtedly literally correct and explains definitely the large increase of capital stock in 1844 and 1845. The reader will undoubtedly compare the statement, "the structure had become so decayed and the track poor," with the encomium in the report of the committee above quoted, "We have reason from experience to be very much gratified with this plan of construction as simple, economical and durable and we can not but feel very much indebted to Mr. Johnson, the engineer, for the ingenuity manifested in its successful application. The whole timber work with the exception of the pine scantlings, is covered with earth which will prevent it from speedily going to decay and as the frame work and embankments mutually support each other it must add materially to the strength of the road."

Unquestionably the men engaged in building the Tonawanda were some of the best and most experienced in Western New York. They were aided by the expert advice of their own local engineer and the judgment of John B. Jervis, one of the ablest and most experienced engineers of the day. They felicitated themselves upon the strength and durability of the track they had constructed and yet in eight years after commencing operation, saying nothing of intermediate repairs, that track must be rebuilt under operation at great expense.

This experience was one of the tribulations of the early railroad builders.

In 1844, by Chapter 50 of the laws of that year passed March 19, the Company was empowered to connect its road in the city of Rochester with the road of the Auburn and Rochester upon a route to be determined by three commissioners named in the act. The gap between the two roads at this point was the only remaining one on the line between Albany and Buffalo. The act limited the time for the completion of the connection to the first day of September, 1846. The date of completion has not been ascertained but undoubtedly it was well within the limiting period.

In 1846, (Chap. 292, passed May 13) an act was passed entitled, "To regulate the price for transporting freight on the Tonawanda railroad." At whose instance this was done has not been learned, nor has it been ascertained what situation gave rise for the interposition of legislation. Whether the company procured it to crush the complaints of dissatisfied shippers or whether shippers asked it to reduce exorbitant charges by the carrier is a question which remains unsolved. At all events the law was passed and is unique in being probably the first attempt in this country to regulate freight rates by statute, and as such it deserves and shall receive full transcription at this place.

§ 1. The Tonawanda Railroad Company shall supply sufficient accommodation for conveying, and shall convey over their road or any portion thereof, passengers and their ordinary baggage, goods, wares and merchandise, salt, grain, flour, wool and all other produce, on the payment of the tolls provided for by this act.

§ 2. The said railroad company may receive for conveying goods, wares and merchandise, from the city of Rochester to Wardville, in the town of Bergen, Genesee county, or to any intermediate place, at the rate of eight cents for every one hundred pounds, and ten cents for every one hundred pounds from Rochester to Batavia, and from Rochester to any place between Wardville and Batavia, and ten cents for every one hundred pounds from Rochester to any place west of Batavia and they shall receive no other or further charge whatsoever for such services, except that they may receive for transporting household furniture from Rochester to Wardville, two dollars per carload of three tons, and from Rochester to any place west of Wardville, three dollars for such carload, and at corresponding rates on furniture as aforesaid, going to the city of Rochester.

§ 3. The said railroad company may receive for transporting wheat and all other grain, from Attica, Alexander and Batavia to the city of Rochester, three cents per bushel; and from all places east of Batavia, two and a half cents per bushel; and the said company may receive for transporting flour from Attica, Alexander and Batavia to the city of Rochester, twelve cents per barrel; and from any place east of Batavia, ten cents; and for pork, pot and pearl ashes, lard, butter, grass and clover seed, from Attica, Alexander and Batavia to the city of Rochester, or from Rochester to those places, eight cents per one hundred pounds; and from any place east of Batavia, six cents; and for wool, twelve cents, for each hundred pounds from Attica, Alexander and Batavia to the city of Rochester, and ten cents for every one hundred pounds east of Batavia; and for salt, ten cents per barrel from the city of Rochester to Wardville, and sixteen cents for any place west of Wardville; and the said company shall not receive any further compensation for receiving and forwarding the above named articles, than the prices named in this section.

Wardville was probably the present village of Bergen. The precise distances from the Rochester terminal, as it was situate in 1846, are not known, but they could have varied but little and that negligible, from Rochester to Wardville 17 miles; to Batavia 31½ miles; to Attica 43½ miles; from Wardville to Batavia 14½ miles. Using these distances for translating the rates named into the rates per ton mile for the purpose of comparison with the rate unit in common use, the results are as follows:

			Per Ton Mile
Rochester to Wardville,	17 miles	wares and merchandise	9c.
Rochester to Batavia,	31½ miles	" " "	6⅛c.
Rochester to Attica,	43½ miles	" " "	4.6c.
Attica to Rochester,		wheat and other grain	2.3c.
Batavia to Rochester,		" " " "	3¹/₆c.
Wardville to Rochester,		" " " "	4.9c.
Attica to Rochester,		flour	2.8c.
Batavia to Rochester,		"	3.88c.
Wardville to Rochester		"	6.00c.

The following examples are probably sufficient to comprehend the principle or lack of principle running through the whole list. Certainly there is a recognition of classification and of length of haul, but the application is interesting. Attica, 12 miles west of Batavia, pays the same flat rate per hundred pounds, per bushel and per barrel, as Batavia. Batavia, 14½ miles west of Wardville, pays 2 cents per hundred pounds, one half cent per bushel and 2 cents per barrel, more than Wardville.

Having stated the facts, it seems well to leave to everyone the opportunity to draw his own conclusions and make his own comments on this first legislative effort to handle the intricate and perplexing problem of freight rates. The point most likely to attract attention is the general level of rates per ton mile with those obtaining in our own day.

The next blow which fell upon the financial fabric of the Tonawanda was the Act of 1847, elsewhere discussed, requiring the laying of heavy iron rail. Then for the second time, if it was rebuilt in 1844, the track had to be rebuilt. March 29, 1848, that Act was amended in behalf of the Tonawanda (Chap. 151) so as to extend the time of performance to January 1, 1851, but only on condition it should expend for the general purpose at least $150,000 in each of the years 1848 and 1849. In its report for the year 1849, is found the following:

The road is laid with a heavy iron rail. The relaying was commenced in the year 1847, continued through the year 1848 and completed in September, 1849. About 6 miles of the road is laid with rails weighing 64 pounds per lineal yard, the remainder with rails weighing 61 pounds per lineal yard.

In this report it is said that capital stock to the amount of $950,000 had been called and paid in. It also had a bonded indebtedness of $150,000 which included the state loan. The total amount which it had charged to construction was $1,150,968.23, which exceeds what the road had cost up to the time it was opened for operation to Batavia, a little over twelve years previously, by over $775,000. Of this excess it seems the stockholders found over $600,000 in their own pockets. Not a cry of complaint from them has come down to us, but the fact speaks for itself. And the public had for its benefit a link in a great through line of railroad.

Chap. 226 of the laws of 1850 (passed April 9), authorized a consolidation with the Attica and Buffalo which was completed the latter part of the year and will be elsewhere described.

The following table is a summary made from the reports of the Company filed in the office of the Secretary of State for the years named:

Year Ending Dec. 31	Operating Revenue				Operating Expenses	Net Income	Operating Ratio
	Passenger	Freight	Other	Total			
	$	$	$	$	$	$	%
1843	59,663.02	11,750.66	4,813.34	76,227.02	43,606.04	32,620.98	57.21
1844	92,639.06	15,722.00	5,816.22	114,177.28	38,311.93	75,865.35	33.55
1845	89,896.98	20,311.12	6,462.50	116,670.60	37,006.12	79,664.48	31.72
1846	111,583.09	23,779.97	8,455.14	143,818.20	45,184.49	98,633.71	31.42
1847	157,738.28	27,684.15	9,743.40	195,165.83	55,719.90	139,445.93	28.55
Total for 5 Years	511,520.43	99,247.90	35,290.60	646,058.93	219,828.48	426,230.45	34.03

CHAPTER VIII

THE ATTICA AND BUFFALO RAILROAD

THE Attica and Buffalo Railroad Company was incorporated May 3, 1836, by Chapter 242 of the laws of that year to construct and maintain a railroad between the village of Attica in the then county of Genesee and the city of Buffalo; to commence at the termination of the Tonawanda road in Attica and running thence to the city of Buffalo on such route as the majority of the directors should determine to be best adapted to the public accommodation. No location for the Buffalo terminal was fixed in the charter.

Commissioners were named in the charter to open subscription books and receive subscriptions to the capital stock, within one year from its passage, giving thirty days notice of the times and places in one of the newspapers in Attica and Buffalo and in the state paper. Ten dollars were required to be paid on each one hundred dollars of stock at the time of subscription. The capital stock was fixed at $350,000 divided into shares of $50 each. When the capital stock should have been fully subscribed, the commissioners were required to call a meeting of the stockholders for the election of thirteen directors. Section 9 of the charter provided, "The said corporation shall not charge or receive a greater sum than at the rate of three cents per mile for the transportation of any passenger and his ordinary baggage." Subject to this limitation the

Company was authorized "to fix, regulate and receive the tolls and charges by them to be received for transportation of property or persons on the said road." There was in the charter no restriction on the right to transport freight. That came later in 1844.

There seems to have been much delay in organizing the Company, but no minute books or other records survive to tell us what was done. It is likely the panic of 1837 affected the situation very materially. However that may be, work does not seem to have started on construction until 1840 or 1841, and the only record which has been found relative to the construction, character of track, etc., is a report made by Tracy McCraken, the chief engineer, dated September 14, 1841. From this we extract the following:

As all the work requisite for the completion of the road from the Summit, 2 miles west of Attica, to Buffalo has been placed under contract in such a manner that requires the contractors to become stockholders and make large advances in its prosecution, it may be as well to first ask your attention to matters therewith connected.

The parties with whom these contracts have been entered into, agree to take their pay, one half in cash, and one half in stock of the road to be paid monthly as the work proceeds. They are composed of gentlemen of intelligence, responsibility, and long experienced in the construction of railroads; they would not consequently enter into any contract involving so large an amount of their own means, until they had made a full examination of the alignments, grades, radii of curvatures of the road, probable cost of construction, etc., etc.

After this careful examination, proposals were received from them, and contracts entered into for the clearing, grubbing, bridging, furnishing materials, and completing the road ready for the iron from Attica to Buffalo, including also the laying of the iron, to be furnished by the company and excepting the grading of the 2 first miles as has been stated. These contracts require the roadbed to be done by the 1st day of January next, and the superstructure laid and ready for the cars by the 4th day of July, 1842.

That the work has been let at low prices, and the stock valued as fully equivalent to cash will appear sufficiently evident by referring to the contract or estimated cost of the work hereinafter submitted. The prices for excavation and embankment 10 and 12 cents, viewed in connection with the small amount to be done and of course the proportionably large amount of trimming, ditching and dressing are as low as desirable; since to let work for less than it will cost, is usually attended with delays, non-fulfilment of contracts and increased expense.

The grading from Attica to the summit (2 miles) could not well be placed under contract till the survey of the Tonawanda road from Batavia to Attica had been made; this was necessary in order to fix upon a suitable place for connecting the two roads, and as it is now completed, the residue of your road should be, placed under contract with as little delay as possible. The point supposed to be most eligible for connecting the two roads is on the table of land at the foot of the hill on the bank of a small ravine, in the rear of Mr. Seward's house, about half a mile north of the center of the village of Attica. The distance from thence to the summit is about 2 miles, the ascent 68 feet; this it is proposed to surmount with a grade of 37 feet per mile, which is the maximum as represented on the profile.

Superstructure:—The superstructure to be composed of mud sills, 4 by 15 inches in length, as long as can be conveniently obtained, with ties, 4 by 6 laid flatwise upon the sills 5 feet apart, with blocks of wood of the same size at equal distances between them, with rails 8 inches square, fastened in their proper position, with cast iron knees at every crosstie. By varying the form of the ties, these knees may be dispensed with, and the rails fastened in a different manner, if it should be advisable. The timber of which the superstructure is composed to be of oak, red beech or hemlock.

Cost of one mile of road, being an average of the whole, at contract prices:—

Clearing, grubbing, grading, culverts, bridges and road crossings...............................	$ 2,000.00
Furnishing materials, and laying superstructure...	2,200.00
Plate rail ¾ × 2½", spike and splicing plate....	2,000.00

Brought forward........................... $ 6,200.00
Right of way................................. 1,000.00
Add for Engineering, water stations, turnouts &
  contingencies............................... 800.00

Total per mile...... $8,000.00
Miles....... 30
Total.... $240,000.00

Total amount of Excavation   141,000 yards
"   "   " Embankment   210,000 "

Should the edge rail be adopted, weighing about 50 pounds per yard, the additional expense, including the necessary chairs and fastenings would be about.................$4,000.00 per mile.

It was found necessary in 1838, owing to delays in organization to obtain an extension of three years in the time required by the charter for the commencement of construction and completion of the road (Chap. 283, laws of 1838). The commissioners appointed to receive subscriptions to stock do not seem to have proceeded in accordance with the law, probably did not receive subscriptions within one year and hence in 1842, it was found necessary to obtain an act legalizing their proceedings (Chap. 80, laws of 1842).

The location of the terminal in Buffalo was, of course, a matter of contention, thus establishing a greatly respected precedent, and on this the power of the legislature was invoked, which April 3, 1843, passed an act (Chap. 169, laws of 1843) authorizing the company "to lay out and construct the western portion of their road in the city of Buffalo from any point where the same is now finished to and upon either Eagle or Clinton streets as far west as Ellicott street or to and upon Exchange street as far west as a point five hundred feet west of the west line of Michigan street, provided that the common council of the city of Buffalo shall hereafter sanction and permit the laying out and construction of said road."

The legislature anticipating such sanction might not be given, and realizing the necessity of a properly located terminal, in the second section of the act enacted the following:

In case the said common council shall not sanction and permit such a location, to and upon either of the streets in the preceding section mentioned, as shall be satisfactory to the company, it shall and may be lawful for said company to lay out and construct their road to and along a route to be designated by the directors of said company, between the Main and Hamburgh street canal and Exchange street to a point west of Michigan street and not more than five hundred feet west of the west line of Michigan street and to establish their passenger depot upon the south line of Exchange street west of Michigan street.

It was upon the route thus authorized in the second section that the road was constructed. The original right of way east of Michigan street was but 40 feet in width. West of Michigan it was 80 feet in width and 210 feet southerly from Exchange street. The lot used for the passenger depot had a frontage of about 60 feet on Exchange street and was located 240 feet west from the west line of Michigan street, the old Continental hotel lot and a passage way lying between them. This lot extended to the right of way. Such were the narrow first dimensions of the Buffalo terminal.

May 7, 1844, the Company was made subject to the act (Chap. 335, laws of 1844) requiring the several roads of the line to pay canal tolls on property transported during the suspension of canal navigation. This is elsewhere discussed and need not be further mentioned at this place.

March 19, 1847 (Chap. 29, laws of 1847), the Company was authorized to increase its capital stock by the addition of three hundred and fifty thousand dollars in shares of fifty dollars each for the purpose of laying its track with heavy iron rail. This act also authorized the construction of a branch from any portion of the main track to the harbor or Big Buffalo creek in the city of Buffalo, at any point easterly of the foot of Washington street which branch should be used exclusively for the transportation of merchandise or other freight and not for the transportation of passengers. This branch had also been authorized by Chap. 169 of 1843, provided the sanction and permission of the Common Council of Buffalo were given. The act of 1847, contained no such requirement which induces the conjecture that the Common Council would not give its permission. It is difficult to understand why the act of 1847, contained the provision without imposing the consent except upon this view and indeed why the second action of the legislature was necessary unless the consent had been refused. This act was the authority for what is now known as the Ohio street branch. Just when it was constructed has not been ascertained. It was in existence in 1853 at the time of the consolidation.

Chapter 236 of the laws of 1850, authorized the consolidation of this Company with the Tonawanda, and such consolidation was made in November, 1850, the consolidation agreement being filed in the office of the Secretary of State, December 7, 1850. The name of the consolidated company was The Buffalo and Rochester Railroad Company and the consolidation and further history of the road being treated in connection with that Company.

On September 26, 1842, the road from Seneca street, Buffalo to Darien in the county of Genesee, a distance of 25 miles was completed and put in operation. From Darien to a junction with the Tonawanda at Attica, the road was completed and put in operation November

24, 1842. Owing to difficulties nothing had been done beyond Seneca street in Buffalo in constructing the road. During the year 1843, the road was completed to the terminus on Exchange street and a passenger station erected fronting on that street on a parcel of land lying next westerly beyond the alley at the westerly end of the old Continental hotel at the corner of Exchange and Michigan streets. The total length of the road thus completed was about 31⅓ miles. There was but a single track. The annual report for 1845 shows the cost of the road, including equipment, was $336,211.37. The report for 1842 shows $201,217.40. These figures are given to show how little meaning is possessed by one date taken alone. The work of constructing, adding facilities, new buildings and the like is going on constantly with a progressive road and without knowing the exact condition of the plant at a given date, one can not say to just what the figures relate.

The following operating statistics are taken from the annual reports filed in the office of the Secretary of State at Albany:

Year Ending Dec. 31	Operating Revenues				Operating Expenses	Net Income	Operating Ratio
	Passenger	Freight	Other	Total			
1842				None reported	None reported		
1843	42,836.88	3,061.67	—	45,898.55	19,149.80	26,748.75	41 72
1844	64,339.97	5,592.74	3,315.43	73,248.14	25,215.05	48,033.09	34.42
1845	58,975.93	6,602.16	4,719.45	70,297.54	30,974.67	39,322.87	44.06
1846	72,405.55	8,185.64	5,025.37	85,616.56	33,564.98	52,051.58	39.20
1847	104,010.22	15,000.00	4,800.00	123,810.22	49,000.00	74,810.22	39.58
Total for 5 Years	342,568.55	38,442.21	17,860.25	398,871.01	157,904.50	240,966.51	39.59

CHAPTER IX

THE BUFFALO AND ROCHESTER RAILROAD

THE Buffalo and Rochester Railroad Company was formed by the consolidation of the Tonawanda and Attica and Buffalo companies. Such consolidation was authorized by Chapter 236 of the laws of 1850, passed April 9. In addition to the usual powers conferred upon a railroad corporation, the act gave the consolidated company the power;

To render the line of railway between Buffalo and Rochester shorter and of more feasible and easier grades by constructing and maintaining a branch or branches, or second line of railway between any two points on the route of the present railroad between Rochester and Buffalo which shall effect that object, but without power to discontinue the railroad already constructed, except as provided by section four of Chapter two hundred and seventy-two of the Laws of eighteen hundred and forty-seven.

Also to increase the capital stock or borrow money for the purpose of covering the expense of the construction of such branch or second line of railway; also to enlarge the width of the existing road between Rochester and Buffalo to not exceeding six rods.

The new Company was required to commence the construction of the branch or new line of railway and expend at least one hundred thousand dollars thereon within two years and complete the same within three years on penalty that the special power to construct the same should be deemed to be revoked and held null and void.

The agreement of consolidation was dated October 8, 1850, executed by the Tonawanda, October 22, by the Attica and Buffalo, November 18, and filed in the office of the Secretary of State December 7, 1850. It provided that the name of the consolidated company should be The Buffalo and Rochester Railroad Company; the number of directors, thirteen; the capital stock thirty-six thousand five hundred shares of fifty dollars each ($1,825,000); of this joint capital, the capital of the Tonawanda was to be taken to be the sum of $1,025,000 or twenty thousand five hundred shares, the capital of the Attica and Buffalo as the sum of $800,000, or sixteen thousand shares of fifty dollars each, the Tonawanda being at liberty to increase its capital to the stated amount before the election of directors. Meetings of the stockholders were to be held at Attica on the 18th day of November for the purpose of passing on the agreement.

The debt of the Tonawanda to the state for the loan of its credit then amounting to $82,000 was assumed by the new corporation. There were other provisions regarding matters of no importance at this time.

The consolidated company promptly commenced the construction of a new line west from Batavia to a point near Depew on the Attica and Buffalo, 8 miles east of Buffalo, which line is now a part of the main line of the Central. Just when this new line was completed has not been ascertained, there being a total absence of information thereon in such of the records of the Company which have been preserved, but it must have been prior to the sale of 23 miles of the Attica and Buffalo hereinafter detailed.

The cost of this new line, judging from the reports of all the companies, to the state engineer, must have been approximately $613,000.

March 31, 1851 (Chap. 76 Laws of 1851), the legislature authorized the Company to sell to the Attica and Hornellsville Railroad Company the whole or any portion of its road from Attica to Buffalo. Pursuant to this authority, it sold 23 miles of the road from Attica to a point near Depew on the 1st day of November, 1852, for $322,000 of which $3,000 was paid in cash and the balance in bonds of the purchasing company, the Buffalo and New York Railroad Company.

CHAPTER X

THE ROCHESTER, LOCKPORT AND NIAGARA FALLS RAILROAD

THE Lockport and Niagara Falls Railroad Company, the predecessor of the Rochester, Lockport and Niagara Falls, was incorporated April 24, 1834, by Chapter 177 of the laws of that year to construct a railroad between Lockport and Niagara Falls, with a capital stock of $110,000 divided into shares of $50 each. It was given the power to transport both persons and property and fix the tolls therefor, subject to the restriction that it should not charge or receive a greater sum than four cents per mile for the transportation of a passenger and his ordinary baggage. By Chapter 99 of the laws of 1837, passed March 23rd, the Company was authorized to increase its capital stock to $175,000. By Chapter 122 of the laws of 1841, passed April 22, the Company was authorized to extend its railroad to the western termination of the Auburn and Rochester railroad in Rochester or to the Tonawanda railroad at Batavia, as a majority of the directors should decide and for the purpose of constructing such extension, the Company was empowered to increase its capital stock as might be necessary not exceeding, however, $500,000 in addition to its then present capital. By Chapter 36 of the laws of 1842, passed February 10, it was authorized to increase its capital stock to an amount not exceeding $1,200,000 in addition to the capital then paid in.

None of the books and papers of this Company has passed into the control of the New York Central, and if any exist, that fact is not known. The only record of its transactions which has been found is a report to the State Engineer, dated January 11, 1849, for the year 1848, which being brief and very much to the point is here produced in full:

Lockport, January 11, 1849.

The president, directors and company of the Niagara-Falls Railroad, report: That five years ago, on the first instant, their railway being only a section on the great thoroughfare, disconnected on the east from the line of travel, and rival railways connected through from Albany to Buffalo taking the greater portion of the through travel, it was found that their road, in the hands of the company, would little more than support itself, until it could be extended from Lockport to Rochester, where it might connect with the great thoroughfare. They therefore leased the road, for fifteen hundred dollars a year, to Henry Walbridge, Asher Torrence and William E. Cooper, the lessees to keep the road in repair; and the company reserved the right to claim it whenever it should be wanted by the companies for the purposes of extension to Rochester, or to renew it with heavier rails. It has ever since been run by the said Walbridge, under the lease. It has consumed the rent to pay the taxes, and discharge debts incurred for surveys of the extension and other purposes.

The length of the old road is 23 miles; of the extension to Genesee river at Rochester, 54.70 miles.

Cost of construction of old road................ $210,000.00
The income to the company as above stated.
No dividends have been made the last five years.

The whole capital for the old road and extension is fixed by the Legislature at $1,200,000.00: over $750,000 have been subscribed for the extension. The grading, masonry, bridging, and completion of the road ready for superstructure, is under contract from Lockport to Rochester, and about 25,000 dollars have been expended for the extension. It is expected to have the whole ready for the iron within the coming year.

The income for the past year to the lessees has been $13,000.00, principally from way passengers. The number of passengers, as nearly as can be ascertained, is through 10,000, way 30,000. Freight, but a trifle. No account of it kept.

United States mail	$ 750.00
Expense of repairs	6,000.00
Running expenses	5,000.00

Number of miles run, 36,000
3 locomotives on the road.
6 passenger cars, capable of carrying 220 passengers.
Freight cars, 5; 1 baggage car.
Average number of men employed on the road, 20.

It is believed the road was completed and put in operation in 1838, from Lockport to Niagara Falls.

Probably some work was done on the extension to Rochester during 1849, but affairs must have got into bad condition since no report was filed for 1849 and by Chapter 111 of the laws of 1850, passed March 28, the legislature took very drastic action and required the president of the Company to sell at public auction to the highest bidder all its real and personal estate including its franchise, the money arising from the sale to be applied on the debts of the Company in a manner particularly prescribed in the act. The act declared that the purchaser or purchasers at such sale should acquire thereby a title to the property as full and absolute as that possessed by the Company.

Section 2 of the act provided that the purchaser or purchasers should have the right: (1) to sell and distribute stock to the full amount authorized by the charter of the Company and the several amendments thereto; (2) to appoint an election to choose nine directors and organize the Company anew by such name as a majority of the directors should adopt and certify to the Secretary of State; (3) that when so organized the new Company should have the same powers and be subject to the same restrictions as the old Company;

Provided, that nothing contained in this act shall be construed to impair or affect the subscriptions for new stock or the obligations or liabilities of said company incurred in the extension of the road from Lockport to Buffalo.

Under the provisions of this act, the road was sold June 2, 1850, at public auction to Samuel Jandon, Joseph B. Varnum and Isaac C. Colton, and December 10th, the title was conveyed to them by deed. On the same day an election of directors was held at the Rochester Bank in the city of Rochester, and Joseph B. Varnum, Edward Whitehouse, Watts Sherman, Freeman Clarke, Silas D. Smith, Azariah Boody, Elias D. Holmes, Roswell G. Burrows and Alexis Ward were chosen as such. At a meeting of this new Board of Directors held the same day, they adopted The Rochester, Lockport and Niagara Falls Railroad Company as the name of the reorganized company. A certification of these proceedings was filed in the office of the Secretary of State, December 14, 1850, and this act completed the reorganization in the manner prescribed by the statute.

For the year ended September 30, 1851, the new Company filed with the State Engineer a very brief report of which the following is a copy:

That the company was reorganized December, 1850. The road was put under contract during the current year and is now in process of construction. It has only the following items to report:

Amount of capital stock as per charter......... $1,375,000.00

Amount of stock subscribed as authorized by resolution of Board upon which payments have been made............................... 1,036,800.00

Amount of capital stock now paid in........... 728,273.75

Funded debt   None

Cost of road and equipment

For graduation and masonry.................. 254,830.83

Total amount expended for bridges............ 10,020.00

Total amount expended for superstructure including iron............................. 87,900.00

Total amount expended for land and land damages and fences............................ 185,339.79

For engineering and agencies................. 18,000.00

Length of road   76 miles

This report shows that the road from Lockport to Niagara Falls could not have been operated during that fiscal year and that work on the extension to Rochester was in progress.

The fiscal year ended September 30, 1852, seems to have been one of great activity. The capital stock has been increased to $1,675,000, of which there had been subscribed $1,447,500 on which there had been paid in $1,446,180, an increase of $717,906.25 during the year. The funded debt according to the Company's report amounted to $711,000, all of which had been incurred during the year. The average rate of interest on the debt was 7 per cent. The length of the road was given as 76.617 miles, the weight of rail per yard 62 pounds, 13 engines, 20 passenger cars, 6 baggage, mail and express cars and 62 freight cars.

The road had been operated for three months and thus must have been opened for operation on or about July 1, 1852. In that time it had carried 86,756 passengers and 1,267 tons of freight; the rate of passenger fare was 2½ cents per mile. The earnings in this three months' period were:

From passengers..................	$64,185.41
From freight.....................	2,132.32
From other sources...............	1,930.00
Total......................	$68,247.73

The report for the ten months ended June 30, 1853, showed large additional changes in the financial situation; increase of capital stock to $2,142,100, all subscribed; amount paid in $2,142,100; funded debt reduced to $389,000. Total cost of construction given as $2,343,388.50. The number of passengers carried 260,000; tons of freight 92,317.

The earnings were—

For passengers.............	$172,086.46
For freight...................	62,850.45
From other sources.............	6,663.36
Total..................	$241,600.27
Operating expenses..............	150,982.34
Gross income..................	$ 90,617.93

It is understood that the line from Lockport to Niagara Falls was changed in whole or in part during these years, but no exact record of such changes has been found.

CHAPTER XI

THE BUFFALO AND LOCKPORT RAILROAD

THE Buffalo and Lockport Railroad Company was incorporated April 29, 1852, by articles of association filed that day in the office of the Secretary of State, with an authorized capital stock of $600,000, divided into 6,000 shares of $100 each. It was to extend from Buffalo to Lockport, an estimated distance of twenty-five miles. It had 13 directors, Azariah Boody, Freeman Clarke, Warren Colburn, Elias B. Holmes, Roswell S. Burrows, Henry Walbridge, Isaac C. Colton, Stoughton Pettibone, John Wilkeson, A. D. Patchin, George W. Tifft, John M. Griffith and David S. Crandall. There were 26 subscribers to the certificate, of whom 5 resided in Rochester, 12 in Lockport, 4 in Buffalo, 2 in Albion, 1 in Greenfield, 1 in Middleport, and 1 in Brockport. The Buffalo subscriptions amounted only to $4,500 or 45 shares; those of Lockport to $6,700, or 67 shares; those of Rochester to $11,200 or 112 shares, of which $7,500 or 75 shares were taken by Azariah Boody, the managing man of the Rochester, Lockport and Niagara Falls. The names of the principal subscribers to this certificate and the number of shares ultimately taken in the Company by stockholders in the Rochester, Lockport and Niagara Falls and the agreement between the two companies for the operation by the Rochester show that this enterprise was undertaken to give the Rochester road an entrance into Buffalo.

All the information obtainable concerning this road is, that at the time of the consolidation, it was not in operation but expected to be ready for it July 1, 1853, that it had a capital stock of $600,000 all paid in and convertible bonds to the amount of $75,000; that the officers reported it would be completed within the capital stock and funded debt.

The passenger terminal of the road in Buffalo was at Erie street on a lot of irregular dimensions, being about 250 feet on the Erie Canal, 175 feet on Canal Slip No. 1, 550 feet on the ship canal and 200 feet on Erie street. This terminal and the right of way from Buffalo to Tonawanda were owned jointly with the Buffalo and Niagara Falls. The junction of the road with the Rochester, Lockport and Niagara Falls was about 2½ miles west of Lockport. The engineer in charge of construction was Warren Colburn.

CHAPTER XII

THE SCHENECTADY AND TROY RAILROAD

THE Schenectady and Troy Railroad extending from Troy to Schenectady presents but few points of interest, but those few are worthy of careful attention. It is the only steam railroad, so far as is known, built and owned by a city not merely as a commercial adventure, but with a view to develop the commercial growth of the city. It is one of the finest examples of the results of locating a road not as justified and demanded by the needs of transportation, but to contribute to another result, namely, the growth and prosperity of a terminal city. It contributes practically nothing to the history of the development of railroad construction and operation with possibly the exception that it was the first railroad in the central system which did not use a strap rail laid on longitudinal wooden stringers. Its first rail was an H iron rail, weighing 56 pounds to the yard. It was a well constructed and well equipped road for its day. In July, 1845, the *American Railroad Journal* had this concerning it: "We passed over this road a few days since and found it uncommonly easy to ride upon. On leaving the Troy House after an excellent breakfast we entered the car which seems to have been constructed with a view to cleanliness and comfort being sustained by 'atmospheric springs' and well ventilated." After some rather highly colored descriptions of the scenery, it predicts it "will render this road from New York to the west a favorite one." Again in July, 1845, the same journal says, "This is one of the best constructed roads in the country. This road is laid with heavy 'H' rail and cost a little over $31,000 per mile. . . . The engines are of the best kind for passenger traffic and the cars made by Gilbert and Eaton of Troy, such as a weary man delights to find." It is certain that the building of this road was the means of forcing the city of Albany to afford to the Mohawk and Hudson the financial assistance necessary for the elimination of inclined planes and stationary power upon parts of its road.

The Company was incorporated by Chapter 427 of the laws of 1836, passed May 21st, and seems to have been in its inception a private enterprise, but nothing was accomplished the first year, except that some stock was subscribed for. Certain it is that the city of Troy was not interested as a municipality, for it had no legal authority so to do. The authorized capital stock was fixed at five hundred thousand dollars and the Company was authorized to charge not exceeding six cents per mile for transporting a passenger and his ordinary baggage. This is the highest legal rate which has been found in New York, except in a few exceptional cases of very short lines of difficult construction. But in the year 1837, by Chapter 174 of the laws of that year passed March 28, the city of Troy was authorized to borrow not exceeding $500,000 on not to exceed twenty-five years' time at 6 per cent interest, the money to be invested in the stock of the Schenectady and Troy to be used in the construction of the road and for no other purpose whatsoever. The road was completed at a cost of over $600,000, and by Chapter 35 of the laws of 1843, passed April 17, additional stock to the amount of $150,000 was authorized. All of this stock was taken and owned by the city of Troy, a heavy load for a little town of but 16,959 population in 1835, which had risen to 19,331 in 1840.

The situation which induced this municipal action was that the Utica and Schenectady and roads to the westward were being constructed which would bring the great passenger traffic of the west through the Mohawk valley to the Hudson. The New York and Albany, a road which was never built, was projected up the Hudson on its eastern side and part of the dream was to extend it as far north as Troy. Efforts were being made finally successful to establish steamboat lines between Troy and New York. Boston capital was pushing the Western railroad toward a point on the Hudson river. The opening of the Erie Canal in 1825 had greatly increased the importance and population of Troy. If it could tap the Utica and Schenectady and secure a fair proportion of the tide of travel from the west, clearly it seemed the city was justified in pledging its credit for the means which would construct so desirable an artery of travel. The road would most likely care for itself and pay for its cost. Also the Mohawk and Hudson which fed the rival city of Albany was burdened with an enormous cost, it was waterlogged with two inclined planes operated by stationary power, it could not transport passengers and property as cheaply as the road from Troy. Commercial rivalry was rife between the two cities. These were the views which led to the plunge which was finally made.

So November 4, 1837, a committee appointed by the Common Council voted it expedient to take stock to the amount of $300,000. November 20th visions grew brighter as the limit was raised to $480,000 and Janu-

ary 28th, it was voted to take all the stock for the
city. And this it must not be forgotten was in the
depression following the panic of 1837. Had it occurred in the booming times preceding that panic, the
wonder would not have been as great.

But notwithstanding the enthusiasm, the matter
lagged for two years and a half, until at a meeting of
the directors of the railroad, held May 25, 1840, the
Mayor of the city in person presented a preamble and
resolution of the Common Council, which summed up
the situation in the following language:

Whereas, this Board are apprised that the directors of the
Western Railroad Company in Massachusetts have taken such
measures to extend their road to the Hudson river as will ensure
the completion of the whole line from the city of Boston to the
village of Greenbush during the year 1841. And believing that
the great interests of the city of New York and the counties
through which the New York, Albany & Troy rail road is to
pass will lead to an early and vigorous prosecution of that important work. Therefore, Resolved; that this board deem the
time to have arrived when the welfare and prosperity of this
city require that the Schenectady and Troy rail road the connecting link between the west and east should receive that attention
which its importance merits and now recommend to the president and directors of said corporation to take immediate measures for the sale of such an amount of the city bonds as in their
judgment can be advantageously expended during the present
year in the purchase of land and materials and in the construction of the road.

Naturally the presentation of a paper of this energetic character by the Mayor of the city, resulted in a
unanimous resolution that the directors would at once
begin operations. Committees were appointed to sell
bonds and to report plan of organization and at a
meeting July 10, the former reported it had succeeded in agreeing for two loans of $50,000 each, one in

New York and one in Boston, both of which cities they had visited. Obviously the facilities for disposing of municipal bonds have improved measurably in the last eighty-five years. July 23, James Laurie was appointed engineer. His salary was fixed at $3,000 per annum and to furnish him a horse and wagon and pay the expense of keeping. The salary of assistant engineer was fixed at $1,200. August 4th the compensation for young men on the engineer corps was fixed seventy-five cents per day. September 10, for reasons unexplained this resolution was rescinded. Probably it was not popular with the young men seeking positions. The Board evidently thought they had secured a very competent man in Mr. Laurie. In a report made to the Common Council, October 15, they say of the appointee, "he having been highly recommended to them and especially by the Road from Worcester to Boston itself, of the making of which he had charge and which is considered by several of our citizens who have travelled upon it, the best piece of work and most economically constructed of any Road in the Country." Nor is there any record that he in any way disappointed their expectations.

August 4, a Commissioner was elected but September 10, the office was abolished from and after October 15. November 14, the route for eight miles from the bridge at Troy was adopted and contractors' proposals were received. November 23, contracts were awarded for grading seven sections. December 14, the president was authorized to contract for 500,000 feet of hemlock timber at $8.85 per thousand. December 21, a contract for 500,000 feet of chestnut timber at $18 per thousand was authorized. This chestnut seems to have been intended for "mud sills" since March 6, the president was authorized to receive on the contract for it, 200,000 feet of tamarack for mud sills of lengths of 21 and 24 feet in the place of chestnut, at $21 for the tamarack.

The report of February 1, 1841, to the Common Council discloses that several routes had been surveyed by the engineer, that the directors after thorough examination had selected the most eligible and that the certificates required by law had been filed. That the greatest elevation did not exceed 50 feet per mile and that only in going toward Schenectady and that no other route could be found with a less elevation than 60 feet and that both going to and returning from Schenectady. That the distance was a little over 20 miles and that another route of about 17 miles had been found but the latter was much more expensive— estimated at $58,919.36, owing to the cuts and fills required.

It also shows that about 9 miles of the Troy end had been divided into ten sections for grading, contracts let and contractors actively at work. The prices for grading per cubic yard are interesting in view of subsequent developments:

Section 1	20	cents	
3	15	"	
4	11¾	"	
5	12	"	(relet March '41)
6	12	'	
7	11	"	(relet March '41)
8	14	'	
9	12½	"	
10	9¾	"	(relet March '41)

Masonry for bridges across the Mohawk river and the Erie Canal had been let for $4 per cubic yard where stone from the lower aqueduct would be proper and should be used, and $8.50 per cubic yard for Amsterdam stone.

The interesting feature of the grading contracts is the number upon which increased pay was asked or the contract wholly surrendered.

The president of the Company seems to have acted as commissioner in charge of the work, since on July 19, 1841, he was appointed commissioner at $1,000 per year "with duties he has been performing." Another man was at this time elected president.

The work seems to have progressed slowly in 1841. Other contracts for grading were let as follows:

Section	Common	Loose Rock	Rock
12	15½ cents	30 cents	60 cents
13	12 "	30 "	40 "
14	13 "	30 "	50 "
15	12½ "	30 "	50 "
16	13¼ "	40 "	70 "
17	15 "	40 "	65 "
18	20 "	56 "	56 "
19	16 "	45 "	60 "
20	12 "	25 "	38 "
21	11 "	30 "	38 "

It is noticeable that unit prices ran much higher than on the first ten sections and that the prices varied with the character of the work and material to be encountered.

It was not until August 10th that any one was authorized to buy iron for the track and in September a committee was appointed to examine what kind of cars and locomotive engines ought to be adopted. This committee reported in December favoring ordering one locomotive from Norris of Philadelphia and one from Rogers, Ketcham & Grosvenor of Paterson, N. J., and the report was adopted. February 9, 1842, a contract was entered into with Eaton & Gilbert of Troy for seven passenger cars. No specifications or description of either cars or locomotives have been found.

As early as May, 1840, Troy felt doubt about its ability to finance the undertaking. It procured the passage of Chapter 299 of the laws of that year, authorizing the issuing of state stock to the amount of $100,000 in aid of the road whenever the Company should have actually expended $100,000 in construction of its road. The event proved the wisdom of this. The bonds of the city were slow of sale and the first $100,000 sold at 6 per cent discount, realizing but $94,000. In August, 1841, the directors accepted the act and made application for the stock, which was in due course granted. A considerable percentage of the contractors were paid with city bonds. Locomotives and cars were paid for in the same manner.

The main line of the road as located terminated on the west side of the Hudson river. The charter contemplated an entrance into the city of Troy over the bridge of the Rensselaer and Saratoga Railroad and Green Island, and gave the Company the power to extend its road into the city on obtaining the right from the other company to cross its bridge and the island. It, however, provided, "but no bridge shall be built by the corporation hereby created between Green Island aforesaid or any part of the west bank of the Hudson river and the city of Troy or otherwise across said river." This restricted entrance to the city over the tracks and bridge of the Rensselaer and Saratoga. In addition to that right, the Company was extremely anxious to acquire land from that company on Green Island on which to erect necessary buildings. There was great difficulty in bringing this about; negotiations for a long time were fruitless. Just what the point of disagreement was, does not appear, the numerous references to the subject in the directors' minutes failing to disclose whether it was merely price, or that and other matters. It was finally adjusted in some manner.

The work of construction proceeded slowly. Iron rails had been contracted for in England. Part did not arrive as contemplated and ultimately some of the rails were bought in America, and when the remainder of the English rails arrived, there was trouble over them. The road was finally opened for operation about November 1, 1842, nearly two years after the letting of the first contracts for grading.

The fare between Schenectady and Troy was fixed by the Board on November 2 at twenty-five cents until November 20 "and that the rates of fare after that time shall hereafter be established." This was an obvious bluff designed to bring the Mohawk and Hudson to some terms, but it failed of its object. May 17, 1843, the fare was fixed at 25 cents, a steamboat association agreeing to pay in addition thereto 25 cents for each passenger from Schenectady delivered at Troy. The twenty-five cent fare was continued until a much later period when it was raised to fifty cents, the Company claiming it was forced to do so in order to obtain privileges from the western roads.

On opening the road, the Board of Directors itself established the wages and salaries and thereby we get information obtainable on no other road. In October, 1842, the minutes show them as follows:

Superintendent $800 per annum; conductor $33⅓ per month; locomotive engineer $50; fireman $30; common laboring man $18; baggage master $25; brakeman $20; track foreman $40; mechanics and repair men $30; attendant at half way station $12.50;

ticket agent Troy $37.50; depot laborers and switch tenders $20; agent and collector at Schenectady $50.

It is of interest to know the prices for labor and materials prevailing in the early forties. Some of these can be picked out from the records of the Company. The unit prices for grading have already been shown, but for some reason many of the contractors made claims for an increased price and some of them received an increase. Apparently the haul was included in the unit price, the excavated material being placed in adjacent embankment, making but a short haul. When circumstances made longer haul necessary, an allowance was made in one case of 9 cents per c.y. on 3600 yards, in another of 35 cents, in another 8 cents on 1,674 yards "hauled from main cut to supply deficiency from cut at station 779." In such cases the distance hauled is not stated. One contractor whose contract price was 14 cents, by order of the directors, received an extra allowance of 5 cents on 15,361 c.y. out of a total of 23,154. Another received an advance of 2½ cents over contract price on all but 292 yards. A. J. Yates claimed $1,040 extra for hard pan excavation. The Board allowed him $700.

The two locomotives with which operations commenced cost about $7,400 each; first class passenger cars, $2,000 each; 8 wheel second class passenger and baggage cars $1,000; 4 wheel freight cars $375 each; chestnut cross ties 35 cents each; posts for fencing 7 cents each.

In masonry, dry rubble cost $1.75 per cubic yard; rubble in mortar, $2.75; limestone corners and coping for bridges and culverts $8.00; limestone covering stone for culverts $6.00; Amsterdam stone delivered but not placed $3.50; earth excavation for foundation, dry, 25 cents per c.y.

The rails seem to have been laid on longitudinal wooden stringers which were laid in trenches about one foot deep; excavation of trenches 20 cents per c.y. in clay; 6½ inch railroad spikes 5⅝ cents per pound. Common labor 75 cents per day; mason's labor $1.50; carpenters 87½ cents, team and driver $2.

The ill success financially of the road induced the Board in November, 1845, to resolve to apply to the legislature for a charter for an extension of the railroad from Schenectady to Utica on the south side of the Mohawk river. A bill for that purpose was introduced into the legislature of 1846, supported by a printed memorandum and vigorous argument before the railroad committee of the Assembly, the Utica and Schenectady answered by printed statements and arguments. Four out of five of the committee reported against the bill and it failed of passage.

In 1852, the city of Troy sold the capital stock to Edwin D. Morgan, then president of the Hudson River Railroad Company and afterwards Governor of the State of New York. Some efforts to ascertain the real nature of this transaction and who were the parties acting in combination with Morgan have met with no success.

CHAPTER XIII

THE MOHAWK VALLEY

THE Utica and Schenectady, incorporated in 1833, occupied a very favorable position in the valley of the Mohawk river and proved to be successful financially from the outset. In consequence, attempts were made to incorporate and construct competing roads through or near this valley. The first attempt which seemed formidable was that of the City of Troy, which constructed and owned the Schenectady and Troy. That road was a financial failure from the first, being unable to divert at Schenectady any substantial portion of the traffic from the west carried by the Utica and Schenectady and which sought an outlet at Albany rather than Troy. It seems to have been thought that if this road were extended to Utica it might succeed in picking up the desired business. Accordingly there were presented to the legislature of 1846, petitions asking for an act authorizing the Schenectady and Troy to extend its road to Utica mainly on the south side of the Mohawk river, but partly on the north side. The Utica and Schenectady filed, January 19, 1846, with the legislature a printed protest. In March following, the Schenectady and Troy submitted a printed statement of 15 pages complaining of unfair treatment received from the Utica and Schenectady as a reason for the proposed legislation. The latter road at once came back with a pamphlet of twenty-four pages containing several affidavits in refutation of the charges made against it. In April, a majority of the railroad committee of the Senate reported to that body the proposed bill which seems to have passed the Assembly, but a minority of the committee filed a vigorous dissenting report. The contest seems to have been vigorous, but for some reason the bill did not become a law.

But the hope of Trojans for a road from Troy to Utica seems to have survived, since the state engineer's report for 1882, states that the Troy and Utica Railroad Company was incorporated as late as 1853 to construct a road from Troy to Utica. The Genesee and Hudson Railroad Company was incorporated in 1852, to construct a railroad from Rochester to Albany. Maps of its proposed location were filed as required by law in January, 1853, and efforts made by it to secure rights of way. On the 21st day of January, 1851, The Mohawk Valley Railroad Company, not the one which entered the consolidation, was incorporated with an authorized capital of two million dollars to construct a railroad from Schenectady to Utica "through the valley of the Mohawk river and on the southerly side thereof when that side shall be deemed most practicable." The president of the Company was Azariah C. Flagg, who had twice been the comptroller of the State of New York and who had a high reputation for ability and integrity. Twelve hundred and five shares of stock amounting to $120,500 were subscribed for and as required by law, $12,050 paid in in cash by twenty-eight subscribers, of whom eight resided in New York City, one in Brooklyn, one in Troy, one in Albany, one in Schenectady, one in Amsterdam, three in Utica, eleven in the village of Mohawk, and one in German Flats, the last two places being on the south side of the river. Among the subscribers were General Francis E. Spinner and B. Carver, who will be later mentioned. Seven of the New York City subscribers took each 100 shares of stock and included such men as Robert and Peter Goelet, C. V. S. and James I. Roosevelt, and Arthur V. Gifford. Spinner took 100 shares and Carver 50. Platt Potter, afterward a justice of the Supreme Court and Ward Hunt, of Utica, later a judge of the Court of Appeals and justice of the Supreme Court of the United States, were subscribers.

There was immediate activity in locating the route. Extensive surveys were made of two possible routes and estimates made of their probable cost. On the 1st of May, the chief engineer made a very elaborate report, describing the routes surveyed in great detail, reviewing the profitable history of the Utica and Schenectady Company, the prospective business and earnings of the new company, and giving the detail of an estimated cost of a complete one track road and equipment, graded complete for two tracks, as $2,126,-107.62, with an additional $580,000 for second track, making a total for a complete two track road of $2,706,107.62.

The Board of Directors, through a Sub-Committee, also made a report on the prospects and advantages of the proposed road, very voluminous, and exhaustively treating these matters, and ordered one thousand copies of the two reports to be printed in pamphlet form.

For some reason not now ascertainable, nothing further seems to have been accomplished in the year 1851. On January 29, 1852, a new board of directors was elected, among whom were John A. Dix and Ward Hunt. Mr. Flagg was re-elected president and Gen. Spinner, secretary and treasurer. We have no account of what happened further until the 28th day of July, 1852, when at a directors' meeting in Albany a complete turn over took place. The Utica and Schenectady had made an arrangement by which it secured control of the company, seven hundred and fifty shares being retained by existing stockholders, the balance being assigned to Erastus Corning and John V. L. Pruyn, or such persons as they might nominate, on paying the amount paid in therefor with four per cent interest from the time of payment.

Messrs. Seymour, Mann, Hunt, Temple, Remington and Flagg resigned as directors and Flagg as president. Messrs. Corning, Pruyn, Vibbard, Townsend, Reynolds, Olcott and Paige were elected directors, Pruyn being treasurer and Vibbard superintendent of the Utica and Schenectady and the others directors of that company. Mr. Pruyn was then elected president of the company.

Evidence exists that in July, 1852, surveying for the route was going on and negotiations for right of way were pending in that year. In September, Mr. Spinner was active in securing the interests of some of the New York promoters for persons connected with the Utica and Schenectady. A file of correspondence now in the possession of the New York Central discloses earnest effort to get the new road under construction. These efforts did not produce results rapidly enough. Under the law the charter of the Company would expire in January, 1853, unless work had been commenced and ten per cent of the capital expended. So in December, 1852, it was decided to incorporate a new company, the Mohawk Valley, the one which entered the consolidation, to take over the assets of the old company and let it go out of existence by operation of law. The new company was incorporated December 29, 1852. Subcriptions were taken to the stock of the new companys and ten per cent paid in as required by law. It is both interesting and instructive to note the names of some of the stockholders and the number of shares taken by them respectively.

B. Carver	110	Thomas W. Olcott	7
F. E. Spinner	67	Robert Goelet	36
A. C. Paige	10	Peter Goelet	36
J. V. L. Pruyn	25	J. W. Hamersly	25
Erastus Corning	25	John A. Dix	18
Ward Hunt	20	Joseph Samson	36
C. Vibbard	6	James I. Roosevelt	36
M. T. Reynolds	20	C. V. S. Roosevelt	36
John Townsend	20	A. Mann, Jr.	18

Those shown in the first column are persons living on the south side of the Mohawk river or connected with the Utica and Schenectady; those in the second column were men who had stock in the original Mohawk Valley and continued with its successor. Corning, Townsend, Olcott and Paige were directors of the Utica and Schenectady, Pruyn was secretary and Vibbard, superintendent. Ward Hunt was a Utica lawyer, hereinbefore mentioned. The Goelets and Roosevelts were well known New York City men, and John A. Dix, the General John A. Dix who afterwards was Governor of the State of New York. The total number of incorporators was 37, of whom 13 resided in villages south of the river, 11 in New York City or its immediate vicinity, 6 in Albany, 2 in Schenectady, 1 in Amsterdam and 1 in Columbia and 3 in Utica. We have given these details in the belief that 37 men of the standing and character of these subscribers, residing at widely separated points, all united in nothing, associated in nothing, except this particular enterprise could not have been brought together in the project had it not been a genuine undertaking to build a new line along the river, partly on the south side to accommodate communities there and incidentally to protect the Utica and Schenectady from competition which it could not control.

On the 5th day of January, 1853, the directors of the old company held a meeting at Albany and adopted a resolution which recited that every railroad corporation was by law required to begin construction of its road and to expend thereon ten per cent of the amount of its capital stock within two years after its articles or association were filed and recorded in the office of the Secretary of State, or in default thereof, its corporate powers and existence would cease; that the said two years in the case of this company would expire January 21, 1853; that it was impossible owing to previous delays, for the company to expend the required amount within the specified time; that a new company had been incorporated composed substantially of the same persons as the present company, for the purpose of building the contemplated road, and authorized the sale to said new company of all the books, maps and papers and other property of the existing company.

On the 17th day of January, 1853, the old company, pursuant to said resolution, sold to the new company all its "maps, charts and profiles of the route of its proposed road and all books, maps, papers and documents owned by it and all personal property and assets of every description" held by it or in which it had any right or interest.

The new company organized with J. V. L. Pruyn as president. A majority of the directors were also either officers or directors of the Utica and Schenectady. Two of the directors were Spinner and Carver. Seventy-five thousand dollars of the stock was taken by the promoters of the original enterprise. On January 20th, President Pruyn issued a circular to the stockholders of the Utica and Schenectady inviting subscriptions to the stock and on January 18 sent a communication to the directors of that road suggesting that road should take a lease of the proposed new road. The new company appointed the Phenix Bank of New York its agent for the registry and transfer of its stock and the Phenix Bank by a resolution of its Board dated February 23, 1853, accepted such agency.

The map and profile of the route were on February 19th filed in the office of the clerk of Herkimer County pursuant to law. A map and profile were filed with the canal commissioners and application made to that body for permission to locate the proposed road at certain points within ten rods of the Erie Canal, which permission was subsequently granted. Among the stockholders of the old company who renewed subscriptions for the new company was Platt Potter of Schenectady, who afterwards was elected a Justice of the Supreme Court, as appears by his letter on file. General Spinner and Mr. Carver are shown by their letters to have been active during the winter in endeavoring to secure right of way. January 24, General Spinner writes to Mr. Pruyn stating that the engineer and two of the directors of the Genesee and Hudson Railroad Company "had been through here and had filed a map of their proposed route through this county in the County Clerk's office. I have found several persons from whom they tried to get title of land but know of none that they succeeded in getting. One of the directors said they were sure of getting the money to build the road without any subscriptions."

The exact relation of the Mohawk Valley to the Utica and Schenectady may be readily ascertained by a consideration of what action was taken by the two companies with reference to constructing the road of the Mohawk Valley, keeping in mind that a majority of the directors of the Mohawk Valley were directors of the Utica and Schenectady; that Mr. Pruyn, the president of the Mohawk Valley, was treasurer and counsel of the other company, and that J. Sternbergh, the secretary of the Mohawk Valley, was a clerk in the office of the treasurer of the Utica and Schenectady.

On February 21, 1853, the directors of the Mohawk Valley adopted a resolution as follows:—

Whereas the greater part of the route of the railroad contemplated to be built by this Company has been located along and in part upon the line and grounds of the railroad of the Utica and Schenectady Rail Road Company and it is desirable that an arrangement should be made with that Company in regard to the construction of said road and if that Company should prefer constructing said road they may also desire to take a lease of and run the entire road to be constructed by this Company.

Resolved, that the Executive Committee be authorized to open a negotiation with the said Utica and Schenectady Rail Road Company on the subject matters aforesaid and to make such agreement in regard thereto subject to the sanction of this Board as they may deem proper.

March 18, Mr. Pruyn presented to the meeting of the directors of the Utica and Schenectady maps and profiles of the proposed road, the originals of which had been filed in the offices of the County Clerks of the counties of Schenectady, Montgomery, Herkimer and Oneida, as required by law and a communication in which he says:

It will be seen from an examination of these maps that the route of the road proposed to be constructed by the Mohawk Valley Rail Road Company runs for much the greater part of its length on the Northerly side of the Mohawk river and along or in part upon the line and grounds of the road of your Company excepting at a few points where it is proposed to straighten and improve the road.

He then presents a copy of the preamble and resolution above quoted and says:

The propriety of an agreement between the two companies as proposed in the foregoing resolution seems obvious to us and we hope will be so considered by you. It may be proper to state in this place what is known personally to most if not all of your number, that in pursuance of the offer contained in the printed circular of this Company of the 20th of January last, a copy of which has heretofore been communicated by me to your Company nearly the entire stock of this Company was subscribed for by the stockholders of your Company in the rateable proportion mentioned in the circular referred to.

The minutes of the Utica and Schenectady show that the directors took the following action on this communication:

Whereupon after considering the matter it was unanimously resolved; That it be referred to the Executive Committee of this Company to make such agreement with the said Mohawk Valley Rail Road Company in regard to the construction of the proposed road and other matters referred to in the said letter and in the resolution of that Company therein set forth adopted on the 21st day of February last as they may deem proper subject however to the approval of this board.

The meeting was an informal one but at a regular meeting of the Board held April 5, 1853, it was

Resolved, that the proceedings of said meeting be confirmed and made the acts of this Board.

It may be confidently affirmed that this action was not in the least surprising in view of the fact that a majority of the directors present at each meeting were also directors of the Mohawk Valley Company. Neither can it be supposed the action was displeasing to the stockholders of the Utica and Schenectady since 533 of their total number of 687 were stockholders in the Mohawk Valley, there being but 586 stockholders in that company.

An agreement pursuant to the aforesaid action of the two boards was executed between the two companies, nor will any one be surprised that it was dated April 5, the day the full Board of the Utica and Schenectady approved the transaction. This agreement is a closely written document of thirteen articles and fourteen pages, drawn with skill and forethought for all probable contingencies and discloses in minute detail what must necessarily have been the plan which induced representatives of the Utica and Schenectady to take hold of the original Mohawk Valley Company, to organize the existing company of that name, to complete surveys of the route, to procure subscriptions by stockholders of the Utica and Schenectady to the capital stock of the second Mohawk Valley Company. It is too long and contains too many details of no present importance to warrant its insertion in full, but a summary of its principal points will substantiate sufficiently the statement just made.

The Utica and Schenectady is to procure and pay for all lands needed for the proposed road in the City of Schenectady and on the northerly side of the Mohawk river in the counties of Schenectady, Montgomery and Herkimer and on the southerly side of the river in Oneida county between its terminal at Genesee street in the City of Utica and the point where the proposed road diverges from its road about three miles easterly from said terminal. Title to all such lands to be taken in the name of the Mohawk Valley Company. It is also to appropriate to the use of the proposed road whatever is needed of its own lands, the proposed road being for the greater part in the territory named but a third track of the Utica and Schenectady located largely upon existing right of way.

The Utica and Schenectady will grade and in all respects construct a first class single track railroad with requisite accommodations over and upon said lands and its own lands where the proposed road is located on them.

The Mohawk Valley will construct a like first class single track road upon the remainder of the route described as beginning at the point of departure from the Utica and Schenectady near Sprakers; thence crossing the Mohawk river to the southerly side thereof; thence through Canajoharie and Fort Plain and recrossing the river to the northerly side a short distance westerly of Fort Plain; also the section of the proposed road which leaves the Utica and Schenectady near the village of Herkimer, crosses the river to the southerly side and continues on the southerly side through the villages of Mohawk, Ilion and Frankfort until it intersects the Utica and Schenectady about three miles east of the terminal of that road in the city of Utica.

If the capital stock of the Mohawk Valley Company ($1,575,000) is insufficient to construct these portions of the road, the Utica and Schenectady will supply the deficiency. If such capital stock is in excess of the amount needed for such construction such excess shall be paid to the Utica and Schenectady to apply on the construction of that part of the road it has agreed to perform. The entire road is to be completed on or before November 1, 1854, and all engines and rolling stock are to be furnished by the Utica and Schenectady.

When completed it is to be used and managed exclusively by the Utica and Schenectady during the corporate existence of the two companies and the Utica and Schenectady is to maintain it in good order and pay all taxes and charges of every kind.

For compensation to the Mohawk Valley, the Utica and Schenectady agrees to pay on all capital stock to the amount actually paid in from and after July 31, 1853, the same rate or percentage of dividends, and at the same time and place, as shall be paid to stockholders of the Utica and Schenectady with the exception that the Utica and Schenectady may distribute among its stockholders any surplus it may have July 31, 1853, without making any dividend to the Mohawk Valley.

Thus it is plain the proposed road was planned to be an integral part of the Utica and Schenectady with two loops on the southerly side of the Mohawk river reaching villages which had for years been clamoring for railroad service. It was to be paid for with either money of the Utica and Schenectady or by money of the stockholders of the Mohawk Valley who were substantially all of the stockholders of the Utica and Schenectady and such stockholders were to be compensated by dividends at the same rate, time and place as dividends to the stockholders of the Utica and Schenectady. Thus as near an actual merger of identity of the two corporations was made as was possible and yet they retain separate corporate existence.

In the consolidation meeting, held April 12, 1853, the same delegates represented both corporations; in the report of the sub-committee, they are bunched and in practical effect treated as one road. The Mohawk Valley was considered as it was an integral part of the Utica and Schenectady.

It is true that while the organization and development of the Mohawk Valley Company was going on in the winter of 1853, a bill was pending in the legislature which ultimately became the consolidation act in which the Mohawk Valley was named as one of the consolidating roads. It may be inquired why with this bill pending the organization of the Mohawk Valley was pushed forward in the manner described. It would seem to be a reasonable and satisfactory answer to such an inquiry that if the bill became a law no one could say with any certainty whatever, that an agreement of consolidation could be made with ten companies involved, having a total of 2,445 individual stock-holders, two-thirds of those of each company being required to assent. If the consolidation proved to be impracticable, the Utica and Schenectady would certainly desire to push forward its own project of improvement.

CHAPTER XIV

THE SYRACUSE AND UTICA DIRECT

A GLANCE at the map of New York will show that the Syracuse and Utica was not constructed on a direct line from Utica to Syracuse, but proceeded in a northwesterly direction to Rome and thence southwesterly to Canastota, in the neighborhood of which a direct line from Utica would intersect it. The direct route was some six or seven miles the shorter and the financial prosperity of the Syracuse and Utica evidently inspired the thought that a road on the direct line could be made equally profitable.

On September 22, 1852, the following item appeared in the Utica *Observer:*

Utica and Syracuse Straight Line Railroad.—

On Saturday the articles for this new road were drawn, and by Monday night about $350,000 had been taken and the ten per cent. paid in. The capital of the company is to be $1,000,000, and from present appearances, it will not take a week to have the whole amount taken up. The directors are among our best business men, and have the means to back up their undertakings. Among those who have already subscribed are the following: William Walcott, James S. Lynch, James Sayre, J. V. P. Gardner, Charles S. Wilson, Willard Crafts, Josiah Case, A. G. Dauby.

The length of the road is to be 46 miles, some six less than the present line. It will pass through New York Upper Mills, Clark's Mills, Verona, Chittenango, &c., thus securing as nearly as possible an air line.

Engineers are to be put upon the line next week and a survey made.

That this road will be soon completed, we do not doubt. The character of those engaged in it, and the importance of the enterprise, prove this. It has been evident for some years, that sooner or later there would be another road between Utica and Syracuse, and the vast increase of travel and business on the old one the past two years proved that the time was near at hand. Even if there was no increase, the business now done, divided between two roads, would give to each a handsome percentage of profits. By the time the line is completed, we believe the business to be done by each will be nearly, if not quite, equal to that on the present road.

On the same day there appeared in the same newspaper a notice of which the following is a copy:

Utica & Syracuse Straight Line R. R. Co.—We hereby appoint Monday, the 27th day of September, instant, at 11 o'clock A.M. of that day, for a meeting of the Directors of the "Utica & Syracuse Straight Line Rail Road Company," at the office of O. B. Matteson, in Utica, for the purpose of fully organizing the Association, and transacting such other business as the said Directors may think proper.—Sept. 20, 1852.

Delos DeWolf	Geo. Curtiss	Geo. C. Tallman
Samuel Beardsley	B. D. Hurlburt	Salmon Case
Hiram Denio	O. B. Matteson	E. M. Gilbert
John Mott	John T. Clark	Eneas P. Clark
	W. B. Welles	

The signers were some of the best men in Utica. Hiram Denio was appointed a judge of the Court of Appeals, June 23, 1853, and was twice thereafter elected to that position, being one of the ablest and most upright judges of that court. Beardsley and Matteson were strong men of their day and John T. Clark was an experienced engineer, who in 1853, was elected state engineer and in 1855, was made one of the Board of Railroad Commissioners.

The fortunes of this project need not be traced further than to say, it was duly incorporated September

28, 1852, with a capital stock of $1,000,000, of which $178,000 had been subscribed and 10 per cent thereof paid in in cash.   It was the active force which stirred the Syracuse and Utica to action, since on the 24th day of January, 1852, Articles of Association of "The Syracuse and Utica Direct Railroad Company" were signed and in a day or two later filed in the office of the Secretary of State, thus incorporating that Company. Its proposed railroad by the articles of incorporation was to "commence on the line of the Syracuse and Utica Railroad in the town of Lenox in the County of Madison and extend eastward through the village of Vernon to the city of Utica in the County of Oneida." Its length was to be 22 miles and the amount of capital stock was fixed at $600,000.

The full amount of the authorized stock was subscribed without delay and 10 per cent or $60,000 paid in in cash.   Surveys were commenced and prior to consolidation $10,206.04 were expended for that and other purposes.

That this was a Syracuse & Utica enterprise is decisively shown by certain facts which need no particular comment.   That road had no legal power to construct the proposed short line.   It was threatened with competition the whole length of its road.   The proposed short line would give it an equally favorable line with the proposed competitor.   Of the 13 directors of the Syracuse & Utica Direct, 9 were directors of the Syracuse & Utica.   Its president, C. Stebbins, was vice president of the Syracuse & Utica and John Wilkinson, the president of that company was one of the directors.   There were 374 subscribers to its stock, of whom 359 were stockholders in the Syracuse and Utica. All of the stockholders of the Syracuse and Utica except 66, took stock in the new company.

That the new company was the result of negotiations of some character with the proposed Utica and Syracuse Short Line may be reasonably inferred from the fact that John T. Clark, one of the promoters of that project, subscribed for fifteen hundred shares, just one-fourth of the entire capital stock and that when matters were finally adjusted, this subscription seems to have been in trust for the leading men in the Utica and Syracuse Straight Line, it appearing that John T. Clark really had 150 shares, Delos DeWolf 175, Samuel Beardsley 130, Hiram Denio 55, O. B. Matteson 515, W. B. Welles 143, and so on, all these persons having been directors of that road. There does not appear to be any reason to doubt that the Syracuse & Utica stockholders assumed three-fourths of the cost of the new road and the promoters of the competing road were taken into the enterprise, they assuming one-fourth the cost and abandoning their original project of a road from Utica to Syracuse.

Such then was the origin and exact status of this corporation, Syracuse and Utica Direct, at the time of the consolidation.

CHAPTER XV

FREIGHT TRANSPORTATION AND RATES

THE treatment extended to the early roads on the line from the Hudson river to Buffalo was not uniform with respect to the carrying of property. It will be recalled that down to the general railroad Act of 1850, all railroads were incorporated by act of the legislature and hence inconsistencies in powers and privileges were likely to occur as different legislatures entertained different notions of public policy or considered that local conditions warranted diversity of treatment. With respect to the transportation of property, a peculiar condition was created by the fact that the line as a whole paralleled and competed with the Erie Canal built and owned by the state and fully opened from the Hudson river to Lake Erie in 1825. Freight was not transported by the state upon the canal, but by boats or boat lines privately owned by individuals, associations or corporations, the state exacting tolls upon the property carried in order to reimburse itself for the money expended in construction. The advantages afforded by railroads over the canal for the transportation of persons and their ordinary baggage were so great as to preclude any limitation upon the right to transport persons. The speed of movement on the canal in the best packet boats was about four miles an hour and the public would naturally insist upon the more speedy conveyance without the burden of double or greatly increased fare. As to property the case was different; the difference in speed was not so great, time employed in transit was not so important and the sections of the state not supplied with railroads probably felt that they were entitled to relief from the burden imposed by canal construction. However that may be, the policy was established of either prohibiting the transportation of property at all seasons, or during the season of canal navigation and where permitted to any extent to exact the payment from the railroads of the amount of tolls which would have been exacted for the transportation of the same property upon the canal. The provisions in this behalf were not uniform as to the roads and accordingly a complete picture can be presented only by taking the roads in detail in the chronological order of incorporation. These tolls were of course added to the rates charged by the railroads and paid by the shippers, hence freight rates during the period tolls were charged appear abnormally high even for those days. Canal tolls on the railroads were finally abolished in 1851, effective December 1, of that year. We may reasonably conjecture that the immediate cause of this abolition was the completion of other roads from the seaboard to the west, notably that of the New York and Erie which was completed to Dunkirk on Lake Erie in 1851.

The roads will now be named in chronological order of incorporation with a concise statement of the provisions of the charter respecting the matter under consideration.

Mohawk and Hudson, April 17, 1826. Power to transport persons and property unrestricted. Rates and charges limited by the following: "Provided that at no time during the existence of this corporation the tolls and charges thus fixed, regulated and received for transportation, shall exceed the amount of tolls and duties together with the charges of freight to which property is subject as the cost of transportation on the Erie Canal, at or before the passing of this act."

Tonawanda, April 24, 1832.   No restriction as to carrying property or rates in charter.   Road extended from Rochester to Attica; canal from Rochester to Lockport, thence to Buffalo.   Railroad not competitive with canal for local freight; in fact a feeder to the canal until construction of connecting roads eastward. Made subject in 1844 to Chap. 335 of laws of that year hereinafter discussed.   Local freight tariff established in 1846 by Chap. 292 of laws of that year.

Utica and Schenectady, April 29, 1833.   Prohibited by charter from carrying property other than ordinary baggage of passengers.   Practically unchanged until Chap. 335 of laws of 1844.   Under that law permitted to take and transport all goods, chattels and other property that may be offered for transportation during the suspension of canal navigation in each year only. On all such property so transported shall pay the same tolls per mile as would have been paid on it had it been transported on the Erie Canal.

Auburn and Syracuse, May 1, 1834.   Power to carry both persons and property.   Shall pay to commissioners of canal fund the same tolls on all goods and other property transported except the ordinary baggage of passengers as may at the time of such transportation be required to be paid to this state on the same kind and description of goods and other property transported on the Erie Canal.   Subject to Chap. 335, laws of 1844.

Attica and Buffalo, May 3, 1836.   Power to convey persons and property.   Not required to pay tolls. Subject to Chap. 335, laws of 1844.

Syracuse and Utica, May 11, 1836.   Power to

convey persons and property. During such portions of the year as the Erie Canal shall be navigable, the corporation hereby created shall pay to the commissioners of the canal fund such tolls on all property transported, except the ordinary baggage of passengers as the canal board shall deem proper, not exceeding the rates of toll charged upon like property upon the said canal. Subject to Chap. 335, laws of 1844.

Auburn and Rochester, May 13, 1836. Power to convey persons and property. "But the corporation hereby created shall not take and transport merchandise or property in such a manner as to lessen the income on the Erie Canal during the time when the canal is navigable." No tolls required. Subject to Chap. 335, laws of 1844.

Schenectady and Troy, May 21, 1836. Power to convey persons and property. No restrictions. No tolls.

Thus four roads in their charters had no restrictions as to property and were not required to pay tolls. One road was wholly debarred from transporting property, except ordinary baggage. One road was permitted to carry property except it must not do so when the canal was navigable in such manner as to lessen the income of the Erie Canal. No tolls were required from it. One road could transport property at all times but was required to pay tolls during times the canal was navigable. One road could transport property but must pay tolls at all seasons of the year.

This was the confused and intolerable situation until after the completion of all lines between the Hudson river and Buffalo with its possibility of through traffic and such it remained for more than a year thereafter. With the prohibition on the Utica and Schenectady through freight traffic was not possible.

This situation received the attention of the legislature of 1844, and resulted in the passage on May 7, of Chap. 335 of the laws of that year which purported by its title to amend the act incorporating the Utica and Schenectady Company. By section 1, that company was authorized to transport "all goods, chattels and other property, during the suspension of canal navigation only." By section 3, it was required to "pay to the Commissioners of the canal fund the same tolls per mile on all the goods, chattels and other property so transported as would have been paid on them had they been transported on the Erie Canal." By section 5, the canal board was given power to prescribe the manner in which such tolls should be collected and to enforce the collection and payment of the same. By section 4, the Syracuse and Utica, the Auburn and Syracuse, the Auburn and Rochester, the Tonawanda and the Attica and Buffalo were required to make returns in the same manner and subject to the regulations provided in the third and fifth sections and to pay the same tolls as were provided in those sections. The section then provided as follows: "but the canal board shall make such rules and regulations regulating the transportation of freight on the same roads west of Utica, so as to continue to the said roads the privilege of transporting local freight without the payment of toll wherever they now enjoy that privilege and to enforce and ensure the collection of tolls on all such freight as shall be carried on the said roads by reason of the privileges in this act granted to the Utica and Schenectady Railroad."

Just where this left the roads west of Utica in view of their differing and peculiar restrictions there is no necessity for considering at this time. No change was made in the status of the Albany and Troy roads by this act. Obviously through traffic which could only be conducted in the winter when canal navigation was closed, which required motive power, cars and other facilities which would stand idle about seven months of the year, could not have been very attractive and must have required high rates as compared with those on which traffic was unrestricted, to say nothing of the tolls exacted which of course were added to the railroads' own charges.

This remained the situation until 1847, when the evils of such a situation became so apparent that the legislature by Chap. 270 of that year, passed May 12, authorized the Utica and Schenectady to take and transport without restriction as to time all goods, chattels and other property that might be offered for transportation. This act continued the requirement to pay tolls upon the Utica and Schenectady and all the roads west of Utica in the language used in the Act of 1844, but adding to that language above quoted, "But no freight passing from any one of said railroads to a connecting railroad to be transported thereon, shall be deemed local freight on either road." Thus freight from Batavia on the Tonawanda to Lancaster on the Attica and Buffalo was treated as through freight and paid tolls although by no possibility could it have been transported over the canal, whereas freight from Attica to Lancaster being carried on only one road was local and paid no tolls.

The annual report of the Syracuse and Utica for the year 1848, dated January 11, 1849, describes very clearly some of the results of the legislation under consideration. After enumerating the freight equipment owned by it, it continues:

This is quite equal to our proportion upon the line and as the most of them stand idle during the summer it is not anticipated there will be required any additional outlay for this service for the year. While alluding to the fact that these cars stand idle during the summer, it is proper to state that it has been found necessary to construct very extensive buildings to preserve them from exposure and decay while not in use. There are covered in these buildings more than 1800 feet of double track (or more than two-thirds of a mile of single track). And these are filled for *five* months in the year with cars that are out of employment. A good covered 8 wheel car for freight such as this company uses costs about $700.

The movement of freight after the act of 1844 took effect can best be seen from a statement issued by John Wilkinson, president of the Syracuse and Utica, April 18, 1848, from which is taken the following table showing the receipts of that road for freight in each month since 1844:

Months	1845	1846	1847	1848
January.....	$2,000.00	$8,299.02	$7,301.82	$7,951.61
February....	2,124.25	329.16	5,478.65	5,066.12
March......	1,500.00	—	9,190.01	11,942.26
April.......	926.32	4,000.00	6,914.12	—
May........	4,280.18	4,498.20	5,814.41	—
June........	69.35	52.63	6,070.09	—
July........	—	472.15	1,001.95	—
August......	—	—	1,002.45	—
September...	10.00	452.16	584.28	—
October.....	—	395.59	—	—
November...	—	313.06	1,253.66	—
December...	2,037.40	811.53	7,883.02	—
Total Freight Receipts	$12,947.50	$19,623.50	$52,494.46	—
Total Passenger Receipts	$182,484.78	$229,708.56	$285,941.61	—

There has been placed under the total freight receipts for each year the total passenger receipts for the same period in order to show the character of the business handled and the relatively insignificant figure cut by freight. The increase in freight receipts in 1847, must be attributed to the Act of 1847, removing time restriction on the Utica and Schenectady.

If this was the condition of a road but 53 miles in length we may easily conjecture what it was on the remaining 281 miles of the line as it then existed. This situation, however, continued to exist for three years more. On July 10, 1851, the legislature (Chap. 497) abolished payment of all canal tolls by the railroads from and after the first day of December, 1851. This act was not passed without a struggle in the legislature, nor did the struggle end with the passage of the act. From time to time propositions were brought forward to renew the tolls and these were favored in the messages of governors. In 1858, the governor said, "I recommend as an equivalent for establishing tolls on freight that railroad companies paying such tolls be allowed to make such equitable increase in passenger rates as the legislature may authorize." In 1860, another governor said, "I cannot doubt the wisdom or justice of reimposing for a few years a moderate rate per ton during the season of navigation upon all freight passing over railroads competing with canals." Others did doubt however.

In 1859, the State Senate submitted to Lyman Tremain, then Attorney General, three questions for his opinion—

First—Whether the act abolishing tolls on railroads passed July 10, 1851, was of a character requiring its passage by a majority of all the members elected to each house, when a three-fifths quorum was present.

Second—Whether said act appropriated public moneys or property in such a sense as to require for its constitutional validity the assent of two-thirds of the members elected to each branch of the legislature.

Third—Whether said act does not conflict with sections 1, 2, 3, and 6 of article 7th of the Constitution.

The Attorney General responded with a long and learned opinion in which he stated his conclusion to be "Upon the whole I am of the opinion that the act abolishing tolls upon the railroads, passed July 10, 1851, does not conflict either with section 9 of article 1, or with sections 1, 2, 3 and 6 of article 7 of the Constitution."

In the winter of 1860, a bitter contest on the subject of tolls was carried on in the legislature, the assembly passing a bill in which the senate would not concur and the conference committee appointed by the two houses also being unable to reach an agreement.

The next Attorney General in 1860, Charles G. Myers, advised that the act of 1851, was unconstitutional and in July of that year, he brought an action in the Supreme Court in the name of the people of the state against the New York Central Railroad Company to recover five millions of dollars tolls accruing upon freight carried by that road since its organization in 1853 up to July 1, 1860, upon the ground that the act of 1851 was unconstitutional and that the acts imposing tolls remained in force. The case went through all the courts to the Court of Appeals but none of them agreed with Attorney General Myers, and so the complaint was dismissed.

An account of the struggles on this toll question with a fairly complete view of the arguments pro and con would be one of the most interesting chapters in a history of the regulation of railroads. All that is proper here is to point out its effect upon the railroads we are considering.

In considering that effect statistics necessary for the study were not required by law until 1848, and the first reports to the state containing them are for the fiscal year ended September 30, 1850. The report for the fiscal years 1851 and 1852, and the ten months ending July 31, 1853, at which date the New York Central took over the roads for operation, are also available and from them may be gathered the ton miles of freight and the freight density each year. The following table is an assemblage of these facts for those roads reporting:

	1851		1852		1853—10 mos.	
	Ton Miles	Density per mile tons	Ton Miles	Density per mile tons	Ton Miles	Density per mile tons
Albany & Schenectady	1,564,986	92,058	2,757,026	162,178	3,500,062	205,886
Utica & Schenectady	5,579,150	71,528	14,579,422	186,916	16,316,762	209,189
Syrcause & Utica.......	3,734,507	70,462	6,493,350	103,069	8,177,466	154,292
Rochester & Syracuse.....	5,416,084	52,078	12,458,640	119,795	4,964,940	268,767
Buffalo & Rochester....	3,010,730	39,615	5,931,856	78,051	7,209,290	90,116

The more easily understood figures are, perhaps, those showing the density of the traffic, that is the average number of tons carried over one mile of road. While the Albany and Schenectady paid no tolls by reason of its location, the greater part of its traffic was through and not local and hence it finds a proper place in the table. Also it should be kept in mind that in the figures for 1852, the year ending with September 30, there are included two months, October and November, 1851, in which tolls were paid. We may now observe the increase in density on the Utica and Schenectady from 71,528 in 1851, to 186,916 in 1852. Like com-

parison can be made on any other road. It is easy to
see what a tremendous jump in freight traffic followed

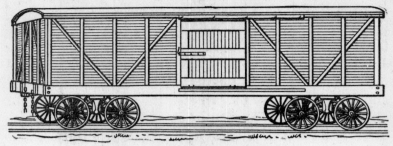

FREIGHT CARS IN USE ABOUT 1844.

the abolition of canal tolls and that such abolition was
the chief cause there is no reason to doubt.

FREIGHT RATES

But very little information is obtainable as to either
specific or average freight rates upon any of the roads
prior to 1853. Some rates charged by the Utica and
Schenectady have been given in the account of that
road. The most important document which has survived is a hand bill tariff sheet issued March 1, 1850, by
the Albany and Schenectady, which bears the caption
"Albany & Buffalo Railroad" and is denominated
"Freight Tariff for the Spring of 1850 for 100 Pounds
including canal tolls from Albany, Schenectady and the
way stations to Buffalo. The Canal Tolls average
one-fourth of the rates."

On this sheet freight is divided into two classes,
first and second. Seventy-eight different classes of
articles are rated as first class with the important
addition, "and all others not enumerated are First
Class." Eighty-seven articles are specified as second
class and in addition there are shown certain "Special
Rates." In very small type near the bottom of the
sheet appears the following:

The several Railroad Companies between the Hudson River and Lake Erie have united together to publish this Tariff of Prices in order to give information to the public, but the control of each Company over property, and responsibility for it, ceases on delivery of the property to the next company at either end of the road.

It is not always easy to determine upon what rule or principle the classification is made. Thus taking common articles of food, dried apples, cocoa, chocolate, eggs at owner's risk of breakage and weather, fruit, figs, fresh fish, ginger, honey, lemons, oranges, oysters, pepper, poultry, dried peaches, pine apples, sweet potatoes, rice, raisins, foreign salt, spices, teas, are rated as first class, while bread, bacon, butter, cheese, coffee, dried fish, lard, meal, molasses, oysters and clams in shell, saleratus, going east, starch, going east, sugar, salt in bags are in the second class. It appears that saleratus and starch going west are in the first class. Ordinary potatoes are first class, while sugar and coffee are second. Hardware is first class; stoves, second; foreign salt is first class; domestic is second; dried apples, first class; dried fish, second; and so on.

The rates are given from Albany to each station on the road and are as follows to the principal points for each class:

| | First | Second | Per Ton | |
			First	Second
	cts.	cts.	$	$
Utica................	33	24	6.60	4.80
Syracuse.............	52	37	10.40	7.40
Auburn..............	61	44	12.20	9.80
Canandaigua..........	78	56	15.60	11.20
Rochester............	88	63	17.60	12.60
Batavia..............	100	66	20.00	13.20
Buffalo..............	100	66	20.00	13.20

Some articles, flour, wheat, apples, potatoes, were not charged by weight but by the barrel. The rate per barrel from Albany to Buffalo was $1. and to all stations Rome and west the rate per barrel was the same as the first class rate per 100 pounds. Fresh beef and pork paid per 100 pounds to Batavia or Buffalo 73 cents or $14.60 per ton. Furniture, feathers, teazels and all light and bulky articles under the heading, special rates, paid ½ cent per mile for every 100 pounds, or 10 cents a ton mile. Piano fortes paid, each, 4 cents per mile, irrespective of weight. Horses in lots of 6 or more, 4 cents per mile each; in smaller lots 6 cents per mile each. Live cattle, not less than one car load and entirely at owner's risk of damage or loss, were charged 2 mills per mile per 100 pounds or 4 cents per ton mile.

The companies refused to take or carry gunpowder, camphene, friction-matches and like combustible articles on any terms; nor would they carry bank bills, drafts, notes, deeds or other writings or be responsible for their loss.

For handling freight at Albany across the Hudson river to or from the railroad station at East Albany a charge of 25 cents per ton was made.

As elsewhere noted as soon as the payment of canal tolls was abolished December 1, 1851, freight rates were reduced accordingly. According to this tariff sheet the railroad rates were about 75 per cent of the rates above shown. It is to be noted that coal does not appear in this tariff.

Legislative Regulation of Passenger Fares

As has been pointed out, the legislature conferred upon these early roads the power of fixing passenger fares up to a maximum amount per mile, such amount not being uniform for all the roads. This was done in ignorance of the cost to the company either of the actual cost of transportation, or of maintenance of the property, or of the depreciation and even of the capital required to construct the road. The companies accepted the limitation in equal ignorance of all these details. The proper theory of rate making was in as great confusion then as it is to-day after nearly one hundred years of experience. As soon as the annual reports of a company showed that it was able to pay fair dividends, its permanent prosperity was assumed by some portion of the public and demands were made upon the legislature to reduce the maximum limitation to a smaller rate per mile. Such demands were supported in some cases, at least, if not in all by the argument that a lesser rate would induce more travel and hence, without any substantial increase in operating expense, the gross operating receipts would not be diminished and the company's net would not be impaired.

The view that the increased travel would protect the companies against loss was termed by them mere theory and they countered against it by the assertion that they had tried the experiment and that travel did not increase measurably. They did not, however, content themselves with this reply alone, but advanced other considerations which in the main can best be stated in their own language.

Efforts to reduce fares were made in 1843 and 1845, both of which were met by vigorous remonstrances and failed. Another attempt was made in 1846, and was met by the Syracuse and Utica with a pamphlet of thirteen pages which covers thoroughly the general position of the railroads. It is worth while to give some attention to the earliest skirmishes of a battle which has continued with but few truces down to the

present time. It is to be regretted that the arguments
of those favoring the measure have not been preserved.
We may very likely assume them to have been based
upon the theory above stated and the further contention
that the profits of the companies were unreasonably
large. Those certainly are the positions which the
remonstrances attack.

The first answer of the railroads was that in issuing
the charters and authorizing the companies to charge
any fare their discretion might dictate not exceeding a
certain sum, the legislature invited citizens of the state
to invest capital in a new and hazardous, but greatly
needed enterprise and thereby placed the state in a
position which good faith demanded should not be
changed. That in short to invite the public to invest
on certain clearly defined terms estopped the state
from changing those terms to the disadvantage of the
investors after an unreclaimable investment, had been
made. This contention was sustained in a report of
the railroad committee of the Assembly of 1845, in the
following language:

> This great state occupies too lofty a position and entertains
> too just a sense of her imperial character, to repudiate any of
> the obligations fairly inferable from legislative enactments in
> which her citizens and citizens of other states have placed im-
> plicit and unwavering confidence.

Citing the statute, the Syracuse and Utica by its
President John Wilkinson, said in its remonstrance:

> The provision above cited is as plain a legislative promise as
> words can make. It means, we insist, precisely what it says
> that this company may charge four cents per mile as long as it is
> for its interest or until the State shall take the road under a subse-
> quent provision. The men who subscribed to the stock, who

paid their money and who made the road, believed that they did so, subject to but one contingency, and that is contained in the 17th section of the Attica and Buffalo charter in which the State reserved the right to take the railroad at any time after ten and within fifteen years from the commencement of its operation on paying the proprietors the cost of the same with ten per cent. interest, deducting the dividends received. The proprietors have the solemn faith of the state held out to them and they are sure it will not be violated when they present it.

The right to alter, modify or repeal does not allow the Legislature to destroy the guaranty upon which the investment was made. It may be exercised when there is fraud or abuse of privilege by the company but can not be exercised in an arbitrary manner without cause. If the power is possessed by the Legislature to reduce our fare where is it to stop? We think we have learned that it can not be reduced without depriving us of profit and that practically destroys the value of the property: though brokers might still speculate in the stock as they do now in unproductive railroads. If the fare can be reduced to a nominal sum, that of course, it will be claimed, is done for the interest of the public. Thus the people or the public or the state will in fact take it without paying us for it, according to the section above cited. The railroad will not be annihilated but it must be used without profit: and thus in place of a valuable property acquired under a reliance upon the laws of a just people would become a burthen to the proprietors.

And so the argument runs on in a lively and interesting manner for pages. We are not concerned with the validity or force of these contentions, although it may be observed the remonstrance wholly fails to discuss the effect upon this argument of the power reserved in the charter to the legislature to amend or repeal it at any time, but only in presenting a complete and faithful picture of the problems these early companies had to face and how they faced them. The remonstrance was not, as I have already said, confined to the presentation of this one point. Any claim that the fare was excessive was met in the following manner:

We have been nearly seven years engaged in the transportation of passengers and in that time by the most careful examination of the business and a comparison of one year with another have sought to find a point at which the interests of the company as well as of the passengers meet. We have no motive to charge any fare but that which will produce to the company a reasonable remuneration upon its capital. We should most cheerfully charge a low rate if we were not conscious it would not pay. It is to the interest of the company, as well as entirely conformable to the feelings and inclinations of the directors individually, to charge the lowest rate that will pay. In pursuance of this we have heretofore charged low fares but the number of passengers was not materially increased. We have found that there were more passengers in 1839 and in 1841, than there have been since. There is a strong competition with us upon the canal: and to all those who do not value their time that is a favorite mode of traveling. There are several routes through the southern and middle states that compete with us for the western travel. The Erie road soon to be in operation is still further to divide our business. All these matters are very carefully considered by us. We have endeavored to ascertain what the whole amount of travel is and how far our numbers can be increased by any reduction. The whole through and way travel is equal to about ninety thousand passengers over our road in the year. A reduction of 75 cents would be a diminution of an aggregate of near $70,000. There are about twenty thousand through passengers upon the packet boats and if we could get all these by the reduction, their fare would be less than thirty thousand dollars. Thus we should lose 70 and gain 30. This is four per cent upon our capital; and of course would sink its value and place a renewal of the road beyond hope. But it would be as impossible to get a moiety of this twenty thousand passengers as it has been heretofore.

The passenger fare of this company has never been above about three and three-quarters cents per mile and we maintain that when all circumstances are considered that is a reasonable fare. It has never produced extraordinary profits. . . . This company some years back fixed the dividends at eight per cent annually. They have neither the expectation they can increase the amount or the disposition to attempt it, because they know how much is required to keep up this work.

Nor did they stop with the considerations but briefly sketched in these excerpts. They refer very pointedly to the authority given them in 1845 to incur indebtedness to renew the track with iron rails.

The last session of the Legislature not only rejected all these propositions to reduce our fare, as has been stated, but it encouraged us to go on and prepare for a reconstruction of our road and authorized us to borrow money for that purpose. Under the faith of this last law, we have gone on preparing for a new track and have expended a large sum for that purpose. We suppose that all agree that these roads should be reconstructed as soon and as thoroughly as possible. . . . The imperfect and unfinished nature of this line of railroad is obvious and this consideration ought to influence our fellow citizens to exertion in our aid rather than in ruinous attacks upon our business and our credit. We consider that nothing is now more important than the thorough reconstruction of the railroad from Buffalo to Schenectady. The cost of iron to lay that part of it from Syracuse to Utica at the present prices will be at least $400,000 and the other material necessary and the labor would make the whole cost of this section not less than half a million of dollars. Where is this amount to be derived? What is the inducement for incurring this great expense?

It is obvious from this last language that the company had begun to reflect seriously upon that great problem of railroad operation which had begun then and has continued to this day involved in the constant necessity for renewing and replacing the physical property. It first presented itself in large form in removing the wooden track and replacing it with an iron track; it has continued without intermission to our own day in track, locomotives, cars, bridges, buildings and is now struggled with as fiercely as ever under the term depreciation. And now the railroads are threatened with as great a loss in the treatment extended it by public authority as was feared by the Syracuse and Utica eighty years ago.

The remonstrance of the Auburn and Syracuse against the same bill is brief but clear and presents the condition of that road as follows, after explaining that its capital stock of $400,000 had all been paid in and that for the purpose of considering an interest account, the payments might be averaged as paid January 1, 1837.

The first dividend that was made by the company was on the 1st day of August, 1841, since which time dividends of 4 per cent have been made by the company every six months making in the whole 10 dividends of 4 per cent up to and including the 2nd inst. (Feby., 1846). A statement of an interest account from the 1st January, 1837, to the 1st day of August, 1841, and an allowance of the excess over seven per cent divided since that time, will show the original stockholders still in arrear, nearly 25 per cent upon their original investment.

Here is the distinct claim that stockholders are entitled to be paid interest upon the money paid in from the time of payment until dividends are paid. This claim is recognized in part by present day commissions by allowing such interest during the construction period only, assuming that the road will at once after being put in operation earn an adequate return upon the investment, without any evidence as to whether it would or could. The construction period allowed on such a road as the Auburn and Syracuse is usually about a year or a year and a half and not four and a half years as claimed in the remonstrance for the interest period. This is one of the first instances where we have found this question raised, which is yet a matter of contention eighty years later.

The proper method of fixing rates of fare is set forth by the company as follows:

Practical railroad men have found that the true rate of fare is to be arrived at by experience and observation, by which the greatest remunerating profit will arise. An increase above that price diminishes the income and a descent below it by so much percentage as the price descends, involves an increase of cars and engines and a diminution of profits. This experience is to be arrived at on this line of railroad by considering the question in connection with the competition of the Erie Canal and other routes during seven months of the year. It is believed that neither this entire line or road, nor any part of it, can secure even the half of the entire travel passing between Albany and Buffalo except at a dead loss.

The bill failed to become a law.

These two remonstrances concur in the statement that even as late as 1846, the Erie Canal still remained a serious competitor for the passenger traffic; that the cheaper rate of fare which could be afforded on it was not overridden by the greater speed of the railroads. As to the relative comfort afforded by the two, we have no means of determining. Probably opinions differed on that interesting point. Certain it is that the present generation would find no comfort in either.

The remonstrance against the bill of 1845 was a long document signed by all the roads except the Attica and Buffalo. We may gather from its contents an accurate notion of the claims put forward by those petitioning for the bill. Some of the relief asked for was a reduction of fare, the appointment of a commissioner to operate the roads, to compel the roads to run their trains at night at all seasons.

There seems to have been a feeling against the companies because they were corporations and had a monopoly character; also, the remonstrance says, "It is frequently objected that there are too many companies to manage the business well: that there are divided counsels and clashing interests." That this last objection was well taken, the companies themselves were forced to recognize a few years later and even then they cautiously refrained from a complete denial in reply to it, saying, "While it is quite possible there may be some weight in these objections, yet we apprehend there is another view of the question." They then call attention to the fact that the directors are distributed along the line of the road, are generally thirteen for each company, are engaged in business and interested in the prosperity of their several localities and will in the nature of things be watchful of the interests and demands of the public; that a convention of their representatives would act like any representative legislature and embody all the information necessary to the most judicious management. Obviously they had not then discovered as they did later that one recalcitrant road possessed as much or more power than all the others combined.

They point out with reference to a single board, "Such a single board would be gradually concentrated in the large cities (perhaps in a single one) and be practically strangers to the multiplied interest of the various sections through which the line extends. We think that the public opinion is now much quicker heard and better fulfilled and obeyed than it would be were there but one board of directors and but one individual controlling." There they place a finger exactly upon what later became the source of complaint and discontent. It has been very difficult for mankind to learn that no possible system of organization of human affairs can possess all the attributes of perfection. Organizations do not act; they are only the methods by which men act and the character of the act depends upon the character of the men acting rather than on the machinery by which they act.

To the charge of being corporations the answer is

made that only through a corporation can a railroad be carried on through a long term of years whether that corporation be the state or an association of individuals. Eighty years later the enormous multiplication of corporations in all classes and branches of business activity has disposed of this objection as public regulation has of the charge of monopoly.

The next criticism treated is that "Many have the mistaken idea that an engine might be started at Buffalo and run through to this city (Albany) continuously and that from this arrangement great benefits would follow." The answer made is, "Experiment has shown that about 100 miles of daily service is a fair use of an engine and of men; and such use is more discreetly and properly derived if it is not continuous. Both the engine and the men can more profitably perform the service if there can be a rest at the end of 50 or 80 miles to examine the engine, to allow it to cool for such purpose and thus have the requisite time for repair and to guard against accident." We must remember they were speaking of the engines of eighty years ago and of the duties then required of a train crew and could not foresee present operating conditions. The criticism of operations of which the critic has no personal knowledge or experience, however, obtains to-day with as great energy and persistence as in former days.

Another point dwelt upon by the remonstrants was the imminent necessity of additional capital for the reconstruction of the track. Their language is emphatic.

The want of capital in our State induced the necessity of a perishable form of structure upon this line of railway. We have for the whole distance west of Schenectady a wood track. The want of strength in this structure, the constantly decaying nature of its material, the manifest advantages of the iron tracks in New England, and the strong impulse that is accumulating in the public mind to compel us to a higher speed, show that we must calculate also upon an iron track on this line; and that it must be laid down as quick as practicable. We believe that the true interests of the public are in this direction and seek this end, rather than to embarrass and delay it by the various propositions made by the petitioners. This line of railway is unfinished and not equal to the public exigency and until such a structure should be laid and in use upon it as will admit of greater speed, less hazard and less expense. A wood structure will endure but about six years when the process of renewal must commence. We can not suspend the use of the railway until the new track shall be laid, hence when decay commences it is from that moment forward, as long as the wood structure is maintained, a constant breaking up and renewal of some part of the track. This business is to go on while the road is in use for travel and thus a perpetual succession of interruptions will occur. Under this conviction we believe that we ought to arrange for a permanent structure at as early a period as practicable; that in so doing we shall best consult the public interests and those of the stockholders and thus soonest be able to test the question at how low rates persons and property can be transported upon the railway.

The truthfulness and wisdom of these remarks can not be gainsaid. So far as has been discovered there had been no strong public movement to force the needed improvement. This plain statement of its imperative necessity made in March, 1845, shows that the companies themselves were not backward in realizing what they ought to do and were not wholly forced by later legislative action into undertaking the work. Indeed the two strongest companies, the Utica and Schenectady and the Syracuse and Utica, and at the session of the legislature to which the remonstrance was addressed, procured legislation, as is elsewhere shown, to enable them to finance the work they so strongly urged.

Thus was presented for the first time in the state of New York, at least, what has ever since been an acute feature of the railroad problem, the imperative necessity for expensive improvements in order to handle business with the dispatch and safety justly demanded by the public coupled with an insistent demand that the rates of service should be reduced contemporaneously therewith. In times of financial distress or dull business tendency to insist upon both is especially manifest. Even experienced legislators have been known to urge the wisdom of abandoning improvements in order to cheapen transportation, recognizing the impracticability of meeting both demands at the same time. Whether such a policy as this can be justified is as much a matter of debate as it was in 1845, although to many it may seem the height of foolishness even to consider such a question. We may on the basis of long experience agree with the remonstrants that proper and adequate facilities efficiently served are first in importance and that public policy requires the very best service obtainable in the existing state of railroad development.

But the remonstrants did not stop with the statements already quoted. Evidently they felt that the very existence of their roads was at stake for their language is susceptible of no other interpretation. They continue:

Upon those parts of the line where the companies were engaged in the transportation of heavy materials to renew or improve the track, the structure so yields under the use as to require a double force of men and increased material to keep up the road fit for use. The roads by reason of their wood structure are entirely incompetent to sustain the business (if it were capable of increase) which at reduced rates of fare, would be necessary to remunerate the stockholders. To relay this line with a permanent rail would at the present cost of iron require about three millions of dollars. From the facts that we have stated it will be perceived that a large amount of capital is required for this object. Where is it to come from? Who is to advance it? What is the guaranty that it will not be rendered valueless? We believe that the petitioners for a reduction of our fare have not well considered the proposition and are not well advised of the consequences.

We are aware that many are of the opinion that it would not affect our business unfavorably if the fare was reduced to three cents per mile. Upon this subject we have to say that we have learned to the contrary. That our population is not sufficiently dense to justify a low fare. . . . The several companies have heretofore reduced their fares to about three cents per mile and for a while to less. It was found that there was no increase of passengers but that the receipts of the companies were so reduced as to make it impracticable for them to go on at such low rates. The same experience was had between this city (Albany) and Boston.

In the course of their argument upon this point, they submit a table which is well worth reproducing. They state it to have been compiled from legislative reports of several companies for the year 1844.

Name of Road	Length in Miles	Rec'd Per Mile From Freight	Rec'd Per Mile From Passengers	Gross Receipts Per Mile
		$	$	$
Utica and Schenectady	78	120	3,927	4,047
Syracuse and Utica....	53	65	3,427	3,492
Auburn and Syracuse..	26	423	3,098	3,521
Auburn and Rochester.	78	100	2,760	2,860
Tonawanda..........	43	366	2,154	2,520
Attica and Buffalo.....	31	180	2,075	2,255

The interest of this table lies in the relative receipts per mile for freight and passenger business, the variations in receipts per mile on the different roads, and the gross receipts per mile from all business.

The objection to the failure to run night trains during the winter is treated as follows:

It has been objected that we stop over night in the winter, that we thus delay passengers and the mails. This again we feel assured is matter with which the petitioners are not fully acquainted and have not considered in all respects. So far as regards the mails the arrangement is made with the full approbation of the postmaster general. He understands the severity of our winters and he has said to us that it was better for the public to fix such an arrangement in winter as we could most profitably perform rather than to undertake to do that in which we might fail. We have considered this to be in all respects the most proper course: and we submit that the manner in which the line is operated in winter through snow and storm has been such as to entitle it to commendation rather than opprobrium. The travel is very limited in winter; so much so that a single car daily each day upon a part of the line is sufficient. There is not travel enough for more than one line. The route is so long that it cannot be run through continuously in the day time. We consider that it is at all times more hazardous to run in the night than in the day time. In the night the engineer can not as well detect any failure in his machine as in the day time. Generally in winter it requires two or more engines to overcome the snow. These can not be worked so well in unison in the night as in the day time. In winter by reason of the cold the liability of the engine, of the axles and wheels to break is much greater than in the summer. All these considerations make it very certain, we believe, that our course in not running in the night in the winter best consults the safety and comfort of passengers. We think that the great majority of passengers approve of it—and should it be found that a limited number residing a few miles beyond the point where the train stops do feel inconvenience and would prefer to go on, they should reflect that an equal number may be put to the same, or indeed, more difficulty being compelled to get up and travel in the night because such persons desire to get home before morning. We should very often run the hazard of being stopped in the night by the snow and it may well be questioned whether it would not be such an act of indiscretion to attempt to run all night in the winter as to subject us to serious liabilities. As soon as the conditions of the tracks will justify us in running in the night, we uniformly commence in the spring.

Nothing reveals to us so vividly as the attacks upon the roads and the answers thereto, the actual conditions of operating and the real state of transportation in the early days. By liberal quotations from their own language we are sure of getting the point of view of the transportation men and if we could get the contentions of the other side we could make up a pretty accurate picture of what was done and what was left undone. At the present time a contention that trains should not be run at night would be received with derision by railroad men but when we take into consideration the enormous differences in track, in locomotive engine power, in safety applicances between the present day and 1845, we certainly are called upon to reflect whether there may not have been much truth and sense in the companies' contention on this point.

The quotations given from the remonstrance show that some of the roads at least had not charged a uniform rate of fare per mile for first class passengers. They had at times made reductions in the hope of either satisfying the public or of increasing their revenue. The fare for emigrant or second class passengers was notoriously low, not much more at times than one-half the first class rate. It has been found impossible to obtain data showing these changes or the effect they produced on travel.

The statutory maximum per mile for each road has already been given in the chapters relating to them respectively, but is here repeated for reasons of convenience.

Mohawk and Hudson, no restriction; Schenectady and Troy, 6 cents; Utica and Schenectady, Syracuse and Utica, Auburn and Syracuse and Lockport and Niagara Falls, 4 cents. On the Auburn and Rochester it was first fixed at 3 cents but this hindering the construction of the road it was the next year made 4 cents. On the Tonawanda there was no restriction until 1844, when it was made 4 cents. Attica and Buffalo, 3 cents.

Assembly document No. 69, dated February 29, 1848, gives the rates in use November, 1847, as follows:

Railroad	Length in Miles	Through Fare	Cents Per Mile
		$	
Albany and Schenectady....	17	0.50	2.94
Troy and Schenectady......	20½	0.50	2.43
Utica and Schenectady.....	78	3.00	3.84
Utica and Syracuse........	53	2.00	3.77
Auburn and Syracuse.......	26	1.00	3.84
Auburn and Rochester.....	77	3.00	3.89
Tonawanda...............	44	1.56	3.54
Attica and Buffalo........	31½	0.94	2.98
Lockport and Niagara Falls.	24	0.75	3.12

At this time the through fare from Albany to Buffalo was $12.

The local rates were probably the same per mile, or nearly so, as the through rates. The Schenectady and Troy, although authorized to charge 6 cents per mile had the lowest mile rate which was brought about by its almost frantic efforts to attract business.

RECONSTRUCTION OF TRACK WITH HEAVY IRON RAILS

A short period of use demonstrated the inadequacy of a track composed of a flat iron bar of small dimensions fastened upon the top of longitudinal wooden

stringers which was used upon all the roads constructed
prior to 1842.   In that year the Schenectady and Troy
used a heavy iron rail weighing 56 pounds to the yard.
The adjective heavy at the present time seems ludicrous
as applied to a 56 pound rail, but it was universally used
at that time, the comparison being with the light strap
or flat bar rail and is still appropriate in treating of track
in the forties of the last century.   A descriptive term
then in use which has since disappeared is *H* rail.   The
paucity of reliable records makes it impossible to trace
the exact course of substitution of heavy iron rail on the
roads under consideration.   The slowness of the process
was undoubtedly due, principally, to the, for those
days, enormous expense involved requiring fresh capital and also to the difficulties attendant upon com-
pletely making over the track under traffic.

The first that can be found of record is that September 25, 1844, only eight years after the opening of the
road the Board of Directors of the Utica and Schenectady requested their superintendent, William C.
Young, to report to it an estimate of the probable cost
of laying a heavy rail on the road in place of the present
rail with such other information on the subject as may
be in his power.   The superintendent made report
November 16.   What his estimate of cost was can
not be learned, but we can judge very well from the
resolution which the Directors adopted at once directing application to the legislature for authority to
increase the capital of the company, not exceeding
five hundred thousand dollars, and for authority to
borrow money for the purpose of laying down a heavy
iron rail.   This action resulted in Chapter 342 of the
laws of 1845, by which the company was authorized
to borrow not exceeding five hundred thousand dollars
on its bonds, "for the purpose of purchasing and laying

down on the track of their road, heavy iron rail of such description as the said directors may deem most advantageous." A most significant paragraph is as follows: "And the moneys so expended shall be deemed a part of the amount expended in the construction of said road and of permanent fixtures for the use thereof," thus establishing by law that the new track was construction and not maintenance. The Board was informed of the passage of this act at its meeting held June 2, but no action was taken thereon until December 17, when the executive committee was authorized to contract for heavy iron rail weighing not less than 60 pounds per yard "as soon as in their judgment it shall be expedient to do so."

The executive committee did not for some reason deem it expedient to move with undue celerity, and the first contract for rails was made with Peter Cooper, December 16, 1846, and on December 17, the Board approved an agreement with the New Jersey Iron Company for 4000 tons of rails at $71.75 per gross ton. The same day the president was authorized to issue bonds of the company to an amount not exceeding $500,000 and to execute a mortgage on the company's property to secure the same. These dates establish the fact that laying heavy iron rail on this road did not begin until 1847. The report of the company for 1849, says, "The tracks were laid in 1847, 1848 and 1849, with heavy iron rail, weighing 65 pounds per lineal yard, except about 13 miles of heavy flat rail weighing about 45 pounds per lineal yard laid previously. The heavy flat rail, although in many respects a good and substantial one, will probably be replaced during the present year, 1850, by the heavy rail." It reported the cost of "iron (heavy rail) for new track" as $825,646.27 and cost of "superstructure for new track," $339,296.71, a total of $1,164,942.98, which varies somewhat from the original estimate of "not exceeding $500,000."

The Syracuse and Utica seems to have taken up the subject contemporaneously with the Utica and Schenectady for May 14, 1845, the same day Chapter 342 was passed, Chapter 343 was passed by the legislature authorizing that road to borrow $250,000 on its bonds "for the purpose of relaying the railway with a substantial iron rail." This act contained the following: "The amount expended in laying such new track or tracks shall be deemed as expended in the construction of the railroad." In its report for 1848, dated January 11, 1849, may be found a very interesting account of the track reconstruction which is well worth reproducing in full.

This new track was commenced in 1846, and about two miles of it was laid that year. The grading for such track had been commenced and executed to some extent in the year 1845.

When this new track was commenced, it was determined to prosecute the work in reference to an entire double track of iron, to be laid down as soon as the demands of business should require it.

In the laying of the first track, therefore, a considerable amount has been expended, in the substitution of masonry for wood in the abutments, and piers of bridges; in culverts, in covered drains, and in grading and in opening drains on both sides of the road. The new track is laid mostly upon a gravel bed, on cross ties, or sleepers, without any other wood in the structure.

Several bridges have been rebuilt, with a double track over them. The Erie Canal is crossed twice with bridges, both of which are new, one having been built in 1847 and the other the last year. They are each covered, of approved kind, and well built.

The Mohawk river is also twice crossed with bridges, both of which have been rebuilt within the last two years.

Considerable sums of money have been expended in rebuilding water stations permanently, and in obtaining supplies of good soft water. Originally the importance of this was not understood.

There will be required a large additional expenditure in like rebuilding of other stations, and in obtaining further supplies of water.

At several of the stations new freight houses will be required the next year.

When the reconstruction of the road was entered upon, the great importance of improving the grades was apparent, and it was resolved to improve them wherever it could be done within the reasonable means possessed by the company.

As this road was originally located upon a low tract of land, in order to obtain the most level and direct line, a considerable part of which is swampy, it will require a large annual outlay in gravelling across these low lands, in order to make a firm road bed.

Our experience has shown that the nearer it is possible to come to the level, in the grade line of the road, in that proportion is the business upon it carried on with economy and certainty. A large amount of money has therefore been expended to reduce the grades wherever it was practicable to do so.

About twenty-two miles of new track was laid before the year 1848. During that year about thirty-one miles of single track has been relaid, besides a considerable extent of branches and the commencement of the double track in three places. In all about four miles of the second or double track has been laid during the past season, so that there has been equal to 35 miles of single track laid, exclusive of branches and turnouts, during the year.

The relaying of the track at the same time that the regular passenger business of the line was kept up, and which required six trains daily over the road, has required the steady employment of five engines, with working trains, in the grading and gravelling of the road and in the moving of materials.

The number of men employed daily upon this work during the season of laying the track, has generally not been less than 500, and a portion of the time much above that number.

The iron first laid upon this road was the flat bar of $2\frac{1}{2}$ inches wide by $\frac{3}{4}$ of an inch thick. It has been used about nine years. As fast as the new rail was brought into use, the flat bar was taken up and sold. It was found that the loss by wear upon this rail was about 300 tons out of 2,000.

Safety also demands a double track as soon as the business of any road will justify it. With a double track from Syracuse to the Hudson river, the trains may be divided, thereby lessening their great weight and increasing the accommodation to the public.

It will require about 5,000 tons of iron additional to lay this track. This iron is all contracted for in England, and over 1,000 tons of it has arrived in New York. The contract price on delivery, free of all charge, is equal to about $48, per ton. The weight of this bar is nearly 70 pounds to the yard.

The iron for the first track was all made in this country. . . . The cost of the 5,000 tons contracted in England and now arriving, is more than $100,000 less than that of the same quantity made in this country. The iron last purchased has been subjected to such tests as to give confidence in its quality.

It is intended to proceed in laying down this track as soon as the weather will permit, in the ensuing spring, and it is hoped that the whole may be laid during the year.

In another part of the report is shown $302,313.76 "for construction of new track" and $46,000 for "construction of second track." As elsewhere shown this road commenced operation July 3, 1839, hence its original track lasted only about nine years before it became necessary to discard it.

These two roads seem to be the only ones in the line which on their own initiative started the work of reconstructing the track. Chapter 272 of the laws of 1847, passed May 12th, was a general law providing that "Any railroad company whose track is now laid in whole or in part with the flat bar rail on which steam power is used in propelling cars, are hereby authorized to issue their capital stock or to borrow on the security of said road, its appurtenances and franchises, as the directors of the company may determine, subject, however, to all previous incumbrances to the state or individuals, an amount sufficient to enable such company to substitute upon their track or tracks the heavy iron rail, every lineal yard of which shall weigh at least fifty-six pounds, for the flat iron rail now in use." Another provision was to the effect that no increase of capital or indebtedness should exceed in the aggregate ten thousand dollars per mile for the entire length of the road.

All the foregoing was permissive and not mandatory, but the second section clamped down the screws in a curious but effective manner on the roads of the central line. "Any railroad company hereinafter mentioned" it said, on whose road steam power is employed in propelling cars having the flat bar rail in use which should not commence to relay the same by or before January 1, 1848, with the heavy iron rail, should not be allowed to divide more than three per cent per annum on their capital stock paid in, for the year 1847, and if one track be not completed within two years from January 1, 1847, they should not be allowed to divide more than one per cent. per annum for the year 1848, nor annually thereafter until they should have relaid at least one track of the entire length of their railroad with heavy iron rail. "And the neglect or refusal on the part of any such railroad company so to substitute the heavy iron rail for the flat bar rail on their railroad track or tracks for the term of three years from and after the passage of this act shall be deemed to work a forfeiture of their Charter." And then the act named specifically the eight roads then constituting the line from the Hudson river to Buffalo.

This act further provided that no road should thereafter construct its track except with iron of at least fifty-six pounds weight to every lineal yard and contains other provisions not pertinent to the rail question. From the annual reports of the several companies it appears that the act was complied with by them in the time and manner shown in the following summary

statement.   The Utica and Schenectady, and Syracuse
and Utica have been given above.

	Years	Weight of rail per yard
Albany & Schenectady	1844, 1848, 1849	58 & 63
Auburn & Syracuse	1847, 1848	61 except 2 miles 65
Auburn & Rochester	1848	67 average
Tonawanda	1847, 1848, 1849	61 & 64
Attica & Buffalo	1847, 1848, 1849	62

It has been found impossible to assemble from the
records accurate figures showing the cost of this work,
but beyond all doubt it amounted to several millions
of dollars.

It does not come within the purview of the present
work to discuss either the merits or demerits of the
heavy iron rail laid at so great an expense, other than
to remark that use developed many defects, its tenure
of life very short occasioning great expense for renewals.
In about twenty years Bessemer steel rails began to
supplant iron which rapidly passed out of use.   Since
the contour or sectional area of the T rail of to-day is a
growth from that first used in the iron rails, it is a
matter of interest to know what the first contours
were.   In 1855 a considerable variety of iron rail was
in use on the New York Central and most of it must
have been laid at the time we have been reviewing.
Accordingly the accompanying cuts are reproduced to
illustrate them without knowing upon which roads they
were laid.   They are taken from the report of the State
Railroad Commission for 1855, a body which had a brief
existence for about one year.   They possess interest as
showing the first attempts to solve the problems connected with the use of a heavy iron rail—problems
which required the careful and scientific study for years
of Dr. P. H. Dudley in the employment of the Central.

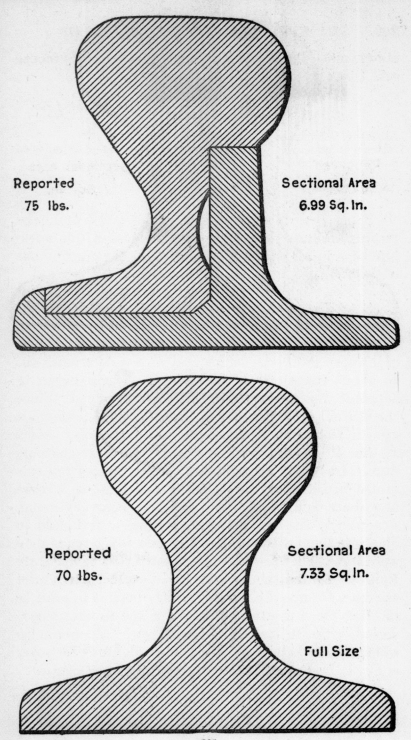

Reported
75 lbs.

Sectional Area
6.99 Sq. In.

Reported
70 lbs.

Sectional Area
7.33 Sq. In.

Full Size

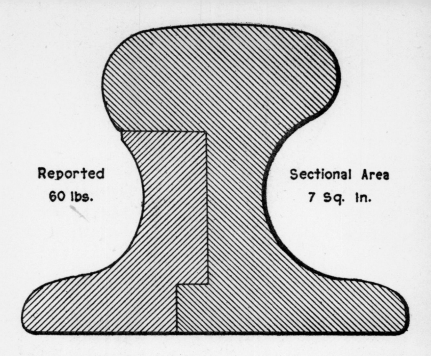

Reported
60 lbs.

Sectional Area
7 Sq. In.

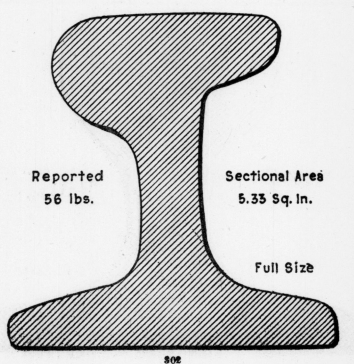

Reported
56 lbs.

Sectional Area
5.33 Sq. In.

Full Size

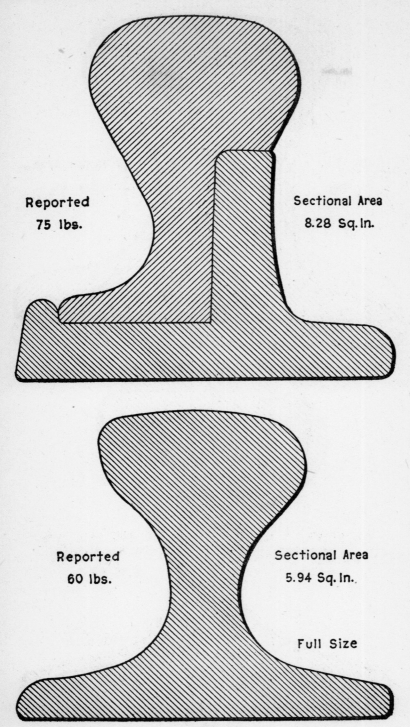

Reported
75 lbs.

Sectional Area
8.28 Sq. In.

Reported
60 lbs.

Sectional Area
5.94 Sq. In.

Full Size

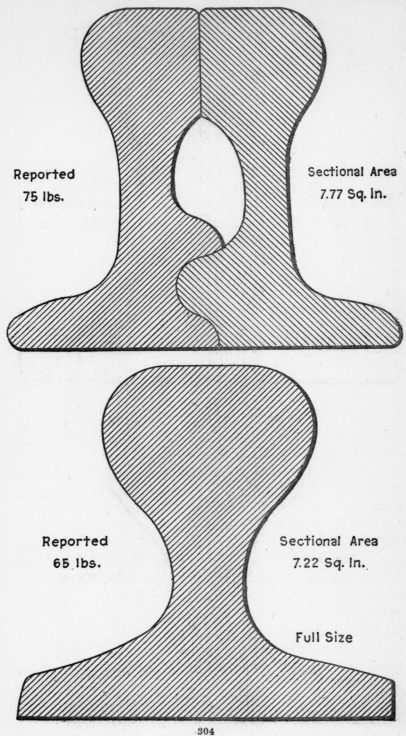

Reported
75 lbs.

Sectional Area
7.77 Sq. In.

Reported
65 lbs.

Sectional Area
7.22 Sq. In.

Full Size

CHAPTER XVI

PASSENGER CARS

IT is a matter of great regret that careful and extended research has been unable to bring to light reliable contemporary data or information from which an adequate description of the passenger cars upon the central line of roads, can be prepared. What we know about them may be readily stated. Those first in use upon the Mohawk and Hudson were in effect but the old form of horse drawn stage coaches placed upon a single four wheel truck instead of the ordinary running gear. Their appearance is quite familiar from the reproductions of the Brown silhouette and their reproduction in the so-called DeWitt Clinton train is faithful to the originals. The use of these was speedily abandoned. In an inventory of that road made in 1840 the principal passenger cars are described as "24 gothic coaches for 20 passengers each, less depreciation 40 per cent $13,341.60." This shows the cost to have been $22,236 or $1,111 each. A foot note shows that the depreciation is reckoned at 10 per cent per annum and hence they had been in service four years and were bought in 1835 or 1836. What gothic means in this connection is unknown. It is obvious that a car accommodating only 20 passengers was not a two truck car and that as late as 1840 one truck cars were in use on the Mohawk and Hudson. The inventory also shows eleven thoroughbrace cars, nine carrying nine passengers each and two but six passengers each. The depreciation charge of 60 per cent shows that they were put in use in 1833 and that as late as 1840 this road was still using its original stage coach type to a limited extent.

The next real view of what was in use on the line is found in an account of six passenger cars put on its road by the Auburn and Rochester at its opening in that year to be found in the *American Railroad Journal* for June 15, 1842, page 380.

MODERN LUXURIES—MAGNIFICENT RAILROAD CARS:—Yankee ingenuity is rarely more pleasantly exemplified than in the luxurious arrangements for railroad travelling of which we now have in Rochester, a magnificent specimen—in the splendid train of passenger cars just launched for the service of the sovereign people, on the *Auburn and Rochester Railroad.*

There are six cars designed to form two trains. The cars each are 28 feet long and 8 feet wide. The seats are well stuffed and admirably arranged—with arms for each chair, and changeable backs, that will allow the passengers to change "front to rear" by a manoeuvre unknown in military tactics. The size of the car forms a pleasant room, handsomely painted, with floor matting, with windows secured from jarring, and with curtains to shield from the blazing sun. We should have said rooms; for in four out of six cars, (the other two being designed only for way passengers) there is a ladies apartment, with luxurious sofas for seats, and in recesses may be found a washstand and other conveniences. The arrangement of the apartment for ladies, we consider the greatest improvement; and it will remedy some serious objections that have hitherto existed against railroad travelling on the part of families, especially where any members are in delicate health. The ladies can now have their choice either of a sofa in their own apartment, or a seat in the main saloon of the cars, as their health and inclination may require.

These cars are so hung on springs, and are of such large size, that they are freed from most of the jar, and especially from the swinging motion, so disagreeable to most railroads.

The lamp of each car is so placed as to light inside and out;

and last though not least, the breakers are so arranged as to be applied readily and with great power, thus guarding against the danger of collisions, etc.

On the whole it would be difficult to imagine any improvements that could be desired though we dare say these down-easters will rig out some new "notions" ere long, which will furnish "board and lodging" as well as mere passage on the railroads. The cars are worth a sight, even if one has neither time nor money (as some of us printers have not) to indulge in the luxury of a ride.

We mention these matters with satisfaction as indications of the strong desire manifested by the Auburn and Rochester railroad company to render their line of conveyance as satisfactory as possible to the travelling public.

N.B. We almost forgot to mention that these beautiful cars were made by Davenport and Bridges of Cambridge, Massachusetts, and cost at low prices about $1,700.00 each or $10,000.00 for the six. This firm keeps about 100 men in employment and have orders on hand now for some 800 cars of all sorts.

It will be noted that these cars were made by Davenport and Bridges of Cambridge, Mass., and the enthusiasm of the writer and his highly colored description indicate they were of the very best type then in use. The accompanying cut and plan of these cars is taken from a contemporary advertisement of Davenport and Bridges.

Another cut shows cars in use about 1844. Such cars were equipped only with hand brakes at each end, with open platforms, vestibules not coming into ordinary use until many years later. The wheels in the cut have spokes, but these must have soon disappeared, since solid cast iron wheels were in use in the fifties. The roof was slightly curved to carry off rain readily and was what would now be called very low inside. Such cars were furnaces in hot weather and refrigerators in cold, except as they were heated by

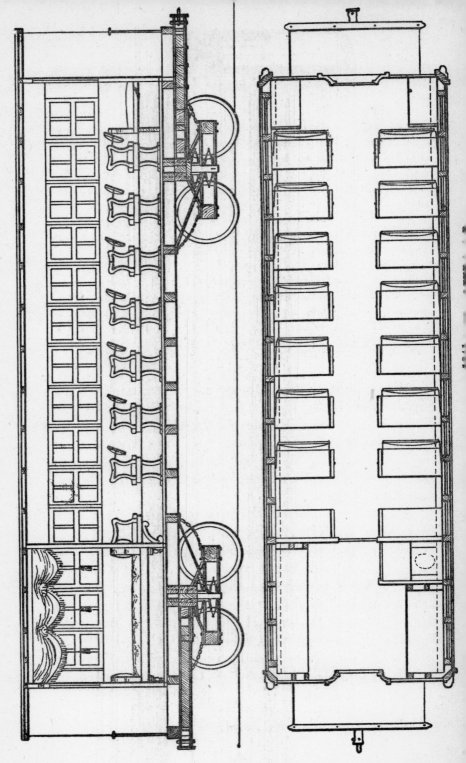

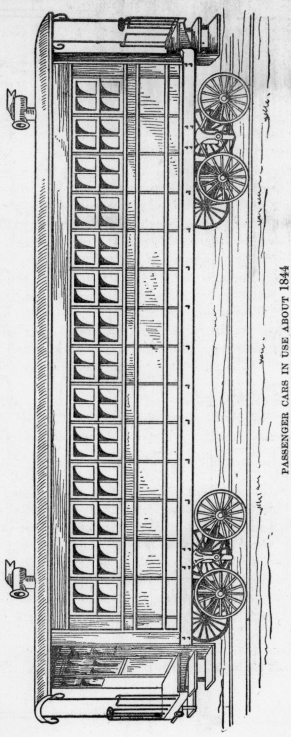

PASSENGER CARS IN USE ABOUT 1844

stoves, one in each, which used wood for fuel, that being piled high in boxes by the stoves. When the brakeman or one of the passengers filled the stove and the wood became fairly ignited, the car would become greatly overheated. When the stoves were not well fed, the car would become very cold and so the temperature alternated according to the attention given the fire. Passengers would frequently crowd around the stoves for warmth and again would open the doors or windows to let in cold air, which last generally gave great dissatisfaction to some of the passengers. There was a notable absence of screens at the windows to keep out cinders and as the locomotives used wood for fuel and spark arresters were not particularly efficient, a liberal supply of cinders generally assisted freely in preventing the cars from being over comfortable and luxurious. The cars were of light weight and could not well be otherwise with the braking facilities then in use.

As the train approached a station, depot as it was generally called, or when the engineer desired to stop at other points, the whistle was sounded and then ensued a scene of great activity and excitement. The husky brakeman, standing on the platform, would seize the brake wheel, turn it with all the speed and strength he could command and when the brake was set he would rush on the run through the car and set the brakes at the other end, generally yelling out as he ran, the name of the station. The lamps of those days barely served to render the darkness visible and occasionally leaked their contents into the aisle. Smoky lamps at times added to the pleasures of the passenger. The light weight car always took advantage of irregularities in the track, never as well surfaced as those of high class roads of the present day, to dance and frisk about vigorously, which process was styled as jolting. All these discomforts were usually borne cheerfully, the general condition of the passenger being far superior to what had preceded in the old stage coaches—dust in summer and deep mud in spring and fall and rough dirt roads at all times.

There is one episode connected with all eight wheel cars, both passenger and freight which was of great importance to all the roads of the central line, as well as to all the roads of the country, which deserves notice at this point. October 1, 1834, one Ross Winans of Baltimore, was granted letters patent on 8 wheel cars. He claimed that the idea had originated with him as far back as the year 1831, at which time a car called Columbus was first run by Mr. Winans' direction on the Baltimore and Ohio railroad. He also claimed that from 1831 to 1834 he had built several experimental cars, the Dromedary, the Comet, the Winchester, and finally, the Washington cars, and that his invention was not perfected until 1834 at about the time he applied for a patent. The patent ran for fourteen years and would have expired October 1, 1848, but on September 25th of that year, the commissioner of patents extended it for seven years, making its expiration October 1, 1855, thus giving a term of twenty-one years for which he claimed royalty.

The validity of the patent was denied by the New-castle and Frenchtown Turnpike and Railroad Company, which was using 8 wheel cars and in 1838, Mr. Winans brought against it his first suit for violation of his patent. This case was tried before Chief Justice Taney of the United States Supreme Court in the Circuit Court for the district of Maryland. The trial resulted in a disagreement of the jury. The case did not proceed further, for the defendant saw fit to make a settlement. But railroads generally refused to compromise, and July 14, 1847, Winans brought suit against the Schenectady and Troy in the Circuit Court of the United States for the northern district of New York. The suit was defended but continued from term to term until June, 1850, when it was tried and resulted in a verdict in favor of the patent and fully sustained the claims of the plaintiff. At the June term, 1851, the defendant made a motion for a new trial which was heard before Judge Conkling of the district court and Judge Nelson of the Supreme Court. A new trial was denied, an elaborate opinion being written by Judge Nelson and final judgment was entered in favor of Winans, October 13, 1851. This judgment seemed to make everything clear sailing for him. In September, 1851, his attorney issued a notice in writing to railroad companies setting forth his claims, the judgment of the court in his favor and calling upon all companies using eight wheel cars to settle for past damages and to pay for future licenses. This circular did not have the desired effect upon the railroads of the central line. Thus at the meeting of the directors of the Utica and Schenectady held October 14, 1851, it was brought to the attention of the Board and the curt entry in the minutes is, "A circular from Charles D. Gould of Albany and J. A. Spencer of Utica as attorney and counsel for Ross Winans in regard to the use of the 'eight wheel railroad car' for which Mr. Winans claims a patent, was referred to the executive committee with power."

The minutes of February 17, 1852, show the following: "The subject of the claim of Ross Winans the patentee of the eight wheeled railroad cars was considered and the matter was referred to the executive committee with power and with the understanding that they may if they deem proper unite with any of the other roads interested in defending the claim."

The executive committee under the advice of J. V. L. Pruyn of Albany decided to resist the claim as did the other roads of the line and in consequence, Mr. Winans brought suits against the Albany and Schenectady, Utica and Schenectady, Syracuse and Utica, Rochester and Syracuse, and Buffalo and Rochester. These suits were pending at the time of the consolidation into the New York Central in 1853, and their defence was assumed by that Company.

Mr. Winans also brought a suit in equity in the U. S. Court against Eaton, Gilbert & Co., carbuilders of Troy, who had built 8 wheel cars for most, or all, the roads of the line, to obtain an injunction restraining them from building such cars. If an injunction could have been obtained in any of these suits, the courts would undoubtedly have granted injunctions against all railroads and all car manufacturers violating the patent. Accordingly counsel for Winans moved for a preliminary injunction against Eaton, Gilbert & Co., and hearing was appointed at Cooperstown in August, 1853. The railroads of the central line assumed the defence of that company's suit. William Whiting, a patent attorney of Boston, was employed to take charge of the defence.

The motion for a preliminary injunction was heard by Mr. Justice Nelson of the Supreme Court who at the opening of the case stated all the facts in relation to the Schenectady and Troy case and remarked "that it could hardly be worth while to argue a similar case again as he had already overruled the motion for a new trial and decided the case in favor of the complainant; and that the granting of an injunction was a matter of course." Counsel for the defence insisting they had a good defence, the court heard the argument of Mr. Whiting. The hearing occupied about ten days. Justice Nelson held the motion under consideration for about eleven months and in the summer of 1854 decided it in favor of Eaton, Gilbert & Co., the defendants.

Mr. Winans now had to elect whether he would abandon further claims under his patent or commence anew and endeavor to obtain another jury verdict, which would support an injunction. He was a bold and determined man with ample means and promptly decided upon the latter course. He had in 1852, commenced suit against the Eastern Railroad of Massachusetts and preparations for trial were made with Whiting in charge of the defence which cost the railroad company upwards of $20,000. Finally the plaintiff declined to bring it to trial and it was ultimately dismissed with costs. He had determined to test the matter in an old suit which he had brought against the New York and Harlem some years before and which had been allowed to slumber. The railroad companies joined in bearing the expense of the defense and Whiting had charge for them. The case came to trial before Judge Betts and a jury in the Circuit Court of the United States in New York City, March 5, 1855, and the trial lasted sixty-two days until May 7. The jury disagreed, but with a large majority in favor of the defendant. The case was tried again before Justice Nelson in November, 1855. The jury was out for three days but was unable to agree, although it stood ten or eleven for the defendant. This trial occupied about thirty days and although indecisive encouraged the railroads to believe no jury would ever render a verdict sustaining the patent.

Winans was plucky and continued the contest.

He brought a new suit against the New York and Erie Railroad Company which was defended with Mr. Whiting still in charge of the defence. It being believed this suit would settle whether the plaintiff could ever succeed before a jury, ample preparations were made for the defence and new testimony hunted up. The trial came on at Canandaigua, New York, June 18, 1856. After it had lasted about thirty days, Judge Nathan K. Hall, of Buffalo, who presided, stated that he was prepared to make several rulings of law which he thought might terminate the action or at least resolve it into mere questions of law which could be finally settled in the Supreme Court of the United States. The proposed rulings being stated, the counsel for Winans admitted that under them, they could not sustain their case. The rulings were accordingly made and a verdict rendered by the jury in favor of the defendant, in the same court house and on the same patent where five years before a jury had rendered a verdict in favor of the patent and for $5,000 damages against the Schenectady and Troy.

The expenses of this trial were very great. It occupied between four and five weeks. There were four counsel on each side, several of whom had devoted nearly a year to preparation for trial. There were between eighty and one hundred witnesses residing in different states examined by commission and some testifying at such length as to require from three to four hours to read a single deposition. The fees of the commissioners taking the evidence for the defence amounted to nearly $1,000, board of witnesses for the defence during the trial between $600 and $700, reporting the evidence between $1,400 and $1,500, models and drawings some thousands of dollars.

When the case came on to be heard before the

Supreme Court at Washington in the winter of 1858, the
New York and Erie was in a bad way financially and
could no longer employ Mr. Whiting. This becoming
known to Erastus Corning, president of the New York
Central, he at once for that road assumed the responsibility of employing him and Whiting made the closing
argument for the defence. The court unanimously
sustained the rulings of Judge Hall and the long
controversy was ended.

In 1860, Mr. Corning requested Mr. Whiting to
prepare a statement of the points involved in the
controversy and of the facts developed by it. In his
letter of request he said "and in making this request,
I beg to express the opinion shared in by all who are
acquainted with the facts, that to your energy, industry
and ability the railroad interests of the country are
most largely indebted for the successful issue of this
matter. On you the responsibility of the defence
mainly fell and that responsibility was faithfully and
ably met, vindicating the well earned reputation you
had already acquired as one of the most clear minded,
thorough and able patent lawyers of our country."

Mr. Whiting acceded to this request and prepared
an account from which the foregoing narrative has been
drawn. He in turn gave due credit to other counsel
associated with him and makes one statement which
should be given in full at this point.

This determined resistance to the claims of Winans, prosecuted with unflinching resolution and backed by ample wealth,
was due mainly to Hon. Erastus Corning, Charles Henry Warren
and Albert Thorndike, acting in concert with the Presidents of
other railroads in New York, New England and Pennsylvania.

To develop and explain the facts and the theories
involved in these remarkable cases would, as Mr.

Whiting observes, require a volume and is wholly outside the purview of this work.

The financial importance to roads whose history is being developed may be appreciated when it is stated that Winans demanded a royalty of $100 a year for each and every 8 wheel car used by a company during a period of twenty-one years.

Another matter of interest relating to the early days of transportation is the kind of fuel used. On the central line it was wood, bought along the line of the road and piled at the stations designated as stopping places for wood and water. Before the country adjacent to the road was denuded of all the timber it could spare and while it was necessary to clear woodland of timber for the purposes of cultivation, this demand for fuel was of considerable advantage to farmers along the line who employed the comparative leisure of the winter months and the facilities for hauling afforded by snow in earning what was for them a very welcome addition to the small cash returns yielded by their farms. The wood was cut in three foot lengths as a rule and every fuel station required a large area of land for its piling. On the roads of the central line, many woodsheds were erected to preserve the wood from the effects of sun and rain. Their number and extent may be learned from the annual report of the New York Central for 1855, which states the number to be 115, although the passenger houses numbered but 50 and the freight houses 56. Their length is stated to be 24,398 feet, over $4\frac{3}{5}$ miles, most of them being substantially roofed.

THROUGH TRAINS FROM BUFFALO TO ALBANY

The completion of the Attica and Buffalo in the early winter of 1842-43, afforded an opportunity for running practically through trains from Buffalo to Albany with only one change, that at Rochester, the Tonawanda and the Auburn and Rochester not being then connected, nor until some time thereafter, when a special act of the legislature made it possible. So marked an improvement, both in the interest of the roads in attracting travel to and from the west in competition with more southern routes and in the interest of the public by way of more expeditious travel freed from the many annoying incidents of dealing with various roads should have been brought about without friction and opposition, but it did not escape the lot of most proposed changes. As illustrating a serious railroad problem of the present day and as a memorable incident in the past, the event is worth considering in detail. The situation was of enough importance to lead to a contest in the legislature and apparently to some disturbance of feeling among some stockholders of the various companies, since it was deemed necessary to issue a pamphlet addressed to the stockholders from which the principal facts have been drawn. The introduction to this pamphlet bears irrefragable evidence of being addressed to a rather serious upheaval and is worth printing in full.

The undersigned, being Directors in several of the above mentioned companies, deem it their duty to lay before you some facts bearing upon the management of these roads, with the view of promoting their prosperity, and ensuring the substantial and permanent value of their stocks.

It would seem hardly necessary to assert that the interests of these rail-roads should not be made subservient to those of competing lines, were it not well known that some persons connected with some of the above companies, are interested in competing lines, and labor incessantly to make all the arrangements upon the rail-roads serve their particular interests in those lines, without reference to the immediate or ultimate effect of such arrangements upon the rail-roads.

Feeling the necessity of unanimity and concert upon the whole line, from the Hudson river to Buffalo, and the justness of the complaints of the public, and the diminished receipts arising from the want of harmony produced by the action of those who sought to control the direction of some of the roads to serve their own interests, and with the view of drawing the travel from the far west over this line of rail-roads, by the comfort, expedition and cheapness of the transit, the following communication was made to the President, Directors, &c. of the Utica and Schenectady Rail-road Co.

Then follows the request of the roads west of Utica hereinafter described.

The directors of the Syracuse and Utica on November 15, 1842, adopted resolutions that their road would enter into arrangements with the several companies upon the route between the Hudson river and Buffalo for the establishment of uniform fare at the rate of three cents a mile for first class cars and for such other rates for a class of cars as would command the emigrant and other travel. That it would tend to reduce expenses upon the several roads to stock the cars between the Hudson river and Rochester and also to Buffalo when the rails should be connected at Rochester. In December following, all the roads west of Utica united in a request that all the roads send delegates to a meeting at Syracuse, January 5, 1843, to consult and agree upon a schedule of time of running the several trains for the year 1843. This seems to have been the first general active recognition of those necessities which ten years later forced a consolidation of all these roads. Apparently because no meeting of the Board of Directors of the Utica and Schenectady was held between the time of issuing the request and the day suggested for the meeting, no meeting was held.

At a meeting of the Directors of the Utica and Schenectady on the 17th of January, 1843, the subject was taken up and being favorable to a meeting the Board proposed a convention at Albany to be held January 31, sent invitations to all the western roads and appointed their executive committee as delegates.

All the roads accepted and the convention assembled at Albany, January 31, and was attended by twenty-three delegates, all the roads being represented. After organizing, a committee of one from each road was appointed to report upon the subjects to be acted on by the convention. The committee reported six resolutions which were all adopted. The first one is so illuminating as to the condition of railroading at that time as to deserve quoting in full.

Resolved; that it is expedient to run two daily lines between Buffalo and the Hudson river, connecting with the morning and night boats out of Albany and Troy and that each line be run in twenty-five hours, including stops; and that the same be apportioned as follows: Buffalo to Rochester, 6 hours; Rochester to Auburn, 6 hours; Auburn to Syracuse, 2 hours; Syracuse to Utica, 4 hours; Utica to Albany and Troy, 7 hours;—25 hours. And that the times of starting from each end of the line be as follows: Buffalo, 6 A.M. and 4 P.M.; Albany and Troy, 6 A.M.; Schenectady 8 A.M.; Albany and Troy, 7 P.M.; Schenectady 9 P.M.

In interpreting this resolution, it should be borne in mind that the route then existing is not the same as the main line of the Central at this time between the same termini. From Buffalo to Batavia, the route was by way of Attica, the direct line now used not being then built; from Rochester to Syracuse, the route was by way of Canandaigua, Geneva and Auburn, the direct line now used not being built until some ten years later. Hence it becomes at least helpful, if not essential, to show the distance for each division named in the resolution.

			Average Miles Per Hour
Buffalo to Rochester	6 hours	75 miles	12½
Rochester to Auburn	6 hours	78 miles	13
Auburn to Syracuse	2 hours	26 miles	13
Syracuse to Utica	4 hours	53 miles	13
Utica to Albany	7 hours	94 miles	13½
Utica to Troy	7 hours	100 miles	14
To Albany		326 miles	13

The fifth resolution declared it expedient to run a third train between the Hudson river and Buffalo, leaving the Hudson river at 1 P.M. and Buffalo at 12 noon, at uniform prices of 2½ cents per mile "for one description of cars" and 1½ cents per mile for emigrant cars. It was referred to the superintendents of the several roads under the direction of the executive committees to arrange the running time of this train and other matters in connection therewith. It has not been found what running time was agreed upon. It would be interesting to know considering that of fast express trains averaged thirteen miles an hour. But it should not be forgotten that all of these roads but the Schenectady and Troy just opened were using the wooden stringer supporting the strap rail, that stops for wood and water were frequent, that no dining cars were in existence and all food for passengers was found at station restaurants, that there was no telegraph system, no signal system, no air brakes for controlling fast and heavy trains, and in fact every device and arrangement essential to the fast trains of to-day was unknown.

The second resolution was that passengers ought to be allowed to pay their fare and direct their baggage to such places on the route as they deem proper—a most inexplicable determination until one recalls the competitive contest between the Mohawk and Hudson and the Schenectady and Troy roads, when it is seen to be the first attempt of the associated roads to deal with that perplexing problem. But the third resolution veered away slightly from the perpendicular attitude of the second by providing that baggage masters be employed at the joint expense of the several roads between Albany and Buffalo, thus leaving Troy to care for itself on its own line. The fourth resolution was directed toward an interesting habit of the general public, it declaring "it is expedient that the car houses (meaning passenger stations) on the line between Hudson river and Buffalo inclusive be closed and the passengers relieved from the press and inconvenience of being crowded in the several car houses by persons who may resort there from curiosity." The sixth resolution directed the superintendents of the several companies under the direction of the executive committees to devise and carry into effect a system of taking fare through the line each way for all the trains, of carrying and ticketing baggage and such system for securing the emigrant travel as might be necessary.

The difficulties attendant upon handling through traffic over seven different roads were apparent. The method of overcoming them was yet to be devised.

On motion of individual delegates, resolutions were adopted to appoint a committee to devise a plan of stocking the passenger, baggage and freight cars on the line between Albany and Rochester and ultimately when the line is completed to Buffalo; that the two fast lines commence on the 15th of March next and the third line on the opening of the canal; that the convention deprecate the practice of employing runners (at a distance from the respective railroads) as destructive to the interests of stockholders and vexatious to the traveling public, and that so far as in their power, they would use their influence against any company which should hereafter indulge in that practice.

This last resolution was directed at the Schenectady and Troy and throws some light on the Albany and Troy contest elsewhere narrated.

Two other resolutions should be given in full,

Resolved, that the several companies upon this Rail Road line will not employ persons in the business of transportation who ever drink intoxicating liquors.

Note that the prohibition is unqualified and absolute; not those who drink to excess, but those who drink at all. The other casts a brilliant light upon winter traveling under the conditions then existing,

Resolved, that during the winter months the train shall leave Buffalo at 7 in the morning and reach and remain over night at Syracuse; and leave Albany at 9 o'clock in the morning and stay over night at Auburn; so that a passenger may make the passage between Albany and Buffalo in two days; and that it be referred to the superintendents of the several roads under the direction of the Executive Committees to carry this out; and this to take effect on Monday, the 6th of February instant.

All the foregoing acts of the convention appear at the present day to be wise and sensible and springing from a desire to make the roads as efficient and useful to the public as conditions would permit. But they did not so appear to some that day. Persons interested in freight and packet boats on the canal and steamboats

BUFFALO & ALBANY
Rail Road.
THREE DAILY LINES.

FARE. Mail Trains.		
	1st Class	Miles
Rochester,	$2,00	75
Auburn,	5,00	153
Syracuse,	6,00	179
Utica,	8,00	224
Schenect'dy	11,00	310
Albany or Troy,	11.50	326

FARE. Accommodation Trains.		
	1st Cl.	2d Class
Rochester,	$1,75	$1,00
Auburn,	2,65	2,25
Syracuse,	4,31	2,08
Utica,	5,62	3,45
Schenect'dy	7,50	4,65
Albany or Troy,	8,00	5,00

Through to Albany in 25 Hours!

Cars will leave Buffalo for Rochester and Albany, at 6 o'clock, A. M. and 4 o'clock, P. M.

Fare to Rochester, - - - - - $2 00
" Albany or Troy, - - - - 11 50

THE ACCOMMODATION TRAIN,

Will leave at 12 o'clock, noon.

Fare, 1st Class Cars, to Rochester, - - $1 50
" " " to Albany or Troy, - 8 00
" 2d " to Rochester - - 1 00
" " " to Albany or Troy, - 5 00

One Train only will leave on Sundays, at 6 o'clock in the morning.

N. B.—Agents and Baggage Wagons will *always* be in attendance upon the arrival of Steam Boats to convey *Baggage* to the Depot FREE OF CHARGE.

Wm. WALLACE,

Buffalo, June 1, 1843.   Superintendent A. & B. R. R. Co.

A. M. CLAPP, PRINTER, BUFFALO.

POSTER SHOWING FIRST THROUGH TRAINS FROM BUFFALO TO ALBANY.

on Lake Ontario were very much dissatisfied with the proposed arrangements, as crude as they were, from our point of view, and proposed to go to the legislature to obtain a law preventing their being carried into effect. As early as February 15, persons in Utica, Troy and Oswego, prepared and presented to the legislature a petition, the first paragraph of which is as follows:

The petition of the undersigned, inhabitants of the county of Oneida, respectfully represents: That they are informed that efforts are now making on the part of the different rail-road companies between the Hudson river and Lake Erie, to form a combination and union of interests, in such manner as to create one great powerful monopoly out of many small monopolies. We believe it was the intention of the Legislature in chartering the different railroad companies, to confine and restrict each company in its general operations, especially in the use of its passenger cars and motive power, to the limits of its own road; and we also believe, that the interests of the travelling public and of the community in general will be better promoted by an adherence to what we suppose was the original intention of the Legislature than by permitting a departure from it.

The petition was referred in the Assembly to a committee of which a member from Oswego was chairman and that committee reported a bill so extraordinary that it was never brought to a vote. Some of its provisions in their practical working would have produced the following results. A passenger who had bought a through ticket on arriving at the junction point of two railroads could surrender his ticket and his baggage labels and demand and receive his baggage and the return of the amount he had paid for his fare over the line or lines over which he had not been transported, provided he made such demand within twenty minutes after his arrival at the junction point in question. At Schenectady no train could leave until the expiration of

thirty minutes after the arrival of a train on a connecting road. Every railroad company was required to
admit and suffer to remain in and to have free ingress
and egress to and from its car houses and depots on the
arrival of passenger trains, the agents and servants of
every other railroad company and of any and every
steamboat, packet boat or line proprietor or proprietors
and of every stage proprietor, company or association,
not exceeding two of each owner, for the purpose of
taking and receiving and conveying the baggage of
passengers to and from the car or depot. Any violation of this provision was made a criminal offense.
This was in answer to the resolution of the convention
relative to runners. The pith of the proposed law,
however, was in a section which forbade railroad
companies to allow their passenger cars to run on any
other road than their own, to own, hire, use or run
passenger cars or motive power in common or in connection. Every company was required to confine the
use of its passenger cars and motive power to its own
line of road and every violation of any provision of the
act by any railroad company, its servants or agents,
subjected the offending company to a penalty of $250
to be recovered in an action of debt in the name of the
people of the state "by any person who will sue for the
same." The ingenuity of some modern seekers for
legislation has scarcely improved on this first effort of
tyros.

For the regulation of through traffic and business
generally in which all were interested, conventions of
the roads were held from time to time as seemed
required, and through time tables were agreed upon,
but unfortunately the records of such meetings for
several years have disappeared. The speed of trains
seems to have been gradually increased, particularly

after the replacing of the strap rail by iron rail in 1847–49. After this work was substantially completed, a convention of superintendents held at Syracuse, November 26, 1849, adopted the following time table for the winter of 1849–50. This table is of interest as showing the running time as well as the number of trains run, three passenger and one through freight and one between Syracuse and Albany daily.

On motion, it was Resolved, That the trains during the winter of 1849 and 1850, be run as follows:—

ON AND AFTER MONDAY, DECEMBER 17, 1849—PASSENGER TRAINS

	Express	*Mail*	*Night*
Leave Albany......	7 A.M.	10 A.M.	7 P.M.
Schenectady..	7:45 "	11 "	8 "
Utica........	11:15 "	3:30 P.M.	12 "
Syracuse.....	2:00 P.M.	7 "	2:30 A.M.
Auburn......	3:15 "	8:45 "	4:30 "
Rochester....	6:30 "	2 A.M.	9 "
Arrive Buffalo......	10 "	6 "	1 P.M.
Leave Buffalo......	7 A.M.	10 A.M.	7 P.M.
Rochester....	10 "	2:30 P.M.	11:15 "
Auburn......	1:30 P.M.	7:45 "	4:30 A.M.
Syracuse.....	3:15 "	9:45 "	7 "
Utica........	5:45 "	1 A.M.	10 "
Schenectady..	9 "	5 "	1:45 P.M.
Arrive Albany.......	9:45 "	6 "	2:30 "

FREIGHT TRAINS

Leave Albany...............	2 P.M.	7 A.M.
Schenectady..........	3:20 "	8 "
Utica................	11:00 "	1:30 P.M.
Syracuse.............	7 A.M.	6:30 "

Freight Trains—*Continued*

Leave Auburn...............	9:30	A.M.		
Rochester.............	4:30	P.M.		
Arrive Buffalo...............	10	"		
Leave Buffalo...............	1	P.M.		
Rochester.............	6	"		
Auburn...............	1	A.M.		
Syracuse.............	3:30	A.M.	6	A.M.
Utica................	9	"	10:30	"
Schenectady...........	3	P.M.	5	P.M.
Arrive Albany...............	4	"	6	"

Such data as these derive their greatest interest when taken in connection with present day performance. In 1925, twenty-three passenger trains left Albany on each week day, running through to Buffalo, six of which go through Buffalo to the west without stopping to receive or discharge passengers and eleven other local passenger trains operate in like manner over parts of the route. The number of trains by no means tells the whole story. The seating capacity of the train must also be taken into account, but of this we have no record for the 1849 list. So many of the present day trains run in sections. As many as six sections of the Twentieth Century have been known, and the Empire frequently goes in two.

The through fare was at the outset divided between the roads on the basis of the length of road, each taking such per cent of the whole as its length bore to the whole distance, with some differential to the two roads east of Schenectady due to their unequal length. When the short lines were completed from Batavia to Buffalo and from Rochester to Syracuse in consideration of the duplication of roads, in February, 1851, the old distance of 75 miles from Rochester to Buffalo was used and the distance from Rochester to Syracuse was fixed at 100 miles, although in fact its length was only 80½ miles.

The through fare varied from time to time. In 1843 it was $11.50 for first class. It was in the power of one road to dictate the amount. Thus in November, 1850, nearly all the roads desired to make the through fare from Buffalo to Albany on express trains $8.25, and other first class trains $6.70, but the Rochester and Syracuse bluntly refused to acquiesce, and accordingly the others were obliged to agree to $9 and $7.50 respectively, although in their resolution they felt constrained to say, "That although in the judgment of this convention the rates of fare are not sufficiently reduced in the proposition of the Rochester and Syracuse Rail Road Company, yet for the purpose of securing the favorable action of that Company the rates which are proposed in their communication be adopted as follows," etc. This was at the rate of about 2¾ cents per mile while the majority desired to fix it at 2½ cents. Yet in the following February (1851) the Convention unanimously fixed this fare at $6.60, which was at the rate of two cents per mile, using the old distance, the reduction to take place April 1, 1851. Nothing is said in the report of the meeting why this action was taken, but one can not fail to recall that the New York and Erie, now the Erie, was completed to Dunkirk in 1851, and western travel was greatly sought by it. At this meeting the time between Albany and Buffalo was reduced to 12½ hours, this also to take effect April 1, the half hour to allow "for dinner at such point as the train may arrive in proper season." In May following, it was voted, beginning May 19th, to run two morning express trains from Buffalo, one at 7 and the other at 8 o'clock; also a through freight from Albany, leaving at 6 P.M., and running through in twenty-seven hours.

In November, 1851, there was a revision of the schedule for winter. Three passenger trains left Buffalo at 7:30 A.M., 10 A.M. and 5 P.M. and two freight trains at 12 M. and 6:30 P.M. Three passenger trains left Albany at 7:30 A.M., 2 P.M. and 8 P.M.; two freight trains at 12 M. and 5 P.M. Freight trains were to be run through in 27 hours, passenger trains with way mail 17 hours, without way mail in 13 hours.

At this meeting a freight tariff for the winter was considered on the report of a committee of one from each road and adopted as follows for the through rates:

1st class westward	70	cents per 100 lbs.
2nd class westward	54	" " " "
3rd class westward	44	" " " "
4th class westward	40	" " " "
1st class eastward	70	" " " "
2nd class eastward	50	" " " "
3rd class eastward	40	" " " "
4th class eastward	33	" " " "

Flour 60 cents per barrel; carload of hogs and cattle, small, $50, large $60; carload of sheep, small $40, large $50.

Terminal charges were beginning to attract attention in the case of the short roads at the eastern end. Fifteen cents per ton were allowed them for loading and unloading to be apportioned west of Schenectady.

STOCKING OF CARS

Upon the completion of the Attica and Buffalo the several companies operating along the route thoroughly realized the necessity and importance of through operation, but, of course, found many difficult and serious problems to solve, especially in regard to the furnishing and management of passenger and baggage cars, the selling of tickets and handling of baggage. It is not proposed to go into these matters in detail at this time but to develop the somewhat curious history which resulted in an agreement made February 17, 1848, by which the Mohawk and Hudson bought the baggage, emigrant and mail cars of all the roads west of Schenectady and then, for an agreed compensation, furnished them for common use in a through line.

Representatives of all the companies met at Albany January 31, 1843, and agreed to run regular passenger trains over the whole line from Buffalo to Albany, beginning the ensuing 15th of March, but did not arrange the terms on which cars were to be furnished by the several companies, only adopting a resolution that a committee of one should be appointed to consider and digest a plan of stocking them on the line between Albany and Rochester, and ultimately when the line was completed to Buffalo. An agreement for stocking cars was not finally formulated until about September, when a difficulty between Albany and Troy roads over fares gave much trouble. The Mohawk and Hudson was charging fifty cents fare from Schenectady to Albany; the Schenectady and Troy but twenty-five cents from Schenectady to Troy. This latter rate did not pay the cost of transportation and if adopted by the Albany road would have brought it to ruin. The merits and indeed the details of this contest need not be entered into here except to the extent of noting that the Troy road claimed in a printed publication that the Utica and Schenectady, "have entered into combinations or arrangements with the Mohawk and Hudson and other companies with regard to fare, by which arrangements have been charged the same fare to Schenectady as to Albany with the avowed intention not to change such course until the Schenectady and Troy Company should raise its fare to fifty cents; and this gross injustice to the

Schenectady and Troy road and to the public was continued and persisted in until the Schenectady and Troy Company was compelled to submit to the condition imposed and raise its fare to fifty cents as required by these chartered guardians of the interests of Albany." This it should be observed as the claim merely of one party to a quarrel. The other side had a different story. The Schenectady and Troy insisted upon a separate baggage car for Troy baggage, in charge of its own agent, or as we would now say baggage master. This it would seem was granted it for a time but the roads west of Utica finally would not carry it on their roads for the alleged reason that the Troy road kept a body of so-called runners all along the line soliciting passengers and thereby greatly annoyed the public. Just what the situation was at any one time, it is difficult to trace. Finally about 1846, the Troy road was out of the deal altogether. Chiefly it would now seem over the runner difficulty.

Later in 1847, it went to the legislature and procured the passage of an act, Chap. 222 of that year, ostensibly directed at the Utica and Schenectady requiring it to give equal facilities to the Troy and Albany roads and providing for the appointment of three commissioners on the application of an aggrieved road, who should summarily inquire into the matter and prescribe such regulations and facilities as would in their judgment secure the enjoyment of equal privileges, accommodations and facilities to all the roads. The award of the commissioners when approved by the Supreme Court was to be binding on the parties for two years and the court was given the power to enforce it.

At the time of the passage of this act, the roads other than the Troy were operating under an agreement, stocking, as they termed it, the cars used in passenger service, which meant they were joint owners on a basis determined by the agreement. The Troy road, of course, procured the appointment of commissioners under the act. The commissioners made their award September 7, 1847, and the award was confirmed by the Supreme Court, December 7, 1847. The award contained twelve provisions, only a few of which are material to the question in hand. The first and second were as follows:

1. Whenever the Utica and Schenectady Railroad Company shall own any interest in passenger, baggage or freight cars in which the Albany and Schenectady Railroad Company shall also own some interest or share, they shall allow the Schenectady and Troy Railroad Company to acquire a like interest to be acquired and paid for by the contribution of suitable eight wheel cars and by payment of any balance over, if any there shall be.

2. If the owners of any other portion of such cars shall on request of the Schenectady and Troy Railroad Company refuse to allow the said Company to acquire and hold such an interest, it shall be the duty of the Utica and Schenectady Railroad Company to give the proper notice on or before the first day of January next, that any contract for joint ownership in cars will be terminated on the first day of April next, pursuant to the terms of such contract.

The eighth provision was as follows, "The Utica and Schenectady Railroad Company shall not permit any person either in their employment, or in or about their depot at Utica to solicit passengers to go either by way of Albany or Troy."

The ninth was as follows, "The Albany and Schenectady Railroad Company, the Utica and Schenectady Railroad Company and the Schenectady and Troy Railroad Company shall neither of them employ or have any agents or runners for the solicitation of passengers at any Rail-Road depot in this state west of Utica nor shall either of said Companies, by any bill or publication attempt to produce prejudice against any other of said companies or their routes, or allow any person in any manner in the employment of either Company to make, offer or use such publications."

The first two provisions quoted were a victory, the last two a defeat for the Troy road, it being the only one desiring to use such runners. It was, however, a Pyrrhic victory. There are signs that the other roads had been anticipating the award and had made ready for it. At all events on the 17th day of February, 1848, all the companies between Albany and Buffalo entered into an agreement by the terms of which the Albany and Schenectady bought all the baggage, emigrant and mail cars of the other roads and became the sole owner thereof. It also agreed with all the other roads except the Utica and Schenectady to supply them during a term of five years from March 1, 1848, with all the baggage, mail and emigrant cars needed on such roads at an agreed compensation of twelve mills per mile for each of said cars so run upon the roads of the respective parties and for every mile so run. In March following, the Albany road entered into a contract with the Utica and Schenectady by which it agreed to furnish for it all the passenger, emigrant, mail and baggage cars that it needed in its business or would need during the next five years. The agreement also contained various provisions designed to meet the situation presented by the demands of the Schenectady and Troy under the statute and award. At the same time, the Utica and Schenectady sold to the Albany road all its passenger cars as well as the emigrant, mail and baggage cars specified in the agreement of February 17th.

These several agreements took the Utica and Schenectady out of the terms of the award relating to ownership of cars which have been quoted and practically defeated the object which the Schenectady and Troy had in view, and yet left the award in force so far as related to its runners. There is much reason to believe the whole scheme resulting in these two agreements originated with Marcus T. Reynolds, then one of the leading lawyers of Albany and also a director of the Utica and Schenectady. Any one who desires to do so is also at liberty to conjecture that the whole row between the Albany and Troy roads was but an incident in a struggle between the two cities for commercial supremacy. It has already been indicated to what extent Albany was compelled to assist its road in getting rid of the inclined planes, and attention may properly be called at this point to the fact that the entire stock of the Troy road was owned by that city. Perhaps it might be called a city war rather than a railroad fight; but there we leave the subject without any attempt to elucidate the real truth of the matter.

The Troy road subsequently in 1849 on the basis of an agreement by the associated roads with certain parties in New York for the sale of emigrant tickets, brought the question of discrimination again before the legislature by having introduced in the Assembly a bill entitled "An Act to preserve a fair competition between the Albany and Schenectady Railroad Company and the Schenectady and Troy Railroad Company. "The bill was referred to the committee on railroads which considered the matter, reported the facts to the Assembly and asked to be discharged from further consideration of the bill and there the matter seems to have ended.

Fuel.

As above stated, the fuel used during the period we are considering was wood. The magnitude of the amount required is almost incomprehensible to one who has never seen the huge piles of cordwood at each station which were required for locomotive use. Fortunately one pretty complete record of the quantity carried has been preserved in the report of the Rochester, Lockport and Niagara Falls to the consolidation committee in May, 1853. It is well worth preservation as a unique record of an early phase of railroad operation long since disappeared. To make the picture complete we insert the list of wood sheds on this road with their value as well as the number of cords with their value, inventoried at each station. The unit price per cord is given in shillings—8 shillings to the dollar—which at that time were in common use.

Rochester

250 cords, short, 28/	....	$	875.00	
45 " 4 ft. 22/	....		113.75	

Spencerport

20 cords, short, 26/	....	65.00	
350 " 4 ft. 22/	....	952.50	
575 " 4 ft. 20/	....	1,337.50	
Woodshed, 112x24	....		$625.

Adams Basin

240 cords, short, 26/	....	780.00

Brockport

840 cords, short, 24/	....	2,520.00	
105 " 4 ft. 20/	....	262.50	
Woodshed, 208½ ft. long	....		750.

Holley

200 cords, short, 22/	....	550.00	
175 " 4 ft. 18/	....	393.75	
155 " 4 ft. 16/	....	310.00	
Woodshed, 112 ft. long	....		337.

Murray

190 cords, short, 21/..........	$	497.80
250 " 4 ft. 16/............		500.00
Woodshed, 112 ft...............		$337.

Albion

20 cords, short, 24/..........	60.00
150 " 4 ft. 20/............	375.00
350 " 4 ft. 18/............	787.50
15 " short, 20/..........	37.50
250 " 4 ft. 16/............	500.00
Woodshed, 208 ft...............	750.

Medina

740 cords, short, 22/..........	2,035.00
750 " 4 ft. 16/............	1,500.00
400 " 4 ft. 14/............	700.00
Woodshed, 208½ ft.............	750.

Middleport

50 cords, short, 20/..........	125.00
350 " 4 ft. 16/..........	700.00
Woodshed.....................	337.

Mabers

590 cords, 4 ft. 16/............	1,180.00
40 " short, 19/..........	95.20

Gasport

480 cords, 4 ft. 16/............	960.00

Orangeport

890 cords, short, 20/..........	2,235.00
585 " 4 ft. 16/............	1,170.00
Woodshed.....................	337.

Gravel Pit

130 cords, short, 20/..........	325.00

Lockport

125 cords, short, 22/..........	343.75
250 " 4 ft. 14/............	437.50
Woodshed.....................	750.

Pekin

825 cords, short, 14/..........	1,443.75
250 " 4 ft. 12/............	375.00
800 " 4 ft. 10/............	1,000.00
Woodshed, 208 ft...............	562.

Tonawanda

20 cords, short, 16/	$	40.00
540 " 4 ft. 12/		810.00
400 " 4 ft. 10/		500.00

Niagara Falls

50 cords, short, 18/	112.50
20 " 4 ft. 14/	35.00
20 " 4 ft. 16/	40.00

Between Rochester and Spencerport

415 cords, 4 ft. 22/	1,141.25
12,900 cords	$28,221.75

Piled in a single row one cord high, this number of cords would have made a pile 19½ miles long.

LOAN OF STATE CREDIT

To aid in their construction the State of New York loaned its credit to four of the roads under consideration as follows:

Schenectady and Troy	$100,000.
Auburn and Syracuse	200,000.
Auburn and Rochester	200,000.
Tonawanda	100,000.

These loans have been noticed in the history of each road but without that detail which is desirable. Accordingly we shall now give a detailed account of each transaction showing the exact part played by the state therein. The first road to receive assistance was the Auburn and Syracuse which so narrowly escaped destruction in the panic of 1837. It applied to the legislature of 1838 for relief with the result that April 18, 1838, Chapter 293 of the laws of that year authorized the issuing to the company "special certificates of stock," bearing interest at 5 per cent payable quarterly, to the amount of $100,000 whenever the company should have expended $300,000 in the construction of their road and in the purchase of lands therefor and "whenever and as often as the said Company shall have in like manner expended the further sum of $50,000 and the avails of all stock previously issued as aforesaid and shall produce like evidence thereof to the comptroller, he shall issue and deliver to the said Company like certificates of stock for the sum of $50,000 until he shall have issued and delivered to said company such stock to the amount of, not exceeding in the aggregate the sum of $200,000."

Certificates of stock to this aggregate amount were issued to the company in the year 1838 and were made payable in 1858. These certificates of stock were mere promises to pay to the company or their order the sum named in each certificate, not exceeding $1,000, with interest at the times and places specified therein. They were in form and effect state bonds. The company was required by the law to sell these certificates within three months after their receipt, under the direction of the comptroller in the city of New York, at public auction, giving at least three weeks previous notice of the time and place of sale in the state paper and in two daily newspapers published in the city of New York. Any premiums realized on such sale were to be paid into the state treasury for the use of the common school fund.

The company was further required by law to make provision for the punctual redemption of the said stock and for the punctual payment of the interest which should accrue thereon, in such manner as to exonerate the treasury of the state from any advances of money for that purpose, and the revenues of the road after paying repairs and the necessary expenses of conducting the business were pledged for the payment of the interest. The treasurer of the company was required to give a bond to the comptroller that he would faithfully discharge the duties and trusts reposed upon him by the act.

For the security to the state for this loan of credit the company was required to give a first mortgage upon the road, the provisions of the statute in that behalf being as follows:

No part of the said stock shall be delivered to the said company until the acceptance thereof shall be signified to the comptroller by the filing in his office of a certificate of such acceptance under the corporate seal of the company and the signature of their president.

Each certificate of acceptance so executed and filed as aforesaid shall be recorded in the office of the secretary of state and thereupon shall become and be to all interests and purposes a mortgage of the said road and every part and section thereof and its appurtenances to the people of this state for securing the payment of the principal and interest of the sums of money for which such stock shall from time to time be issued and accepted as aforesaid.

In case the said company shall make default in payment of either the interest or principal of said stock or any part thereof, it shall be lawful for the comptroller to sell the said road and appurtenances at auction to the highest bidder, giving at least six months notice of the time and place of such sale by advertisements, etc., etc.

The interest upon these certificates was punctually paid by the Auburn and Syracuse as long as it maintained its corporate existence. At the consolidation the debt, both principal and interest, was assumed by the New York Central, which paid the same in full at maturity. Thus it will be seen the state never advanced a dollar to the company. It loaned its credit, in effect guaranteed the payment of the indebtedness and was never called upon to perform its guarantee.

The foregoing is in all essential particulars the treatment extended to each of the three other roads receiving state aid. Each road was required before receiving any certificates to expend substantial sums of its own in construction. No money was advanced by the state. It delivered certificates of the same general form as those issued to the Auburn and Syracuse. The amount of the certificates was made a first lien on the road in the nature of a mortgage. The company was required to pay both the interest and principal of the certificates and upon default the comptroller was authorized to sell the road and its appurtenances at public auction to the highest bidder. The Auburn and Rochester was required to create by annual payments sinking funds with which to redeem the certificates, such funds to be in the custody of the comptroller. The Schenectady and Troy was required to deposit as additional security bonds of the City of Troy to an amount equal to the certificates delivered.

The payment of these certificates, principal and interest, was assumed by the New York Central in the fifth article of the consolidation agreement, and such payment was punctually made by it at maturity. The state in no case advanced or paid one dollar in cash.

STOCK IN OTHER RAILROADS

The vast importance to the central line of roads of connections at Buffalo and the Niagara river in order to obtain at least a due proportion of the great traffic, both passenger and freight, from and to the rapidly growing west was, from the opening of the entire line from Albany to Buffalo, clearly apparent to and understood by the management of all the roads constituting that line. It was useless to consider such freight traffic so long as the Acts of 1844 and 1847, and imposing canal tolls remained in force, and without reasonable prospect of repeal. The abolition of these tolls by the legislature of 1851, left the railroads in a position to actively engage in the development of such connections which took practical form by investment in the capital stocks of the Buffalo and State Line Railroad Company and the Great Western Railroad Company, Canada West. The Buffalo and State Line was the road running from Buffalo to Dunkirk and thence to the state line of Pennsylvania, and afterwards became the eastern end of the Lake Shore and Michigan Southern. The Great Western of Canada was projected to be constructed from Windsor on the Detroit river opposite Detroit to the Suspension Bridge at Niagara Falls, a distance of 277.89 miles. At Detroit it formed a connection with the Michigan Central subject to ferriage across the Detroit river. The estimated cost of the road was $5,000,000. The authorized stock was $6,000,000. Subscriptions to the stock in Canada were obtainable to only about $1,650,000. The Canadian government agreed to guarantee the interest for an indefinite period upon bonds bearing 6 per cent interest for one-half the cost of the road, and the company was hopeful of obtaining a government guaranty of the principal. It, therefore, was essential to obtain aid elsewhere to the extent of $1,000,000, and an effort was made to get this from railroads in the United States, which would have business connections with the Great Western. To enable this to be done an act was obtained from the legislature of New York, April 12, 1851, authorizing any railroad corporation in the state of New York with the consent of stockholders holding two-thirds in amount of its capital stock to loan its credit or to subscribe to the stock of the Great Western in like

manner and with like right as individuals, not exceeding, however, five per cent of the capital of any corporation so subscribing to such stock, provided that
the eastern terminus of the Great Western should
be at some point on the Niagara river.

A preliminary convention of friends of the Great
Western was held at Niagara Falls, May 5 and 6, 1851,
and a committee was appointed to procure sub-
scriptions. Among that committee were Henry B.
Gibson, president of the Rochester and Syracuse, John
Wilkinson, president of the Syracuse and Utica,
Erastus Corning, president of the Utica and Schenec-
tady, and John T. Norton, president of the Albany and
Schenectady; also John M. Forbes and others of Bos-
ton, largely interested in the Michigan Central, Zachariah
Chandler, Henry Ledyard and others of Detroit.

A report was prepared by a sub-committee of this
committee, printed and extensively circulated, which
gave all the material facts relative to the Great Western
and also an estimate of its probable financial returns,
based on the results which had been achieved on the
Michigan Central. Competing distances were set out
in detail. The result of the committee's examination
is summed up in their concluding sentence.

An examination of the map will show the character this great
route (Chicago to the seaboard) must maintain when the last link
is completed and also how deeply interested are the rest of the
roads in the chain in its speedy completion. This done and no
line of roads can be built from New York or New England to the
valley of the Mississippi whose line will be so short or straight
with such easy grades, or so well adapted in any particular to the
carrying trade between the Atlantic and the growing millions of
the North West.

The central line of roads in New York, however,
took no action until after the bill abolishing the canal

companies to secure business and assist in creating a great through line from the Mississippi valley to the seaboard and the care taken by them to protect their investment so far as that could be done.

Some of the companies took stock in the Buffalo and State Line as follows: Syracuse and Utica, $63,200; Rochester and Syracuse, $105,500; Buffalo and Rochester, $94,500. This stock was also taken over by the Central at the consolidation.

When one reflects upon the burdens these companies had borne in retracking their roads, the Buffalo and Rochester in building the new line from Batavia, the Rochester and Syracuse in then building the direct line between Rochester and Syracuse, and the Rochester, Lockport and Niagara Falls just then completing its road, he will begin to appreciate the enterprise they showed and the risks they were willing to take in developing a larger and better system of transportation.

BRIDGES

Little or no information has come down to us regarding the early bridges. An examining committee appointed by the Board of Directors of the Central in 1859, made an elaborate and valuable report of their proceedings in which they say:

"Among the several railroad corporations consolidated into the New York Central but little regard was paid to system or uniformity in the construction of bridges. Each company erected such structures as it deemed best adapted to its peculiar circumstances. The result has been the bridges, as a whole, proved very defective and but poorly calculated, without large annual expenditure, to withstand the heavy traffic and high speed to which they have been subjected.

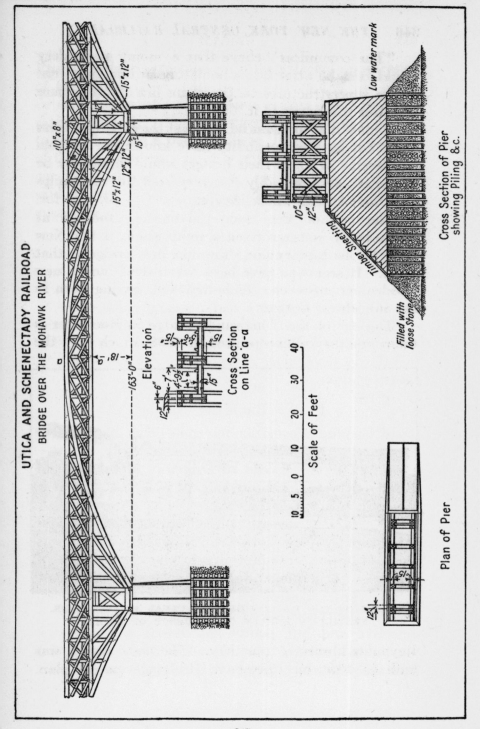

UTICA AND SCHENECTADY RAILROAD
BRIDGE OVER THE MOHAWK RIVER

Low water mark

Cross Section of Pier
showing Piling &c.

Filled with loose Stone

Timber Sheeting

10"x8"

15"x12"

15"x12"

12"x12"

15"

81'-0"

163'-0"

Elevation

Cross Section
on Line 'a-a'

12"   6"

4'-9½"   7"

4'-2"

15"

15"

Scale of Feet

10 5 0   10   20   30   40

Plan of Pier

12"

15"

CHAPTER XVII

THE CONSOLIDATION

IN the year 1853, the railroads between Albany and Troy on the east, and Buffalo and Niagara Falls on the west, by consolidating, created The New York Central Railroad Company. From a very early date each road as it was constructed was regarded both by its promoters and the public generally as part of a through line from Albany to Buffalo. As has been shown in the various reports, each road was constructed in such manner as to fit it for use with other roads in the line. Together they were commonly known as the central line. Upon the completion of the Attica and Buffalo in December, 1842, and before the union at Rochester of the two roads entering that city, arrangements were speedily made for through operation of trains with but the one transfer at Rochester. Conventions of presidents, directors and managers or superintendents, were frequently held to agree upon tariffs, time tables and other details of operation. Agreements were made and carried out for the stocking of cars which have elsewhere been described. The evils of separate management were acutely felt. The Auburn and Rochester and the Auburn and Syracuse were in consequence consolidated in 1850, as were the Tonawanda and the Attica and Buffalo. As early as June, 1842, the Mohawk and Hudson and the Utica and Schenectady were in active negotiation for a common operation of both roads and although they failed to reach a satisfactory basis of agreement, the question came up again and again in the deliberations of the board of directors of the Mohawk and Hudson.

The subject of a general consolidation must have been informally discussed by others who were interested officially in railroad affairs.

The minutes of the directors of the Utica and Schenectady for October 7, 1847, contain the following: "A letter was read from the Rail Road Committee of the Senate on the subject of consolidating the lines of Rail Roads from Albany to Buffalo. The subject was discussed and it was referred to the President to answer the said letter."

Neither the letter nor the answer has been found and nothing appears to have come of the suggestion, whatever it was, but we know from this entry that the thought of consolidation was in the minds of legislators and discussion was taking place.

In a convention of all the companies held at Albany, February 12, 1851, the following resolution was adopted and apparently unanimously: "On motion of Mr. Corning, Resolved, that a Committee consisting of the Presidents of each Company on the main line between Albany and Buffalo, be appointed to make application at the present session of the Legislature for a law authorizing any two or more Companies on this Line to consolidate their stock and become one Company if the stockholders representing in value two-thirds of the value of stock of any such companies shall elect to do so." This was two years prior to the passage of the consolidation act of 1853. When that act was finally passed April 2, 1853, the several companies were thoroughly prepared to act, met in a convention with the leading men of each composing

the delegates in less than two weeks and the question
debated was not to consolidate or not to consolidate,
but the terms on which the consolidation was to be
made. Such unanimity of feeling on the main question
could not have been the result of a sudden springing of
the plan, but it must have been the consequence of long
experience and much reflection. The two consolidations in 1850, of the roads west of Syracuse had been in
effect over two years and their practical working was
known to all.

The action of the stockholders is significant. The
number in each of the companies at the date of consolidation was as follows:

Albany and Schenectady	277
Schenectady and Troy (nominally)	1
Utica and Schenectady	687
Syracuse and Utica	424
Rochester and Syracuse	947
Buffalo and Rochester	262
Rochester, Lockport and Niagara Falls	317
Buffalo and Lockport	36
Total	2,951

The Mohawk Valley and the Syracuse and Utica
Direct are omitted from this list as non-operating roads.
There were stockholders who owned stock in two or
more roads, so that the number of individuals entitled
to and receiving stock in the consolidated company was
2,445, scattered widely along the line of the road and
elsewhere. No individual or combination of individuals
held a controlling monetary influence. Such control
as there was arose wholly from the character and
standing of the men possessing it and the confidence
felt in their ability, judgment and integrity. The
unanimity in the action of this great number of stockholders can only mean they understood the reasons

underlying and the necessity for a closer union of the roads and a unified management coupled with greater financial ability to meet the pressing problems of the future.

The external conditions bearing upon the situation were these. The Boston and Worcester, the Western, and the Albany and West Stockbridge railroads, which later were consolidated in the Boston and Albany, were under one management, had been open to Greenbush opposite Albany since 1841, and afforded an opening to Boston for all the western traffic which could be secured and handled over the line. The Hudson River railroad was opened in 1851, and afforded a like route from Albany to New York City. The New York and Erie, now the Erie, had been completed and opened from New York to Dunkirk on Lake Erie and the line of the Buffalo and State Line, in 1851, thus making it a sharp competitor for the western traffic. The Pennsylvania and Baltimore and Ohio systems were bending all their energies to work into the western states and secure their growing and valuable business. The Buffalo and State Line and its western connections which were ultimately consolidated into the Lake Shore and Michigan Southern had just been opened, afforded a valuable connection at Buffalo for the west, which was, however, tapped at Dunkirk by the New York and Erie. The Great Western of Canada gave promise of making a connection at Suspension Bridge which would command traffic from the Michigan Central at Detroit.

In short the opportunities for a large and growing through traffic were great if the line could be put in condition to handle it despite the keen competition of roads lying to the south. The canal tolls had been abolished so that incubus was removed. The grades were favorable and superior to those of the competitors, thus affording an advantage in cost of operation. The paramount question was whether the roads constituting the central line were in a condition to enable it to handle and hold the through traffic which plainly lay within its power to obtain. They were not.

The facts supporting this statement are easily presentable. The New York Central, according to its reports to the state, in the first year of its operation ended September 30, 1854, expended in construction and new equipment, $3,862,845.16; in the second year ended September 30, 1855, $1,453,356.64; in the third year ended September 30, 1856, $2,425,661.45, a total of $7,741,843.25.

In a report dated December 4, 1855, the chief engineer of the road says:

On an examination of the line of the Road immediately after the consolidation, it was found that on large portions of it the iron was badly worn, many of the chairs were badly broken or none had originally been used and the ties and bridges needed very general renewal; with one or two exceptions the materials and supplies were also of the most limited extent. Since that time, very extensive repairs have been made. A large part of the Superstructure has been renewed and the whole line placed in the sound condition requisite for the transaction of the large business the Company is now doing. The stock of materials and supplies has been largely increased and (maintained at the present point) will be sufficient to meet the constant demand for the uses of the road.

This expenditure in three years time is conclusive evidence as to the necessity for remedying the condition reported by the chief engineer. In the estimate on which the consolidation was based as will be seen later, the committee took into consideration the fact that the road west of Syracuse had but a single track and estimated that $2,281,000 would be required to construct a second track.

Some of the details of these additions and betterments are important. From the first of May, 1853, from which time the real working of the consolidated road dates, to September 30, 1855, a period of two years and five months, locomotives were increased from 139 to 190; baggage cars from 48 to 62; passenger cars from 159 to 222; freight cars from 1028 to 1852. Some retirements were made from the old stock, locomotives 2, passenger cars 13, freight cars 3.

Buildings. At Albany a brick freight house, 180 feet long, two stories high, and an 18 stall brick engine house. At West Albany extensive yard tracks, and cattle pens, three car houses for passenger cars each 335 feet long of brick with slate roofs. At Schenectady a large freight house. At Utica an addition to the engine house equivalent to room for 12 locomotives. At Syracuse an enlargement to the tunnel under the canal so as to permit two tracks, a second track through the city and enlarged freight accommodations. At Auburn, new engine house and shops. At Rochester a new brick freight house 300 feet long, a new engine house of brick, capable of holding 20 engines, addition to the blacksmith shop 100 feet in length, an addition to the machine shop 150 feet in length, a boiler shop, new bridges over Genesee river, Brown's mill race and under St. Paul Street. Previous to the rebuilding, there was but one track for most of the distance across these bridges, rebuilt with three tracks; the passenger depot was also completed. At Batavia, a new brick passenger station, the one now in use there. At Buffalo a large and commodious freight house 600 feet in length and 170 feet in width, fronting on Buffalo harbor, in what is now the Ohio Street yard. The greater part of the land for this yard was purchased at an expense of $260,150. Its dimensions were, on the harbor 816 feet, on Ohio Street 898 feet, average depth 158 feet.   The acquisition of this yard and the erection of buildings and other additions diminished the freight operating expenses at this point about sixty-six per cent. At Suspension Bridge, a passenger station 150 feet in length, a freight house 300 feet in length, another freight house 900 feet long, accommodations for live stock greatly enlarged and improved.   At intermediate stations, 15 passenger stations, 7 freight houses, 13 water houses, and 12,850 feet of woodsheds.

Second tracking.   This had been greatly progressed but not wholly completed.   All the grading, masonry and bridging completed, except about 10 miles between Syracuse and Rochester, and 8 miles between Rochester and Byron.   The original Tonawanda right of way from Rochester to Batavia was not sufficiently wide for a second track and additional land had to be bought. Iron rails had been laid on 72¼ miles of second track. At West Albany 126 acres of land were bought for a yard at a cost of $31,500 and a contract made for 97 additional acres at the same price, $250 per acre.

Of the millions required for all this new work, it is well to note that the following sums were received pursuant to the consolidation agreement—

Mohawk Valley stock.................	$1,559,319.05
Syracuse and Utica direct, stock.......	589,793.96
Schenectady and Troy stock..........	162,500.00
Buffalo and Rochester stock..........	718,750.00
Total.......................	$3,030,363.01

That the strong and experienced business men who made up the directorates of the consolidating companies did not understand the situation requiring the great outlay here outlined and did not enter upon the consolidation as a means of bringing the central line up to the condition required to take care of the growing freight and other business, and thus meeting their duties to the public, must be regarded as surpassing rational belief.

That the individual roads operating separately could not meet the situation is certain. Only five years prior to the consolidation they had strained their resources and credit to the utmost in reconstructing their tracks with iron rail, an indispensable improvement, and now they faced the problem of replacing much of that rail which by reason of its softness had become badly worn. The roads west of Syracuse, having but a single track, required a double track. The Buffalo and Rochester could not be charged with the expense of the Ohio Street yard and freight house designed to care for through business in which all the roads would share, nor could the Albany and Schenectady finance the West Albany yards which were demanded for the benefit of the through business.

Above all that, through business, both passenger and freight, could not be handled as the public demanded by eight different operating roads under different management and superintendence. That experiment had been tried for ten years and had not worked to the satisfaction of either the public or the companies. It is a work of supererogation to discuss the merits of consolidation of small railroads into a larger system in the year 1926. Experience has demonstrated all the advantages and disadvantages during over seventy years, until the public, once suspicious and distrustful, is insisting on forced consolidations, if voluntary ones are not forthcoming. The railroad men of 1853, out of hard earned and costly experience had learned the necessity of union, precisely as the states of 1787, out of a like hard experience had been taught the necessity of a better political union.

The situation, then, in 1853, which confronted the management of the existing roads was a rapidly growing business with every prospect of an indefinite future expansion, facilities inadequate to meet such growth, a practical impossibility for the separate roads to finance the additions and betterments required to meet their public duties, inability of the terminal roads at Albany and Buffalo to provide adequate terminal facilities and yet compelled to prorate earnings from through business mostly on a mileage basis and above all, operation carried on by eight separate roads each under its own management, with its own standards of discipline, repairs and maintenance.

Unification was an economic necessity required by economic causes. It was not a device invented by any one for ulterior purposes. Its consideration was forced by pressing needs which had impressed themselves upon the minds of all dealing with the subject. The total absence of all discussion as to the desirability and the necessity of a union conclusively proves that all were agreed upon that. When the time for action arrived, the only point debated was how the union could be made, upon what terms the several roads should unite their properties, what representation in the new company the stockholders of the existing companies were to receive.

In 1853, there was no general law in the state of New York authorizing the consolidation of railroad corporations. A special act, Chapter 76 of the laws of 1853, was passed by the legislature and became a law April 2. Section 1, authorized the Albany and Schenectady, Schenectady and Troy, Utica and Schenectady,

Syracuse and Utica, Rochester and Syracuse, Buffalo
and Lockport, Mohawk Valley, Syracuse and Utica
direct, Buffalo and Rochester, Rochester, Lockport
and Niagara Falls Railroad Companies or any two or
more of them at any time to consolidate into a single
corporation in the manner following. The directors
of two or more of said companies might enter into an
agreement under their respective corporate seals for the
consolidation of the said corporations, prescribing the
terms and conditions thereof, the mode of carrying the
same into effect, the name of the new corporation, the
number of directors thereof, which should not be less
than thirteen nor more than twenty-three, the time
and place of holding the first meeting of directors, the
amount of capital and the number of shares of the stock
of the new corporation which should not be larger in
amount than the aggregate amount of capital of the
several companies thus consolidated and should not be
increased except in accordance with the general railroad
law, the manner of converting the shares of capital stock
of each of said corporations into the shares of the new
corporation, the manner of paying any shareholder that
might decline taking shares in the new corporation with
such other details as might be deemed necessary.
Such agreement was not to be deemed the agreement of
the corporations until after it had been submitted to
the stockholders of each corporation separately at a
meeting to be called upon a notice of at least thirty
days, specifying the time and place of such meeting
and the object thereof, to be addressed to each of the
stockholders when the place of residence was known and
deposited in the post office and published for at least
three successive weeks in the state paper and in one of
the newspapers printed in each of the counties through
or into which the railroad of the said corporation should

extend, and had been sanctioned and approved by such stockholders by the vote of at least two-thirds in amount of the stockholders present at such meetings respectively, voting by ballot, either in person or by proxy, each share being entitled to one vote. When the agreement had been so sanctioned and approved it should be deemed the agreement of the several corporations.

Section 2, provided that a duplicate of the agreement should be filed in the office of the Secretary of State and that immediately after the first election of directors the corporations should be merged into the new corporation.

Section 3, prescribed the general powers of the new corporation to be those expressed in certain provisions of the Revised Statutes and the general railroad law of 1850.

Section 4, provided that all the property of the old corporations should vest in the new corporation without any other deed or transfer and that the title to real estate should not be deemed to revert or be impaired by the consolidation.

Section 5, provided that the rights of creditors should not be impaired and that the new corporation should be liable for all the debts and liabilities of the consolidating corporations.

Section 6, prescribed the method of appraising the stock of any stockholder who should at the meeting or within twenty days thereafter object to the consolidation and demand payment for his stock.

Section 7, is here transcribed in full:

When any two or more of the railroad companies named in this act are so consolidated, said consolidated company shall carry way passengers on their road at a rate not to exceed two cents per mile.

Section 8, provided that the act should take effect immediately.

The directors of all the companies named in the consolidation act were eager and ready to avail themselves of its provisions. The Albany and Schenectady appointed a committee to represent it April 4th, two days after the law took effect. The only business of the meeting was to pass the following resolution, "Resolved, that a committee consisting of E. C. McIntosh, R. H. Winslow, Thos. Tileston and H. Pumpelly be appointed with full power to represent this Company, to act and conclude an arrangement for consolidation of the stock and interests of this Company in accordance with an Act of the Legislature of the state of New York passed March, 1853."

We may easily infer this resolution was drawn after the bill had passed both houses of the legislature, but before the act became a law, since the date of its passage is left blank, but named as being in March. Laws are identified as having passed on the date they became a law. We should note also that the committee was given full power to make and conclude an agreement without being required to refer a proposed agreement back to the Board for approval. The same power was conferred upon its committee by every other company except the Syracuse and Utica. Evidently there was great desire to have the business done and done speedily.

The minutes of the Utica and Schenectady show that the Secretary on April 5th, laid before the Board a certified copy of the act and that, "The President stated that he had been informed that several of the companies named in the Act had already appointed Committees on this subject." Whereupon the Board appointed a committee of four and because any agreement must be approved by the stockholders before it could take effect, resolved, "that the said Committee have full power on the part of this Company to enter into any agreement for such consolidation which they may deem proper."

A meeting of the committees was called merely by suggestion. John V. L. Pruyn, secretary of the Utica and Schenectady on the same day, April 5th, sent a letter to each of the other companies advising that his company had appointed a committee for the purpose of the act and continued, "and it was agreed to recommend to the several Companies that the Committees appointed by them on this subject should meet at Syracuse on *Tuesday next*, the 12th instant, at Four o'clock in the afternoon."

The committees met at the time and place specified. No delays were to be tolerated. Preliminary conferences were not thought of. Action, prompt action, was the order of the day.

The meeting was called to order by Erastus Corning, president of the Utica and Schenectady, and on his motion Henry B. Gibson, president of the Rochester and Syracuse was made chairman. John V. L. Pruyn was appointed secretary. Twenty-eight delegates were present representing the several companies as follows:

Albany and Schenectady—
Ezekiel C. McIntosh —President
Thomas Tileston   —Director
R. H. Winslow   —Director
H. Pumpelly   —Director

Utica and Schenectady—
Erastus Corning   —President
Marcus T. Reynolds   —Director
Alonzo C. Paige   —Director
John V. L. Pruyn   —Secretary
Chauncey Vibbard   —Superintendent

These delegates also represented the Mohawk Valley.

Syracuse and Utica—
John Wilkinson	—President
Charles Stebbins	—Director
David Wager	—Director
Joel Rathbone	—Director
John Stryker	—Director

These delegates also represented the Syracuse and Utica direct.

Rochester and Syracuse—
Henry B. Gibson	—President
John H. Chedell	—Director
Horace White	—Director
Charles Seymour	—Director

Buffalo and Rochester—
Joseph Field	—President
Dean Richmond	—Director
D. W. Tomlinson	—Director
Asa Sprague	—Director

Rochester, Lockport and Niagara Falls—
J. B. Varnum	—President
A. Boody	—Director
E. B. Holmes	—Director

Buffalo and Lockport—
| Isaac C. Colton | —President |
| J. B. Plumb | —Director |

Schenectady and Troy—
| Russell Sage | —President |

All the committees present had full power to enter into an agreement for consolidation except that from the Syracuse and Utica, which was to report to the full Board then in session in the same city. Each committee reported the capital stock and funded debt of its road and then the following resolution was adopted:

Resolved: That sub-committee be appointed of one from each road to report a plan of consolidation for the consideration of this meeting, and that each Company name its own member of the said Committee.

The following were then named by their respective companies as members of the committee:

Albany and Schenectady	—Mr. McIntosh
Utica and Schenectady	—Mr. Corning
Mohawk Valley	—Mr. Pruyn
Syracuse and Utica	—Mr. Stebbins
Syracuse and Utica Direct	—Mr. Wilkinson
Rochester and Syracuse	—Mr. Chedell
Buffalo and Rochester	—Mr. Richmond
Rochester, Lockport and Niagara Falls	—Mr. Boody
Buffalo and Lockport	—Mr. Plumb
Schenectady and Troy	—Mr. Sage

The meeting then took a recess until 8 P.M. to enable the sub-committee to enter upon its duties.

We may at this point observe that there was an entire lack of discussion as to whether a consolidation was advisable. Every company was committed to that. The only matter open for discussion was on what terms the consolidations could be made. Upon this point it is well to consider somewhat carefully what the problem was with which the committee was to struggle.

Here were ten companies agreed that it was desirable from every point of view to throw all their property into one common ownership. An inescapable condition of such common ownership was that, except dissenters under §6 of the consolidation act each stockholder of each company must surrender his stock and ownership in an existing company and accept in lieu thereof stock in the new company. There were over twenty-four hundred such stockholders. Without the assent of two-thirds in amount of the number present at the ratification meeting no consolidation was possible. It could not be assumed that any stockholder would assent unless he believed he was getting a just equivalent in the company for what he surrendered in the old. If his stock were worth any given sum, say $10,000, he must be made reasonably sure he would get a representation stock worth an equal amount, or else he would know injustice was done him. Accordingly he must be assured he was not getting less than his proper due and also that no one was getting more than his proper share. If the stocks of all these companies had been of equal value and that value was par, the question would have presented no difficulty. One share of the stock in the new company would have been of the value of one share in any one of the old companies. But the shares of the old companies were not of equal value. They did not sell for the same in the market; they did not command the same in dividends; they had not been alike profitable in the past, and the future under the separate managements did not give promise they would ever be of like value. It was not the old companies which were to take the stock of the new company. It was their stockholders and the commonest principles of equity demanded that they should all be treated justly, no one getting either more or less than that to which he was justly entitled. Issuing of stock share for share was absolutely out of the question and as the event proved was so regarded by everyone. It followed that the committee's task consisted in devising some scheme by which each stockholder would get his just proportion in the new company without exchange of share for share. The consolidation act declared that the capital stock of the new company should not exceed the aggregate amount of the capital stock of the old companies and thus in practical effect restricted the number of shares which could be issued by the new company.

All these considerations show that the paramount question to be solved by the committee was how much value was being put into the common pool by each of the consolidating companies, for upon the value of the property of any given company depended the value of a share of its stock. So the primary question was value.

Now at that time economic thought had been developed only to the point where people knew what they meant by value. The idea of value so ineffable that it could not be defined, that the process of ascertaining it was so mysterious and indefinable that it could not be explained, was then wholly unknown. That conception of value, if so it may be termed, did not arise until sixty years later. Whether it will be found practical and workable in present day consolidations, either voluntary or forced, remains to be seen. But surely we must interpret the transactions of seventy years ago by the dim light of those who believed the value of their property was what they could sell it for, or found from the size of the return it yielded them.

While this point is fresh in mind, it is impossible not to wonder what will be the view of one who owns a block of railroad stock which yields him a six per cent return, when he is asked or commanded to put it in on parity with the stock of another which has never yielded and does not now yield any return whatever. Will he or will he not feel that getting, say a three per cent return instead of six, savors very strongly of confiscation, and will he or will he not instruct his lawyer to inquire what remedy he has?

We have pointed out that the sub-committee did not have a free hand, although sent out by the meeting without instructions. They were compelled to meet and deal with certain insurmountable restrictions and limitations. They were forced into a narrow path and if they stumbled therein, their work would be in vain. Unless the situation in which they were placed is thoroughly understood and appreciated, no just judgment can be passed upon the fruit of their labors.

The committee, composed of the ablest and most experienced men in the convention, struggled long and earnestly with the problem before them. They were not able to report until 4:30 P.M. of the 13th. Then Mr. Corning as chairman of the committee submitted a verbal report accompanied by a statement of the amounts proposed to be allowed on consolidation to the respective companies which had been agreed to by all the companies except the Syracuse and Utica and the Rochester and Syracuse, the former claiming an allowance of 55 per cent premium on their stock instead of 45 proposed to be allowed them; the latter claiming 35 per cent premium instead of 30 per cent to be allowed them.

After consultation with his associates, Mr. Gibson, on behalf of the Rochester and Syracuse, announced they would accede to the report. The convention thereupon passed the following resolution:

Resolved; That all the companies heretofore named (except the Syracuse and Utica Company which has declined acceding to the terms proposed) do hereby agree to consolidate their respective companies into one corporation under the Act of the Legislature aforesaid on the general principles reported by the Committee. The value of the Troy and Schenectady road to be determined hereafter in a manner satisfactory to both parties or otherwise the said road not to be included in the consolidation.

Mr. Stryker, then on behalf of the Syracuse and Utica, stated that that company would consent to come into the consolidation provided the premium to be allowed on its stock be increased from 45 to 50 per cent. After considering the same, and Mr. Gibson, the chairman, having, on behalf of the Rochester and Syracuse Company, expressed the wish that the proposition be accepted, the same was adopted and it was resolved that the Syracuse and Utica be admitted into the consolidated company.

It was then resolved that a committee be appointed, one from each company, to prepare for execution the draft of proposed Articles of Agreement, for the consideration of the several companies, and to do all things requisite so far as may be in their power to perfect the consolidation and to decide upon all matters in regard thereto, until the same shall have been finally completed by the election of directors of the new corporation, that four members of the committee regularly convened should be a quorum and that each company name its own member. It was further resolved that the said committee have power to decide upon the terms on which the Schenectady and Troy should be admitted into the consolidation.

The minutes of the convention at this point contain the following:

Mr. Corning moved, which was seconded by Mr. Wilkinson, that the valuation of each road as already agreed upon be reduced ten per cent. Objections were made from several quarters and as the modification proposed required at this time the unanimous consent of all the parties no question was taken upon the motion.

The following is the statement of amounts proposed to be allowed, which was reported by the committee. The first line of figures after the name of each company is the amount of its capital stock outstanding, the second the premium proposed to be allowed thereon:

Albany and Schenectady......	$1,624,865.	
17%......................	276,227.05	
Debt.....................	136,700.	$ 2,037,792.05
Utica and Schenectady and Mohawk Valley............	6,075,000.	
55%......................	3,341,250.	9,416,250.00
Syracuse and Utica and Straight Line with proposed addition of $300,000................	3,300,000.	
45%......................	1,485,000.	
Debt.....................	126,000.	4,911,000.00
Schenectady and Troy........	520,000.	
Debt.....................	100,000.	620,000.00
To be expended (estimated)....		500,000.00
East of Syracuse..............		$17,485,042.05
Rochester and Syracuse.......	$5,605,700.	
30%......................	1,681,710.	
Debt.....................	759,000.	$ 8,046,410.00
Buffalo and Rochester.........	$2,281,000.	
Stock to be issued and paid for at par.............	719,000.	
40%......................	1,200,000.	
Debt.....................	177,000.	4,377,000.00
Rochester, Lockport and Niagara Falls..................	2,093,600.	
25%......................	523,400.	
Debt.....................	476,000.	3,093,000.00
Buffalo and Lockport..........	675,000.	
25%......................	168,750.	843,750.00
		$16,360,160.00
Add for double tracks (estimated)..................		2,281,000.00
West of Syracuse.......		$18,641,160.00

The foregoing is a complete report of the proceedings of the convention, except that the minutes were read and approved.

It is well at this point to consider just what was done and what was not done at this convention. First; it was determined to consolidate, but upon this there was absolute unanimity at the outset, dependent only upon the terms which could be arranged. Second; a committee was appointed to report upon those terms and the only subject it reported upon was the valuation to be given to each road in forming the union. It was this question which engaged the labors of the committee. Upon this question two companies dissented from the report as to the value assigned their own roads, but raised no objection to the value given any other road. One of these companies accepted the report. As to the other, a compromise was made by general concurrence. Third; the Utica and Schenectady and the Mohawk Valley were treated as one, and the same treatment was extended to the Syracuse and Utica and the Syracuse and Utica Direct, without the slightest objection from any one. It would seem to be incredible that in a struggle for a just and acceptable relative valuation, there should have been no objection to premiums on their stock unless there was something in the situation which rendered it equitable as between the companies themselves. Each company was actively endeavoring to obtain for itself a just relative valuation as is shown by the objections to the report. A premium of 55 and 50 per cent respectively to these companies without roads would have been unthinkable under these circumstances unless there was something in their treatment in connection with that accorded to their principals which rendered it acceptable as between the companies themselves. What this something was is clearly a matter to be investigated. Fourth; that we have not erred in considering the report of the committee as a matter of valuation is shown by the consolidation resolution which expressly says, "The *value* of the Troy and Schenectady road to be determined hereafter" &c., and by the motion of Mr. Corning seconded by Mr. Wilkinson "that the *valuation* of each road as already agreed upon be reduced ten per cent."

A further point to note at this time to be developed later is that in taking the value of the roads as the basis of consolidation and not the cost or the capital stock and funded debt, they set an example which is now followed by every court and commission in the country and forms the basis upon which the United States government and the railroad companies of the country must justify themselves for an expenditure of upwards of one hundred millions of dollars in the past thirteen years. Their method of ascertaining value may not have been the same as that now chiefly used, but it certainly accorded with that favored and used by the business world then and now.

We may note further that when this question of value was settled satisfactorily, nothing further engaged the attention of the convention except to provide the machinery for working out the details of the consolidation, giving to the committee appointed full power to settle every question. We must next, therefore, follow the transactions of that committee.

It met the evening of the 13th and consisted of Messrs. McIntosh, Corning, Wilkinson, Chedell, Field, Sage, Plumb, Stebbins, Boody and Pruyn, each with the exception of Chedell and Boody being the president of the company he represented. Mr. Corning was appointed chairman and Mr. Pruyn secretary. The committee then adopted four resolutions and adjourned to meet at Albany the 4th day of May at 7 P.M. The resolutions follow in full:

Resolved; that a circular be addressed to each Company requesting them to close their books on the evening of the 30th day of April, instant, and thereafter to keep all their accounts separate from previous transactions, to the end that when the consolidation shall take place it may take effect from and after the said 30th day of April: and also requesting each Company without delay after that date to furnish this Committee with a particular and detailed statement of its property which will pass to the consolidated Company as the same may exist on that day and of all liabilities, direct and contingent, on the day above mentioned.

Resolved; that it be provided in the agreement for consolidation that the consolidated Company purchase the stocks in the Great Western Rail Road Company, Canada West, and in the Buffalo and State Line Rail Road Company, held by any of the present Companies, the former at par and interest at 6 per cent from 1st January last and the latter at its market value at this time to be ascertained hereafter and that the consolidated Company pay for said stock in its bonds at such time and rate of interest as shall hereafter be agreed upon.

"Resolved; that Mr. Pruyn be requested to prepare the draft of the agreement of consolidation to be submitted to this Committee."

"Resolved; that the Chairman be authorized to call meetings of this Committee at such time as he may deem proper."

The committee met pursuant to adjournment at the office of Mr. Pruyn in Albany on the 4th day of May and continued in session that and the two subsequent days. Mr. E. D. Morgan, five years later elected Governor of the state, appeared as substitute for Mr. Sage and there was also in attendance the whole or part of the time the following persons, directors, or officers of the old roads; Dean Richmond, R. H. Winslow, G. H. Mumford, Horace White, J. W. Drummond, E. Foster, Jr., A. C. Paige, Chauncey Vibbard, J. Rathbone and M. T. Reynolds.

The first evening Mr. Pruyn submitted a draft of the articles of association which was discussed at

length. May 5, at 9 A.M., the committee met and
further discussed the draft prepared by Mr. Pruyn and
made some amendments thereto. The number of
directors was after discussion fixed at thirteen. The
statements of the affairs of the companies requested
at the April meeting were taken up and discussed in
detail. At 2 o'clock P.M., the committee took a recess
for an hour and a half. At 3.30 it met and discussed
the agreement with great particularity until 6 when it
took another recess until 7.30 at which hour it again
convened, and discussed certain car accounts and claims
presented by the Albany and Schenectady. Having
disposed of these, they resumed examination of the
agreement and at 10 P.M. adjourned until 9 the next
morning. At the appointed hour on the 6th, they
resumed examination of the agreement, continued
thereon until 2 P.M. and then took a recess until 3.30,
at which hour they again met, appointed a committee
to procure certificates for the premium allowances, a
committee to accept options for land purchased by the
Mohawk Valley Company, a committee to reduce the
fare of western through passengers, a committee to
negotiate with certain other companies in western New
York on matters not specified in the minutes and finally
completed the examination of the agreement, having
settled all the questions arising in regard to it. Mr.
Pruyn and Mr. Paige were requested to revise the
agreement as finally settled and to have the same
printed without delay. The 17th of May was fixed
upon as the time for signing the agreement, the companies east of Utica to meet at Albany in the morning
and those west of Utica at Syracuse in the afternoon.
The stockholders' meetings to pass on the agreement
were appointed to be held June 29, at such place as
each company might appoint.

On the 17th of May the directors of the several companies met at the cities specified and duly executed the articles of agreement as prepared by Mr. Pruyn and revised by the committee.

The committee also met informally at Syracuse May 17, and transacted some routine administrative business. Among other things Mr. Corning and Mr. McIntosh were authorized to construct an additional freight depot at Albany and Mr. Corning and Mr. Wilkinson were authorized to contract for ten baggage cars. They met again at Buffalo June 8, appointed a committee to inquire into the propriety of extending the passenger and freight depot grounds in Buffalo and to make preliminary negotiations for the lands required for those purposes. Messrs. Corning and McIntosh were appointed a committee to purchase such additional lands at Albany as were in their judgment needed for the purposes of the company. Some other administrative business was transacted.

The stockholders of the several companies duly approved the consolidation agreement. A meeting for the election of directors was held at Albany, July 6, at which the following named were elected:

Erastus Corning	
John V. L. Pruyn	} of Albany
Ezekiel C. McIntosh	
Russell Sage	of Troy
Alonzo C. Paige	of Schenectady
David Wager	of Utica
John Wilkinson	} of Syracuse
Horace White	
John H. Chedell	of Auburn
Henry B. Gibson	of Canandaigua

Joseph Field
Azariah Boody $\Big\}$ of Rochester

Dean Richmond of Buffalo

These persons met at Albany, July 7, and organized by the election of Erastus Corning, as president, Dean Richmond, as vice president, and John V. L. Pruyn, as secretary and treasurer.

Among the resolutions adopted was the following:

Resolved; that the Executive Committee be authorized to take measures for laying a double track on the direct line of road from Syracuse to Buffalo as soon as the same can in their judgment be most advantageously accomplished and to adopt all such measures as they may on examination deem necessary to put the entire line of road from Hudson's River to Lake Erie with its rolling stock and machinery in the very best condition.

A duplicate of the consolidation agreement was the same day filed in the office of the Secretary of State and thus on July 7, 1853, The New York Central Railroad Company came into existence.

In a memorandum made by Mr. Pruyn shortly after the election of directors is preserved a record of some interesting inside information concerning the same. He says,

The new Company (the New York Central) elected its first directors on the 6th of July, 1853. The occasion was one of great interest as the consolidation with its attendant circumstances had largely attracted public attention and was the subject of much comment. Mr. Corning held a large majority of the proxies. The Board he elected lived entirely on the line. I was in favor of taking one director from New York and one from Boston and Mr. Corning had almost down to the last determined to take this course but some of the gentlemen on the line, and particularly Mr. Gibson, urged him strenuously not to do it and he, reluctantly I think, yielded. Mr. Varnum of New York, who had been prominently spoken of as one of the new Board, he informed me had assented to this course.

This memorandum also contains other matter well worth preserving:

I was very laboriously occupied during this spring and summer in the proceedings consequent upon perfecting the Consolidation of the Rail Roads, and the formation of the New York Central Rail Road Company. The labor of drafting the Consolidation agreement devolved upon me, which as it probably involved a larger amount of property than had ever formed the subject of an agreement in our State, was one of great responsibility. I had the draft printed and it was revised by Judge Paige who acted as Counsel, and I also sent it to the different gentlemen who had attended the meetings at my office to settle upon the detail of its provisions, (and some others interested) that they might examine it and make such suggestions as they thought proper before it was engrossed. These gentlemen were Mr. Corning, Mr. M. T. Reynolds, Mr. Gibson, Mr. Richmond, Mr. Wilkinson, Mr. McIntosh, Mr. Plumb, Mr. Winslow, Mr. Morgan of New York and several others.

The question as to the number of Directors was one considerably discussed. Mr. Reynolds took strong ground against more than 13. I advocated a larger number in order properly to represent the different interests—18 I thought would have been better. The smallest number was agreed to. When the agreement was drawn, I kept this clause open, and might have had it altered at the last moment, but Mr. Reynolds objected in the Utica and Schenectady Board to leave the matter open, and we had to close it at the number agreed upon. The sinking fund provided for by the agreement to meet the (nearly) nine millions of dollars of debt certificates was a provision which I thought prudent to meet so large a debt. I believe that this was entirely my suggestion, and it will form a marked feature in the future history of the road. The principle of providing gradually for the extinguishment of the debts of Rail Road Companies is a very important one, and as long as reduction is going on, although very slowly, the Company is benefited and public confidence increased. The fund is based on the calculation that $1\frac{1}{4}$ per cent per annum (its amount) will in 30 years, (at the end of which time the certificates mature,) with accumulated annual interest at *six* per cent, amount to the total of the debt—a result which if proper attention be paid to the matter I think there will be no difficulty in securing.

I was elected Treasurer and Secretary of the new Board. I said to Mr. Corning that I did not wish the appointment as it might interfere seriously with my professional business. The Company needed the services of a lawyer, and one of some experience in the affairs of the line, such as I had acquired while acting as Treasurer of the Utica and Schenectady Rail Road Company, as its organization, the issuing of new stock certificates, etc., etc., would bring up many legal questions. I of course was not with the Board when the question was discussed, but was called upon by Mr. Gibson and Mr. Paige as a Committee and requested to take the office. The question of salary was of course raised. I said that if it took me out of my profession I would not take less than Ten Thousand Dollars per annum, but I wished to retain my hold on my profession and to go occasionally into Court, and if I could do this, would accept Eight Thousand Dollars per annum. I do not wish to give up my profession and therefore only go into this long enough to organize it thoroughly, and see it well started in its operations at least in my department.

Having fully traced out what was done in effecting the consolidation we are now ready to consider upon what basis or bases it was done. It is essential to all consolidations or union of property interests that the union proceed upon some settled principle which the parties believe will ensure to each interest a just and adequate proportion of the whole. Unless each party to the transaction believes this has been substantially secured to him, no voluntary agreement is possible. The more parties there are to the arrangement, the greater the difficulties to be overcome. In the case in hand ten corporations were endeavoring to throw their properties into a common pool and no one could feel sure it was getting its proper per cent of the total without having some definite knowledge as to how the total as stated in dollars was arrived at. If the interest of one party is overstated, it necessarily results in loss to one or all the others. Accordingly, each party, if it proceeds intelligently, must have or think it has, adequate knowledge of what each of the others is justly entitled to for what it brings into the common owner-ship. This necessitates some standard of judgment which applies to all the properties, since if a yard stick of one length is applied to one, and another of different length to another, there can be no test of their relative importance. If a carpenter were to attempt to build a house or a machinist a locomotive, using for some of the parts measurements according to the metric system and for others measurements according to our stand-ards of feet and inches, the result can be readily appre-ciated without any elucidation.

So the great problem at the Syracuse meeting was to agree upon and use some common basis of judgment which would give to the stockholders of each company a just and fair proportion of the securities to be issued by the new company for the property it received from all.

There were several bases theoretically possible; (1) purely arbitrary agreement; (2) cost of property; (3) its appraised value; (4) its earning power; (5) the mar-ket value of its stock and bonds.

As to the first it was literally out of the question. Two parties may do business in that manner, with ten it is practically impossible even if dealing with their own property. In this case the negotiators were merely trustees for thousands of others, the concurrence of two thirds of whom was necessary to give validity to any agreement entered into. The hard headed business men composing the convention could never have reached an agreement except upon a basis which they considered reasonable.

As to the other possible bases, it can not be overlooked that the real question involved was the value of the properties involved. Transfers of property and adjustments relating thereto depend for their terms upon value. Only one notion was entertained concerning value in 1853, and that was power in exchange, what it would command from a desirous purchaser. Hence appraised value would in those days be only an estimate of the extent of such power based upon such evidence as the appraiser considered material. An appraised value which does not take into consideration earning power when exchange value is to be ascertained would be ridiculous. So another test of present value of a corporation is the price its stock will command in the open market. It is obvious that the convention and its committee did not consider an appraisal on the basis of cost of reproduction new, for no such work was undertaken and it is believed cost of reproduction new in such a case was never thought of until some forty-five years later. The cost of a property may be an item to take into consideration, but no one can justly claim that it is determinative. Common experience teaches every one that some properties are worth less than cost, some more than cost.

The foregoing considerations have been sketched with the utmost brevity to call attention to the reasons why the convention through its committee adopted as the standard for measuring the amount of securities which should be issued by the new company for the property turned over to it, the value of the same according to the notion of value universally entertained in those days, and therefore necessarily awarded to each consolidating company the amount which in their judgment represented the fair value of the property it contributed to the new ownership. As things were viewed in those days, no other course was open to them and one may venture to remark the same is substantially true of consolidations to-day and will remain so for all time. If one will ask himself on what basis he would proceed if he were charged with the duty of negotiating such a deal there will be no dissent from this view.

Section 6, of the Consolidation Act has such important bearing on the fixing of the value of the several roads that an omission to notice it would be serious error. It provides that if any stockholder, at the meeting of stockholders, or within twenty days thereafter, shall object to the consolidation and demand payment for his stock, he or the new company may apply on reasonable notice to a special term of the Supreme Court for the appointment of three persons to appraise the value of his stock. The court shall appoint such appraisers who shall meet at the time and place designated by the court and they or any two of them after being duly sworn, shall estimate and certify the value of such stock at the time of the stockholder's dissent. The new company shall pay to the stockholder as directed by the court. Such appraised value and the stock may be held or disposed of by the new company.

Much of the stock of the old companies had a market price largely above par. It is inconceivable that the appraisers would or could have fixed the value of such stock at less than its market value. If they fixed it at say 150 of par value the company would have been obliged to pay $150 for a one hundred dollar share and for it but one share of the stock of the new company could have been issued. If any considerable number of those holding such stock had dissented it is easy to see the new company would have been swamped in the launching. This provision of the act made it compulsory by its practical possibilities, that the stockholders should not only vote in such numbers as to ratify the agreement but that those not so voting or consenting, should not in any substantial number avail themselves of section 6. The consolidation agreement must necessarily give every stockholder the fair value of his stock in some form or one of two things would be most likely to follow; either the stockholders' meeting would not ratify it or if it did a large minority would elect to take the appraised value of their stock with disastrous consequences to the new company.

This is a dilemma which confronts every voluntary consolidation and also every involuntary one unless legislative power is ample to compel a stockholder to surrender his stock for less than its value and become a member of a new corporation against his will.

There may be and doubtless are different ways of attacking the question, what constitutes the exchange value of a property. In arriving at a determination different persons will arrive at different results but unquestionably they will all rely upon earning power and in the case of a corporation the price its stock commands in the open market. These, of course, will be interpreted and modified by surrounding conditions and circumstances. In reaching a final agreement there will be necessarily give and take to some extent.

Just what the roads were valued at is easily ascertainable from the Consolidation Agreement. The new company is required by that to issue securities and assume indebtedness as follows:

Capital Stock, Article 3,.......	$23,085,600.00
Assumed indebtedness, Article 5,	1,956,475.85
Debt certificates, Article 14,..	8,857,091.00
Total.................	$33,899,166.85

It received for the above the following:

Cash
  Buffalo and Rochester....... $ 718,750.00
  Schenectady and Troy....... 162,500.00
  Mohawk Valley............. 1,559,319.05
  Syracuse and Utica Direct... 589,793.96 $ 3,030,363.01

Sinking Funds
  Buffalo and Rochester....... 24,348.46
  Rochester and Syracuse..... 71,652.23   96,000.69
Estimated value of roads...... 30,772,803.15

  Total.................... $33,899,166.85

The question presented is whether $30,772,803.15 was the fair and reasonable value of these properties in May, 1853. The earning power bearing upon this question is that the net income from operation of all the operating roads for the year ended September 30, 1852, was the sum of $2,260,696.50. This sum is equivalent to 7 per cent (the legal rate of interest at that time) upon $32,295,665. In reaching this result of net income, it should not be forgotten that the Buffalo and Lockport was only in construction and had no revenues; that the Rochester, Lockport and Niagara Falls was in operation only three months and its net was only $36,295.13 and that the Schenectady and Troy had a deficit of $5,990.02, which is deducted from the total of the other roads in computing the above net income.

The operating results for the year ended September 30, 1853, were not known at the time of the consolidation, but we presume the several companies knew what they had earned net up to April 1, 1853, during the six months then elapsed of the fiscal year and in any event the net for the entire fiscal year, is cogent evidence on the question of the earning power of the roads. That net income was $2,608,754.50, an increase of $348,058 over the previous year and is the equivalent of 7 per cent upon $37,267,921.

The Consolidation Agreement recites the difference in prices of stock of the various roads as a reason for issuing the debt certificates. Those prices, of course, varied from time to time in 1852, but the maximum quotations which have been found for that year are, Albany and Schenectady 112½; Utica and Schenectady 145; Syracuse and Utica 135; Rochester and Syracuse 125; Buffalo and Rochester 120; and Rochester, Lockport and Niagara Falls 107¾.

It is such evidence as the foregoing that the companies acted upon in reaching a value of $30,701,150 for all the roads and which made it seem just and equitable to over 2400 stockholders that they should have something tangible to represent that value beyond the $23,000,000 of stock. The abolition of canal tolls, effective December 1, 1851, had begun to show results in increasing freight business; the opening of western roads was beginning to show favorable results; the new company was planning to put the three millions to be received from the stock subscriptions into additions and betterments designed to take care of this growth, actual and anticipated. It did not expect to increase rates to meet additional interest or dividends and did not increase them.

Such was the point of view held by the persons directing and planning the consolidation.

The foregoing does not cover the cases of the Mohawk Valley and the Syracuse and Utica Direct. They had no roads to value; the stockholders were to pay only par for their stock, and in and of themselves they were not and could not be entitled to the debt certificates which were issued to them. It is but just and fair to explain as briefly as possible the reasons upon which that action was based.

Taking first the Mohawk Valley, in the sketch of

that road its relations to the Utica and Schenectady have been fully shown. It was practically a part of that road, its stockholders were mainly the stockholders of the Utica and Schenectady. In the convention at Syracuse the two companies were treated as one as is shown by the memorandum reported by the committee. No other road objected to this treatment nor to the allowance of 55 per cent in debt certificates. It is impossible to believe they would have assented to this without a word of objection unless there was some existing reason why they would not be relatively harmed by it. That reason may be readily stated, but first it should clearly appear just how much the two roads together took by the consolidation.

	Stock	Debt Certificates	Total
Utica and Schenectady..............	$4,500,000	$2,475,000	$6,975,000.
Mohawk Valley.....	1,575,000	866,250	2,441,250.
Total received by both.............			$9,416,250.
Deduct cash paid by Mohawk Valley...			1,559,319.05
Balance allowed in stock and certificates............			$7,856,930.95

The net income of the Utica and Schenectady in that year was $724,770.73 equivalent to 7 per cent interest on $10,353,868 and upon the basis of earning power the stockholders of that road would have been entitled to stock and certificates to that amount. So on this basis the account stands as follows:

Value of Utica and Schenectady based on earning power	$10,353,868.00
Actually paid to Utica and Schenectady and Mohawk Valley	7,856,930.95
Difference	$ 2,496,937.05

or taking the Utica and Schenectady alone:

Value	$10,353,868.00
Received in stock and certificates	6,975,000.00
Difference	$ 3,378,868.00

If the Utica and Schenectady chose to allow a part of that to which was entitled to go to the Mohawk Valley, we have a complete explanation why the other roads made no objection to the issue of debt certificates to the Mohawk Valley to the amount of $866,250. If the issue of debt certificates was justifiable, the fact that some of those to which the Utica and Schenectady was entitled went to the Mohawk Valley, is not the subject of just complaint. In fact it made no difference except as noted below to those who were stockholders in both roads. It benefited those stockholders in the Mohawk Valley who were stockholders in the Utica and Schenectady and to the extent of that benefit the amount going to its stockholders were diminished. Why this course was taken must probably always remain a matter of conjecture.

The case of the Syracuse and Utica Direct is precisely like, in its circumstances, that of the Mohawk Valley. It bore the same relation to the Syracuse and Utica all of which has been fully explained in the chapter relating to it. They were treated as a unit in the report of the consolidation committee. The stock and certificates received by both roads were as follows:

	Stock	Certificates	Total
Syracuse and Utica..	$2,700,000	$1,350,000	$4,050,000.
Syracuse and Utica Direct...........	600,000	300,000	900,000.
Total............			$4,950,000.
Deduct cash paid by Syracuse and Utica Direct...........			589,793.96
Balance allowed in stock and certificates........			$4,360,206.04

The net income of the Syracuse and Utica for the year 1852 was $376,024.96 equivalent to a 7 per cent return upon $5,371,785 and upon the basis of earning power the stockholders of that road would have been entitled to that amount in stock and certificates. On this basis the account stands as follows:

Value of Syracuse and Utica based on earning power....................................	$5,371,785.
Deduct debt assumed by new company.........	126,000.
Balance to be paid by stock and certificates.....	$5,245,785.
Actually paid in stock and certificates..........	4,360,206.04
Difference....................................	$ 885,578.96

Here again the introduction of the Syracuse and Utica Direct into the consolidation did not increase the amount of certificates required by the basis upon which the consolidation was made.

The case of the Buffalo and Lockport is not so clear. It received certificates to the amount of $168,750, being 25 per cent upon its capital stock of $675,000. This most likely was in consequence of its relations to the Rochester, Lockport and Niagara Falls to which as heretofore pointed out, it was undoubtedly a subsidiary by reason of the undiscovered contract between them. But just how the Niagara Falls road's value was ascertained and what it was fixed at we do not know. The reasonable inference seems to be that the Utica and Schenectady and the Syracuse and Utica made some concessions to these roads on account of their recent construction and that this was one of the modifications in allocating an agreed total which generally become necessary in concluding difficult arrangements.

NOTE. In concluding this account attention should be called to some matters of minor importance in order to avoid possible misapprehension. The Mohawk Valley trustees were required by Article 10 of the Consolidation Agreement to pay over to the new company without delay the ten per cent already paid in on its stock, deducting, however, all expenses and charges paid or justly incurred. The amount so deducted was $15,680.15 and accordingly the new company received in all on the Mohawk Valley stock $1,559,319.05 as above stated.

By Article 11 a like requirement and deduction were made in the case of the Syracuse and Utica Direct. The deduction made was $10,206.04 and the full amount received on account of this company's stock was $589,793.96 as above stated.

In the reports of the Central for 1855, the amount of Debt Certificates is said to be $8,894,500. Some readjustments were made in consequence of fractional parts of shares of stock and other details so that the amount actually issued was $8,892,600 and is so stated in the report for 1856. The amount stated herein is $8,857,091.

The excess over this amount shown by the report arises from the taking in by the Central of the Rochester and Lake Ontario Railroad pursuant to Article 17 of the Consolidation Agreement, but subsequently to the consolidation, and hence not treated in this book. The amount given in this book is correct for the roads herein covered, and is ascertained by computing on the amounts of capital stock named in Article 3, the percentages fixed by Article 14 of the Consolidation Agreement.

APPENDICES

THE CONSOLIDATION AGREEMENT

The Consolidation Agreement is a long, elaborate document consisting of 24½ closely printed pages exclusive of all signatures. It is believed to have dealt with larger financial interests than any instrument theretofore executed within the state and accordingly was drawn with exceeding care and great skill by J. V. L. Pruyn and reviewed by Judge A. C. Paige. It is unnecessary to print it in full it being a public record on file in the office of the Secretary of State at Albany. Accordingly there is given a summary which faithfully indicates all essential provisions. It consists of a general agreement to consolidate followed by twenty-two articles prescribing the terms and conditions of the consolidation and was dated May 17, 1853.

The General Agreement. This refers in general terms to the consolidation act, recites that an agreement to consolidate thereunder has been made and that the several companies do agree that the several companies shall be consolidated into one corporation under the name of The New York Central Railroad Company which shall continue for the term of five hundred years.

Article 1. Provides that the number of directors shall be thirteen; the first election thereof shall be held at the City Hall in Albany the 6th day of July then next; and minutely fixes the manner of conducting the election.

Article 2. Provides for the subsequent elections of directors on the second Wednesday of December in each year, that each stockholder shall be entitled to one vote for each share of stock, and that vacancies shall be filled in the manner prescribed in the by-laws.

Article 3. Recites the amount of the capital stock and of the convertible bonds of each company then outstanding as follows:

	Capital Stock	Convertible Bonds
Albany and Schenectady	$1,535,800	$86,000
Schenectady and Troy	650,000	
Utica and Schenectady	4,500,000	
Mohawk Valley	1,575,000	
Syracuse and Utica	2,700,000	
Syracuse and Utica Direct	600,000	
Rochester and Syracuse	5,606,700	2,000
Buffalo and Rochester	3,000,000	

	Capital Stock	Convertible Bonds
Brought forward.................	$ 20,167,500	$ 88,000
Rochester, Lockport and Niagara Falls...........................	2,016,100	139,000
Buffalo and Lockport.............	675,000	
	$22,858,600	$227,000

Recites that on the stock of the Mohawk Valley and Syracuse and Utica Direct but $10 on each share had been paid leaving $90 per share unpaid and that on the stock of the Buffalo and Rochester $718,750 remained unpaid.

Fixed the capital stock of the new corporation at $22,858,600, divided into shares of $100 each, subject to be increased by the conversion of convertible bonds to $23,085,600.

Article 4. Provides that one share of each of the old companies shall be exchanged for one share of the new company, except in case of the Buffalo and Rochester whose shares were of the par value of $50 each, two of its shares should be exchanged for one share of the new company. Provision is made for rejecting odd or fractional shares of less than $50 each.

Article 5. Recites the funded debt of each company other than the convertible bonds; the new corporation assumes and agrees to pay the same, as well as convertible bonds which may not be converted into stock. The amounts of such funded debts are as follows:

Albany and Schenectady.............	$226,823.62
Schenectady and Troy...............	100,000.00
Syracuse and Utica.................	126,000.00
Rochester and Syracuse.............	756,000.00
Buffalo and Rochester..............	200,000.00
Rochester, Lockport and Niagara Falls	476,000.00
	$1,884,823.62

Recites that the city of Troy is to pay the interest on the Schenectady and Troy bonds to March 1, 1858; that each company is to pay the interest on its bonds to May 1, 1853; that $400,000 of the Rochester and Syracuse bonds are for state stock issued and are subject to a sinking fund of $71,652.23 in the hands of the comptroller leaving the balance of the whole debt the amount stated. That $100,000 of the Buffalo and Rochester bonds are for state stock. That the comptroller holds a sinking fund of about $23,000 leaving the actual debt about $177,000.

Article 6. Provides that all indebtedness and liabilities of each old company, direct and contingent, at the close of business April 30, 1853, other than the bonds and funded debt, are to be paid by the respective companies or the trustees who may settle their affairs out of their own assets which do not pass to or vest in the new company. This did not extend to equipment, machinery or supplies contracted for previous to April 30, but not then delivered; all such equipment, machinery and supplies to be paid for by the new corporation on receiving the same. No partial payment thereon by an old company previous to April 30, to be refunded to the old company.

Article 7. The trustees of each company appointed pursuant to Article 8, shall account for and pay over to the new company all moneys received by their respective companies since April 30, except calls on stock made previously to that time and shall be credited and allowed all payments out of said moneys properly made in carrying on business operations of the company since April 30 and up to time of accounting. The Rochester and Syracuse also to be credited with the amount expended by it in constructing its straight line road between Syracuse and Rochester not included in the statement of its capital stock and indebtedness, but not in any event to exceed one hundred and twenty thousand dollars.

Article 8. Authorizes the old companies respectively to retain for the payment of their indebtedness and liabilities all moneys which they had on hand April 30, 1853, all amounts and debts due them that day, including payments or installments on stock called for before that time and payable previously to the date of the agreement; and all stocks and securities for the payment of money which they then held. Each company was required to assign to trustees, before the election of directors of the new company, all the property which it was entitled to retain in trust for the purposes mentioned. Also to assign to such trustees all the moneys received by or due to them respectively which under the 7th Article were to be paid over to the new corporation and that the trustees should account for the same without delay to the new company. Also to assign to the trustees all the money and personal assets which was to be turned over to the new company.

Article 9. Provides that shares of capital stock held by any of the old companies in the Great Western Railroad Company, Canada West, and in the Buffalo and State Line Railroad Company, should be sold to the new company it paying par for the Great Western stock, (deducting any installments remaining unpaid) and all accrued interest thereon allowed by the company and remaining unpaid; and for the Buffalo and State Line stock par and twenty per cent premium with interest from April 30, that being the market value of the stock that day. Payment to be made to the trustees of the several companies in bonds of the new company due in thirty years from May 1, 1853 and bearing interest payable semi-annually at the rate of 6 per cent. The amount of the stocks so held was declared by the respective companies to be as follows:

Albany and Schenectady	Great Western	$25,000
Utica and Schenectady	Great Western	200,000
Syracuse and Utica	Great Western	75,000
	Buffalo and State Line	62,300
Rochester and Syracuse	Great Western	125,000
	Buffalo and State Line	105,500
Buffalo and Rochester	Buffalo and State Line	94,950
Rochester, Lockport and Niagara Falls	Great Western	68,500

Article 10. The Mohawk Valley Company agrees that its trustees will pay over to the new company without delay the 10 per cent paid in on its stock, $157,500, less all expenses and charges paid or justly incurred by said company.

Article 11. The Syracuse and Utica Direct agrees that its trustees will pay to the new company, without delay, the 10 per cent paid in on its stock, $60,000, less all expenses and charges paid or justly incurred by said company.

Article 12. The whole amount unpaid on the capital stock of the Buffalo and Rochester shall be paid to the new company.

Article 13. The certificates of stock in the new company to be given to the stockholders in the Mohawk Valley and Syracuse and Utica Direct, shall state that ten dollars only on each share has been paid and that the ninety dollars per share remains to be paid as the same may be called for by the directors. Like provision as to the unpaid Buffalo and Rochester stock. Provisions that any of the stockholders holding these stocks may pay before February 1, 1854, on certain specified terms, but directors may call for payment before that time if they so elect. Stocks paid in part shall receive dividends only on the amount actually paid in but at the same per cent as full paid stock.

Article 14. "The estate, property and franchises of the said companies, parties hereto, which in pursuance of the said act of the Legislature, will vest in the said new corporation on its organization, being relatively of unequal value, and the stocks of the respective companies having heretofore uniformly sold in market at different prices or rates of premium, the parties hereto do hereby, with the view of making compensation to the stockholders of the said companies, respectively, fix upon the following amounts to be allowed therefor by the issue of certificates as hereinafter mentioned, to wit:"

(The following percentages are on the capital stock as hereinbefore stated.)

Albany and Schenectady.............. 17 per cent
Utica and Schenectady................ 55 " "
Mohawk Valley...................... 55 " "
　　on the whole capital stock it being subject to the further payment of $90 per share.

Syracuse and Utica.................... 50 per cent
Syracuse and Utica Direct............. 50 " "
 on the whole capital stock it being sub-
 ject to the further payment of $90
 per share.
Rochester and Syracuse............... 30 " "
Buffalo and Rochester................ 40 " "
Rochester, Lockport and Niagara Falls.. 25 " "
Buffalo and Lockport................. 25 " "

No allowance is made to the Schenectady and Troy "as the stock of that company is not considered to be worth its nominal or par value, and its new stock is made subject to the further payment to the new company of $25 on each share at such times as the directors may require."

Article 15. The new company shall without delay after its organization issue to the stockholders of the respective companies certificates for the allowances made in Article 14 which shall state the amount to which he is entitled, that such amount is to be paid out of the future income of the company after payment of the cost of maintaining and operating the road, May 1, 1883, with interest at the rate of 6 per cent per annum from May 1, 1853, payable semi-annually. Such certificates were to be made in amounts of $500, $1,000, $3,000, $5,000 and $10,000 only, but certificates for a fraction or in excess of any of these amounts might be issued or such fraction or excess might be paid in cash by the new corporation.

But no certificate shall be issued to the stockholders of any company until the trustees of such company shall have given satisfactory security for the payment of debts and liabilities of that company not charged on the new corporation and the new corporation fully indemnified against the same.

Article 16. Provides a sinking fund for securing the payment of the debt certificates at maturity. There is to be set apart annually out of earnings after first paying all expenses of running and maintaining the road and the interest on the certificates, an amount equal to one and one-fourth per cent of the principal of the certificates, which fund with the accumulations thereon shall be invested in the public stocks of the State of New York or in the stocks and bonds of any incorporated city in the state of New York, authorized by law to issue the same or in the purchase of any of the said certificates as the company may deem most desirable. Such fund and the securities belonging thereto to be kept separate and apart from the other funds and securities of the company.

Article 17. The agreement between the Rochester, Lockport and Niagara Falls Railroad Company and the Rochester and Lake Ontario Railroad Company shall be fulfilled by the new company.

Article 18. The several companies grant and release to the new company, when formed, and to its successors and assigns, all their lands and real estate or which may be held or owned by them at the time when they merge into the new corporation.

Article 19. The road of the Buffalo and Lockport Railroad Company shall be in all respects completed by that company at its own expense with all necessary buildings and the title to its real estate perfected on or before the first day of July in the manner agreed upon by the contract between that company and the Rochester, Lockport and Niagara Falls company. If not so completed satisfactory security shall be given to the new corporation for such completion before debt certificates shall be issued to the stockholders.

Article 20. The amount of unpaid and unclaimed dividends of the old companies shall be paid over to the new company which shall pay such dividends whenever legally demanded.

Article 21. Should the stockholders of any company refuse to ratify the agreement on or before July 1 the same shall on and after that day become of full force and effect and be an agreement between the companies whose stockholders shall have sanctioned and approved the same.

Article 22. Should any shareholder in any or either of the old companies decline taking shares in the new company, such shareholder shall be paid for his shares in the manner prescribed by the act authorizing the consolidation.

RATIFICATION BY THE STOCKHOLDERS

Meetings of the stockholders of the several companies were held on June 29, 1853, to pass upon the consolidation agreement and they unanimously sanctioned and approved the same.

The following is the result of the ballot taken by each meeting on the question—

	For	Against
Albany and Schenectady	12,125	None
Schenectady and Troy	6,499	None
Utica and Schenectady	30,801	None
Mohawk Valley	11,940	None
Syracuse and Utica	21,391	None
Syracuse and Utica Direct	4,857	None
Rochester and Syracuse	9,406	None
Buffalo and Rochester	39,297	None
Rochester, Lockport and Niagara Falls	13,950	6
Buffalo and Lockport	5,143	None

The Rochester, Lockport and Niagara Falls meeting after the result of the ballot had been announced unanimously passed a resolution sanctioning and approving the agreement.

BRIEF NOTICES OF LEADING MEN

These brief notices are not even biographical sketches. They are intended to give a mere outline which affords opportunity to anyone interested to follow up the subject.

George William Featherstonhaugh

Born, April 9, 1780, in London, England.
Died, September 28, 1866, in Havre, France.

A brief sketch of Mr. Featherstonhaugh's life up to the time of the severance of his relations with the Mohawk and Hudson has been given in the text of this volume. His subsequent history will now be briefly noted.

He had given much attention to geology. On his arrival in England in 1826, he was elected a Fellow of the Geological Society of London. After 1829 he devoted his efforts to literature, travel, geology and exploration. He removed to Philadelphia, lectured on geology in Philadelphia and New York, translated from the Latin one of Cicero's works. In 1831, he established *The Monthly American Journal of Geology and Natural Sciences*, said to be the first journal devoted to geology published in America. In 1833, he was appointed the United States government geologist and the same year he translated a work from the Italian.

In 1834, he began a series of geological explorations first going to Mexico and after his return publishing an official account of his researches. In 1835, he undertook another journey on horseback and in canoes in the northwest in Michigan and about the great lakes and extended his travels into Minnesota, living for some time among the Indians and learning their language.

On his return after publishing an account of his expedition, he visited the Cherokee nation in Georgia and studied the geological formation of their country.

In 1839, he sailed for England. On his arrival there he found the dispute between England and the United States over the boundary between Maine and Canada in progress. The British government immediately called upon him for information. Finally he and Richard L. Mudge were appointed commissioners to investigate the situation on the ground and early in 1840 they went to Canada for that purpose. In 1844, they returned to England and made their report and received the thanks of both houses of Parliament. Soon after this he was appointed by the British government as consul at Havre in France and this position he held until his death in 1866. He assisted in the escape of Louis Philippe from France after his deposition in the revolution of 1848.

Mr. Featherstonhaugh was a man of marked ability and extensive attainment. He was a friend of many leading Americans, Daniel Webster, Henry Clay and others. His friendship with and influence over a group of New York City capitalists secured the construction of the Mohawk and Hudson and for that service he deserves the remembrance of the American people.

John Jacob Astor

Born, July 17, 1763, in Waldorf, near Heidelberg, in Germany. Died, March 29, 1848, in New York City.

Mr. Astor's place in American life and business during the first half of the nineteenth century, was too great and varied to admit of even a sketch of its extraordinary activities. He was a man of extraordinary mental power and well balanced judgment.

He was one of the chief promoters of the Mohawk and Hudson; was elected a director in 1828, 1829, 1830, and 1831, and during this period he attended fifty-one meetings of the directors, thirty-eight of which were held at his house in New York City. He served upon committees and was chairman of the general or executive committee in charge of the construction of the road. Besides being a subscriber to a large number of shares of stock, he assisted the enterprise financially, at one time loaning it $35,000. He was not re-elected director in 1832, and his name does not appear in connection with the road subsequent thereto. Why he dropped out has not been ascertained.

Lynde Catlin

Born, in 1768, in Litchfield, Connecticut. Died, October 18, 1833, in New York City.

Mr. Catlin was connected with the Mohawk and Hudson, from its inception, being named in the charter as one of the three commissioners to receive subscriptions to its stock. He was also one of the five first directors and with the exception of a short period in 1829, served as such until June, 1833, and was the only treasurer of the Company, up to the time of his death, and was a member of the executive committee.

He was educated as a lawyer and graduated at Yale in 1786. He entered the banking business, became the cashier of the

Merchant's Bank in New York City, was for a time cashier of the New York branch of the United States Bank. He returned to the Merchant's Bank, as its president, and remained in that position until his death.

JAMES RENWICK

Born, May 30, 1790, at Liverpool, England.
Died, January 12, 1863, in New York City.

Mr. Renwick was elected a director of the Mohawk and Hudson in June, 1829, and served as such until June, 1832. He was one of the general or executive committee, which had charge of the construction of the road.

He graduated at Columbia College in 1807, the first in his class. In 1813, he became instructor in natural and experimental philosophy and chemistry in that institution and in 1820, was made full professor, remaining such until 1853. He was the author of a considerable number of books and was also versed in engineering. He is said to have been an intimate friend of Featherstonhaugh.

NICHOLAS FISH

Born, August 28, 1758, in New York City.
Died, June 20, 1833, in New York City.

Colonel Fish was elected a director of the Mohawk and Hudson in September, 1826, and served in that capacity until June, 1832. He was vice president of that company from July, 1829, until his retirement as director and as such seems to have been the chief executive officer, Mr. Van Rensselaer, the president, giving little, if any, attention to company affairs.

Colonel Fish was very active in army service during the revolution, was in both battles at Saratoga, and was at Monmouth and Yorktown. He was a lieutenant colonel at the close of the war. Alderman of the city of New York, 1806–1817, and was active in many literary and religious institutions of that city.

JOHN I. DEGRAFF

Born, October 2, 1783.
Died, July 22, 1848, at Schenectady.

Mr. DeGraff was a director of the Mohawk and Hudson in 1829, 1830, 1831. Although not commissioner for the construction of that road, he seems to have been more in active charge than Cambreling, the commissioner, settled the construction accounts with the company and received a larger compensation for his services than did his principal.

He was a successful merchant in Schenectady and was several times mayor of that city. He served as representative in Congress, two terms, from the Schenectady district.

JOHN B. JERVIS

Born, December 14, 1795, at Huntington, Long Island.
Died, January 12, 1885, at Rome, New York.

Mr. Jervis began his work as engineer in 1817, on the Erie Canal and in 1819, was appointed a Resident Engineer and remained on the canal until near its completion. Appointed Assistant Engineer on the Delaware and Hudson canal in 1825, and Chief Engineer in 1827. Appointed Engineer of the Mohawk and Hudson Railroad in 1830, and later of the Schenectady and Saratoga Railroad. Next appointed Chief Engineer of the Chenango canal. Made preliminary surveys and estimates for enlarging the Erie Canal in 1835. In 1836, he became the Chief Engineer of the Croton aqueduct at New York and in 1846, Consulting Engineer of the Cochituate Water Works. In 1846, he became Chief Engineer of the Hudson River Railroad, planned and located that road and remained in charge of that work until 1849, when he resigned on account of ill health, but was at once appointed Consulting Engineer, without decrease of salary. In 1850, he was appointed Chief Engineer of the Michigan Southern and Northern Indiana Railroad (afterwards a part of the Lake Shore and Michigan Southern Railway and now a part of the New York Central), and was for a time its President. Later he became Engineer of the Chicago and Rock Island Railroad and in 1884, its President. He went to Rome, N. Y., in 1858, and lived a retired life for three years and then became Superintendent and Engineer of the Pittsburgh, Fort Wayne and Chicago Railroad. He retired in 1866, at the age of seventy-one, from active railroad work, but in 1868, became connected with the Merchant Iron Mill at Rome, and was connected with that concern until his death.

Mr. Jervis was one of the distinguished engineers of his day.

GEORGE LAW

Born, October 25, 1806, at Jackson, Washington Co., New York.
Died, November 18, 1881, in New York City.

George Law was elected a director of the Mohawk and Hudson, June 14, 1843, and president at the meeting of the Board, on the same day; re-elected in 1844, and resigned both positions March 8, 1845.

For some time previous to Mr. Law's election to these positions, the affairs of the company had been in a bad way, owing to the difficulties attendant upon the elimination of the inclined planes. June 15, the day following his election as president, the Board adopted the following resolution:

"Resolved, that the President of this Company be and he is hereby authorized and empowered to proceed to the Company's road and organize the business of the Company as in his judgment will best promote its interests and that he have full power in his discretion to remove any of the present officers and agents of the Company and appoint such new officers and agents as he may consider proper and take such other measures as may be necessary to conduct the affairs of the Company as in his judgment will best promote its interests; and that so much of the By Laws and resolutions of this Company as conflict herewith be and the same are hereby suspended for this purpose."

A resolution so drastic as this indicates clearly that for some reason unexplained the operating conditions had become unsatisfactory and needed radical treatment at the hands of a severely practical man. The elimination of the Albany inclined plane owing to its great expense and the inability of the Company to finance it, was also a serious problem, demanding prompt solution. These tasks were committed to Law, a new man on the Board. It would seem certain he was brought into that position for the express purpose of handling and solving certain difficulties and as soon as he had accomplished that task, he retired to attend to his own private business. At all events, negotiations with the city of Albany were promptly undertaken by Law and a committee of directors, with results which have been fully detailed elsewhere. The committee acting with Law, consisted of Banks, Little, King and Pruyn, and was given plenary power.

Law remained president until after the road was changed to its present location in Albany, and for about six months thereafter and his connection with that work is the feature which entitles him to brief notice at this place. He was a contractor for public works, constructed sections of the Croton aqueduct and the High Bridge of that work over the Harlem river. His subsequent activities in building railroads, operating steamship lines, and other work of that character, made him one of the prominent men of his day, so much so that in February, 1855, he was placed in nomination, by the Pennsylvania legislature, as a Native American, or Know Nothing candidate for the presidency.

Erastus Corning

Born, December 14, 1794, in Norwich, Connecticut.
Died, April, 1872, in Albany, New York.

Mr. Corning was a director of the Utica and Schenectady Railroad Company, during its entire existence and also its only

President. He was also a director of the Mohawk and Hudson from June, 1833 to June, 1835; for some years of the Michigan Central Railroad Company; and of the Hudson River Railroad Company, 1849–1863.

He was elected the first president of the New York Central and held that position until 1864, when he resigned, owing it is believed, to ill health. He was a director for a few years after ceasing to be president, his last year of service being 1867.

He held public official positions as follows: Mayor of Albany, 1834, 1835, 1836, and to May 14, 1837, when he resigned; senator of the state of New York, 1842–1845; representative in congress, December 7, 1857, to March 3, 1859, and from July 4, 1861, to March 3, 1863. He was again re-elected but resigned on account of failing health; regent of the University of the state of New York from 1833, and at the time of his death was vice-chancellor of the Board of Regents of the University.

His business activities were very great. He was first a clerk in the hardware store of an uncle in Troy. He removed to Albany in 1814, entering the hardware business there and became the head of the extensive hardware house of E. Corning & Co. He was also interested largely in a rolling mill business, which grew to large proportions. John F. Winslow was associated with him in this concern. His influence in railroad matters was almost controlling and no man's business reputation for capacity and integrity stood higher.

John V. L. Pruyn

Born, June 22, 1811, in Albany, New York.
Died, November 21, 1877, in Albany.

Mr. Pruyn was elected a director of the Mohawk and Hudson Railroad Company in 1835, 1836, 1837, 1838, 1843, 1844 and 1845. In July, 1843, was elected its secretary and also appointed attorney and counsel. July 1, 1843, he was also elected secretary and treasurer of the Utica and Schenectady and held those positions during the remainder of the corporate existence of that company. He was also, during some porton of this period, attorney for the company. On the acquisition of the Mohawk Valley Company he became a director and its president.

He had entire charge of the detail work of the consolidation of 1853, and drew the consolidation agreement, all of which he performed with great ability. On the organization of the directors of the New York Central, he was made treasurer of the company and held that position until 1857, when he was made general counsel and president pro tem. In 1861, in addition to these positions, he was again made Treasurer on the occurrence of a vacancy in that office. In 1865, he ceased to be treasurer but remained general counsel. In 1853, he was elected a director and remained such until Commodore Vanderbilt acquired control of the road in 1866, when his official connection with it ceased.

Mr. Pruyn was an able lawyer, and a very efficient man of business. He was elected to the state senate in 1861, and as representative in congress of 1863 and 1867; was a commissioner for the new capitol building at Albany and as such laid its cornerstone, July 7, 1869. He was elected Regent of the University in 1844, and became its Chancellor in 1862, and served until his death. He was also a president of the State Board of Charities and a Regent of the Smithsonian Institution.

JOHN WILKINSON

Born, September 30, 1798 in Troy, New York.
Died: Date not ascertained.

Educated at Skaneateles until twelve years old and then at the academy in Onondaga. After graduation at the academy he entered the law office of Forman & Sabin as clerk and was admitted to the bar in September, 1819, and opened an office in Syracuse. He is said, in a history of Onondaga county, to have been the first lawyer to settle in Syracuse. In 1820, a post-office was opened in that place and he was appointed postmaster. In 1825, at the first election of village officers he was elected village clerk. He remained postmaster until July 26, 1840.

He assisted in projecting the Syracuse and Utica Railroad, was elected a director and its first president and retained those positions until the consolidation of 1853. He was elected a director of the Onondaga County Bank in 1825, and remained such during its life. In 1838, he assisted in the organization of the Bank of Syracuse in connection with Horace White, was made its president and continued in that positon until his death. In 1834 and 1835, he was elected a member of the Assembly from Onondaga county.

He was elected one of the first directors of the New York Central Railroad Company but his service on the Board was brief. For a time he occupied the position of agent for the examination of legal and other claims against that company.

He was at various times actively interested in various other railroads and it is said that in his latter years he operated the Terre Haute, Alton and St. Louis Railroad, for two years as trustee and receiver.

Mr. Wilkinson was a very active and forceful man and his services for the Syracuse and Utica deserve remembrance.

INDEX